A Perfect Freedom

RELIGIOUS LIBERTY IN PENNSYLVANIA

J. William Frost

THE PENNSYLVANIA STATE UNIVERSITY PRESS
University Park, Pennsylvania

Library of Congress Cataloging-in-Publication Data

Frost, J. William (Jerry William)
    A perfect freedom : religious liberty in Pennsylvania / J. William
Frost.

       p.   cm.
    Originally published: Cambridge ; New York : Cambridge University
Press, c1990, in series: Cambridge studies in religion and American
public life. With new introd.
    Includes bibliographical references and index.
    ISBN 0-271-01091-6 (pbk.)
    1. Freedom of religion—Pennsylvania—History.   2. Religion and
state—Pennsylvania—History.   3. Pennsylvania—Religion.
4. Pennsylvania—Constitutional history.   I. Title.
BL2527.P4F76   1993
323.44'2'09748—dc20   93-18813
                                                    CIP

Published by The Pennsylvania State University Press,
Barbara Building, Suite C, University Park, PA 16802-1003

A Perfect Freedom: Religious Liberty in Pennsylvania was first published
in 1990 by Cambridge University Press

To Bert, Claire, Jane, Kazue, Nancy, and Pat,
my colleagues in the Friends Library
who make work a pleasure.

Nor are we less happy in the Enjoyment of a perfect Freedom as to Religion. By many Years Experience we find, that an Equality among religious Societies, without distinguishing any one Sect with greater Privileges than another, is the most effectual Method to discourage Hypocrisy, promote the Practice of the moral Virtues, and prevent the Plagues and Mischiefs that always attend religious Squabbling.

Lieutenant Governor George Thomas, 1739

The sentiment of entire freedom in religion; of perfect liberty to worship God according to our own views of right.... It is impossible to conceive that there is to be anything *beyond* this which mankind are to desire in their progress toward perfection.

Reverend Albert Barnes, 1845

Contents

List of Illustrations

Illustrations follow page 28

Statue of "Religious Liberty," Philadelphia. (Photo by J. William Frost)

Second Presbyterian Church, Philadelphia. (Courtesy of John M. Decker, Philadelphia, Pa.)

Old Guinston Presbyterian Church, York County. (Courtesy, Department of History, Presbyterian Church (USA), Philadelphia, Pa.)

Merion Friends Meeting House, Lower Merion. (Courtesy of the Friends Historical Library of Swarthmore College, Swarthmore, Pa.)

Bethel African Methodist Episcopal Church, Philadelphia. (Courtesy, Library Company of Philadelphia)

"Peaceable Kingdom," by Edward Hicks. (Courtesy of the Abby Aldrich Rockefeller Folk Art Center, Williamsburg, Virginia)

American Bible Society logo. (Courtesy, Department of History, Presbyterian Church (USA), Philadelphia, Pa.)

Burning of St. Michael's Church, Philadelphia. (Courtesy, Library Company of Philadelphia)

Camp meeting. (Courtesy, Library Company of Philadelphia)

Title page of William Penn, *The Great Case of Liberty of Conscience.* (Courtesy of the Friends Historical Library of Swarthmore College, Swarthmore, Pa.)

Lucretia Mott. (Courtesy of the Friends Historical Library of Swarthmore College, Swarthmore, Pa.)

John Ettwein. (Courtesy, Moravian Historical Society, Nazareth, Pa.)

William Smith. (Courtesy, University of Pennsylvania Archives)

Ezra Stiles Ely. (Courtesy, Department of History, Presbyterian Church (USA), Philadelphia, Pa.)

Francis Alison. (Courtesy, Permanent Collection of the University of Delaware, Newark, Delaware)

James Wilson. (Courtesy, Department of History, Presbyterian Church (USA), Philadelphia, Pa.)

Benjamin Rush. (Courtesy, Department of History, Presbyterian Church (USA), Philadelphia, Pa.)

Gilbert Tennent. (Courtesy, Department of History, Presbyterian Church (USA), Philadelphia, Pa.)

Preface to the Paperback Edition

Before state governments turned over public relations to advertising agencies, license plates attempted to boost their states by the use of mottos with a certain dignity. New York was the "Empire State," Connecticut the "Constitution State," Illinois a "Land of Lincoln." Pennsylvania used its traditional label of the "Keystone State," a slogan used as early as 1802. Since many Americans neither knew what a keystone was nor would be attracted to visit one, a change was necessary. Pennsylvania tried folksiness, "You've Got a Friend in Pennsylvania," before surrendering to the presumptuous, "America Starts Here." Since Columbus never came to Philadelphia, and Plymouth and Jamestown predate Pennsylvania by more than half a century, my suggestion for a more accurate slogan would be either "America's Religious Liberty Began Here" or the more succinct "Pioneer of Religious Liberty."

Pennsylvanians have reason to be proud of their contributions to American history. Pennsylvania was the first state to exhibit what we now see as characteristics of modern America: urbanization, diversity of population, toleration of variety, economic prosperity through agriculture, industry, trade, and mining. Pennsylvania began notable reform movements: Indian rights, antislavery, temperance, women's rights, and peace. This book is the story of an important Pennsylvania reform movement that came to characterize the American experiment in democracy: religious liberty, or, as it is sometimes called, the separation of church and state. Pennsylvania created a distinctive pattern of religious liberty before 1720 that endured with minor changes until the mid-twentieth century. The Supreme Court has now pronounced unconstitutional major elements of Pennsylvania's traditions of religious liberty. Many of the most important landmark cases involved Pennsylvania. The most recent Supreme Court decisions, often by a narrow majority, show a minority of the Court affirming policies that echo Pennsylvania's traditional beliefs and practices. The current debate over Christmas displays in public buildings and prayer in schools shows that many in America would like to retain elements of that earlier synthesis. Even so, on those contemporary issues where the debate is fueled by religious fervor, such as abortion and homosexuality, neither the Court, the opponents, nor proponents see the issues as involving religious freedom. This depoliticization of religion shows the success of the separation of church and state.

The purpose of this book is not to take sides in the ongoing controversy over church and state or to provide historical ammunition for those who advocate strict separation or accommodation. Rather, it is to show that in the past Pennsylvanians consciously adopted policies filled with ambiguities and inconsistencies that met their needs. An ideology tempered by politics often determined the final outcome. So even though Pennsylvania's policies worked well or proved popular in the past, that is not sufficient reason to advocate them now.

America's pluralism today makes the diversity of colonial Pennsylvania look minor league. But the first colonists were surprised by the amount of religious varieties within the Christian tradition and had to learn how to deal with it. We now expect increases in a pluralism that already includes Christians, Jews, Muslims, Buddhists, Hindus, assorted Spiritualists and cults, and those who are either areligious or nonreligious—all of whom must be guaranteed equal rights, the liberty to practice religion, and the freedom from religious coercion. Yet we worry that the common moral elements needed to sustain democracy may be lacking. So the consensus linking civic morality and organized religion that worked in the Keystone State in 1789 or 1900 may not be retrievable in the year 2000.

Religious, political, and social contexts shaped the Pennsylvania patterns of religious liberty that allowed women and men freedom to practice their faith while generally removing religious animosities from the political realm. As recent events in Ulster, India, the Middle East, and the former Soviet Union and Yugoslavia have shown, religious differences can jeopardize political unity and destroy hoped-for compromise. It seems unlikely that any one policy defining all nations as religious, secular, or something in between will bring peace. After three centuries America is still debating the implications of religious liberty, because the policy remains so odd, ill-defined, and confusing. So, finally, I hope that this book teaches Americans caution about advocating our patterns of religious freedom for other countries of the world.

Acknowledgments

Modern research is a cooperative enterprise, and many scholars have contributed to the formulation of the ideas expressed in this book. For years I enjoyed fruitful discussions with the editors of the Papers of William Penn. In 1985–6, under the aegis of the Transformation of Philadelphia Project, Dale Light, Richard Pointer, Michael Zuckerman, Judith McGaw, Doris Andrews, Judith Hunter, and I exchanged information in seminars on the history of religion in the Delaware Valley before 1860. Early drafts of the manuscript received critiques from James Field, Stephanie Wolf, and Jean Soderlund. The editors of the Cambridge Studies in Religion and American Public Life ask an author to submit his manuscript to faculty and students at the University of Chicago Divinity School. They read my manuscript carefully and, in a seminar, provided a helpful analysis of strengths and weaknesses.

At every library where I worked the staff provided efficient service by tracking down obscure sources, helped me to understand law citations, and suggested additional resources. Most of my research was done at the Swarthmore College Library, the Friends Historical Library of Swarthmore College, the Library Company of Philadelphia, the Biddle Law Library of the University of Pennsylvania, and the Presbyterian Historical Society. Additional research took place at Eastern Baptist Seminary Library, St. George's Methodist Historical Society, the Goshen College Library, the Historical Society of Pennsylvania, and the Quaker Collection at Haverford College. Glenn Colliver brought the published proceedings of the Episcopal Convocation to the Presbyterian Historical Society for me to read. I would like to thank Herbert Gilbert for his valuable assistance in preparing the manuscript for the press. Jane Thorson typed the manuscript, offered astute criticism and encouragement, and helped Charlotte Blandford prepare the index.

Support for my research came from a Eugene Lang Faculty Fellowship from Swarthmore College and a Fellowship, funded by the National Endowment for the Humanities and the Transformation of Philadelphia Project and administered by the Philadelphia Center for Early American Studies. Portions of Chapters I and VIII appeared first in articles in the *Pennsylvania Magazine of History and Biography* in 1981 and 1988, and are reprinted here with the permission of the Historical Society of Pennsylvania.

Finally, I want to thank my wife Susan and son James for their patience and support during the many days and weekends I spent researching and writing about religious liberty.

Introduction: The Pennsylvania Traditions of Religious Liberty

Most readers of this book will be seeking insight into the meaning of the religious clauses in the First Amendment. The study of the history of religious liberty is particularly pertinent today because of the increasing debate over original intent and the controversy arising from recent Supreme Court decisions concerning school prayer. The danger is that the contemporary issues sometimes reverse historical priorities. Until the mid-twentieth century, Pennsylvanians held the First Amendment to be a symbolic testimony to the nation's adoption of their beliefs and practices on religious freedom. The Federal disestablishment clause was important for what it showed about the religious clauses in the 1790 Pennsylvania constitution. The First Congress's inclusion of religion in the Bill of Rights had little impact on Pennsylvania's conduct for the next one hundred and fifty years.

In the colonial period Pennsylvania's pattern of separation of church and state paved the way for similar policies in other states and the Federal government. Thomas Jefferson in his *Notes on Virginia,* written in 1781 and published in 1785, saw the postrevolutionary Virginia disestablishment of the Church of England as growing out of a pattern begun in Pennsylvania one hundred years earlier. The radical experiment in religious liberty, wrote Jefferson, took place in Pennsylvania (and New York) and not in Virginia.[1]

Scholars have long recognized that the Founding Fathers incorporated republican ideology and colonial experience in creating the constitutions for the states and the new nation. Pennsylvania was the primary model for the success of freedom of religion in the other states. The delegates to the First and Second Continental Congress and the Federal Constitutional Convention, all held in Philadelphia, saw the results of freedom of religion at firsthand. Philadelphia was the most cosmopolitan city in the colonies, the Athens of North America. Since the 1720s the growth in

1

prosperity of the city and surrounding countryside had been linked to the freedoms the populace enjoyed, particularly religious liberty. James Madison, attending college at Princeton, learned that the lack of governmental tax support hurt neither Pennsylvania nor the Presbyterian church. In 1773, when Madison began his investigation of religious liberty, he wrote to William Bradford of Pennsylvania asking about "the extent of your religious Toleration" and "Is an Ecclesiastical Establishment absolutely necessary to support civil society?"[2]

Today, Virginians can thank the Revolutionary generation for establishing religious freedom; New Englanders can look back to the First Amendment and Baptist agitation as goads prompting Connecticut, New Hampshire, and Massachusetts to question direct tax support for religion. Even before the War of 1812 the alliance between magistrates and ministers in New England was an anomaly, such policies having been repudiated by the rest of the nation. Connecticut in 1818 and Massachusetts in 1833 finally disestablished the Congregational church.

By contrast, Pennsylvanians could claim that their land was born free. The factors that created and sustained the colony's religious liberty can be understood in isolation from similar practices elsewhere. Pennsylvanians looked to their own history for precedents and procedures and saw themselves as models for others. From its founding in 1682 – long before the influence of factors like the Great Awakening, pietism, and the Enlightenment that historians often cite as the antecedents of the American pattern of separation of church from state – Pennsylvania stood for non-coercion of conscience, divorce of the institutional church from the state, and the cooperation of the church and state in fostering the morality necessary for prosperity and good government. Pennsylvania first encountered the dilemmas that separating churches from the state entailed for both institutions. Her citizens and churches early learned how to live under and then rejoice in conditions of religious freedom. This book is the story of that adjustment.

Until the Revolution, most colonists outside the Middle Colonies knew little about the distinctive religious patterns of Pennsylvania. Between 1775 and 1790 reformers in those states that levied taxes to support the Church of England (the South) or several churches (New England and New York) contrasted Pennsylvanians' voluntary gifts with their situation. Pennsylvania became a symbol of a new republican pattern of religious liberty in opposition to a single or multiple establishment. The policies that New York and the southern states adopted before 1800 and that eventually came to prevail in New England resemble Pennsylvania's. After 1800 it was not that other states sought to emulate Pennsylvania so much as that it had already provided a solution to common problems of church and state, religious pluralism, and civic virtue. Pennsylvania pioneered American religious liberty.

Considering the importance of Pennsylvania's experience in religious freedom, it is surprising that there has never been a full study of its evolution.[3] Historians have produced excellent books on how Massachusetts, Rhode Island, Virginia, Connecticut, and New Hampshire separated church and state.[4] The contributions of James Madison and Thomas Jefferson are well documented. Biographies of William Penn and monographs on individual denominations abound. Three recent excellent books on religious liberty exemplify the neglect of serious research on Pennsylvania's continuing traditions of religious liberty. Thomas J. Curry's *The First Freedoms: Church and State in America to the Passage of the First Amendment*, Leonard Levy's *The Establishment Clause and the First Amendment*, and William Lee Miller, *The First Liberty: Religion and the American Republic* find little to say about Pennsylvania, perhaps because drama and significant events are seemingly found in persecution and politics in New England and Virginia.[5]

Pennsylvanians wanted the freedom to attend worship services or to stay at home, to pay a minister or to ignore him. The entire populace made religious liberty succeed, but those who addressed the theoretical issues and implications were white males – politicians, clergy, trustees, lawyers, judges, and editors. Only rarely can we glimpse the contributions of blacks, lower-class whites, and women. In the decade of war between 1755 and 1765 – the French and Indian War and the so-called Pontiac's rebellion – the frontier settlers opposed Quaker pacifism as an infringement of religious equality. After the Revolution, Jews sought to end restrictions on their holding public office and succeeded in having their synagogues and charitable organizations incorporated. Even after the 1780 law that declared gradual emancipation of slaves, blacks experienced various legal disabilities. Still, they created black congregations within predominantly white denominations, like Episcopalian and Presbyterian, as well as autonomous black churches. By obtaining legal incorporation, black Christians demonstrated that religious liberty extended to all Americans. Women did not constitute separate churches, but they did receive charters for their moral and philanthropic organizations. Lucretia Mott and Sarah Grimké in the 1840s opposed clerical power and Sunday legislation as destructive of religious freedom. After the 1844 anti-Catholic riot in Philadelphia, nativist women founded a newspaper in which they advocated immigration restriction as a measure to preserve religious liberty against the Pope. Mechanics, frontiersmen, Jews, blacks, Catholics, Protestants, clergy, laity, politicians, judges sought to preserve and extend religious liberty. The history of church and state in Pennsylvania took place within a consensus created in the early years of settlement.

This book emphasizes five themes of religious liberty: (1) autonomy for the churches, (2) separation of the institutional church from the state, (3) freedom of conscience for the individual, (4) the informal support of religion as a creator of the morality necessary for good citizenship, and (5) natural law as the intellectual basis for policies in the colony and state.

The subject is neither church and state nor toleration in Pennsylvania, because the colony was not autonomous and the Quakers who founded it had a sectarian mentality. William Penn and the Friends created the initial pattern of freedom. After 1700 Pennsylvania's sectarian policies on religion had to be approved or acquiesced in by authorities in England who consulted with officials of the Church of England. The practices followed in the eighteenth century represented a compromise between Quaker and Anglican positions. England after 1689 had a form of toleration; New England and the South enjoyed toleration. A state practicing toleration recognized the legitimacy of dissent, but labeled it as a variant that could legally exist without having full rights. By contrast, Pennsylvanians sought religious liberty.

From the 1680s until the Revolution the praxis of religious liberty was a source of political acrimony in Pennsylvania. The controversies occurred among Quakers, between Quakers and Anglicans, and among the sectarians (Quakers, Mennonites, Moravians, German Brethren) and church people (Anglicans, Presbyterians, Lutherans, and Reformed). At first religious freedom contributed to instability in the colony; eventually it became a source of strength. By 1720 virtually all Pennsylvanians accepted the virtues of religious liberty, but now battles arose over whether the Quaker definition of religious liberty was discriminatory and a threat to security. The debate over whether to support the Revolution and the treatment of pacifists during the war also involved the definition of religious liberty.

Religious liberty forced eighteenth-century immigrants from established churches in Europe to create mechanisms that would bring order within their churches, settle clerical disputes, and provide financial stability. The clergy had to learn how to operate in an environment of religious pluralism, governmental neutrality, and lay power. Both laity and clergy created new roles for addressing moral and political issues in the general society. The political authorities needed to improvise laws to protect church property, preserve morality, regulate marriages, and define the status of ministers. All of these subjects brought controversy.

In the eighteenth century Pennsylvania was the most liberal American colony on religion. For example, only in Philadelphia was there a legally functioning Roman Catholic Church protected by authorities. On two occasions magistrates moved against anti-Catholic mob violence. Only in Pennsylvania were religious objectors to war not penalized. Only in Pennsylvania did those who ran the assembly learn in time to defend the rights of minorities such as slaves and Indians. Only in Pennsylvania did the government allow virtual autonomy to sectarian communities such as Ephrata and Bethlehem, where inhabitants modified basic institutions, including private property. Pennsylvania's churches remained separate from the government, and its ministers were free to criticize the colony's politicians. The history of religious liberty in Pennsvylania before 1776 shows how different that colony was from the rest of the emerging nation.

The first three chapters of this book will describe the emergence of religious liberty in Pennsylvania: the vision of William Penn, the adjustments made by the early settlers, the controversies over pacifism, and how the later immigrants and ministers who created the Presbyterian, Lutheran, and Reformed churches came to support freedom of religion.

The impact of the American Revolution in altering the Pennsylvania traditions of religious liberty is the theme of Chapters 4 and 5. The sectarians and their allies who dominated the colony lost power and their replacements had a new perspective on what religious liberty entailed. Pacifism, equal rights for sectarians, and anticlericalism disappeared as Pennsylvanians fought to secure their independence. Catholics achieved equality; the state disenfranchised Quakers and other sectarian pacifists from 1776 to 1786. Laws mandated the legal equality of denominations and the separation of the institutional church from the state. The Presbyterian church became dominant in Pennsylvania, and the Scots-Irish and Germans came to power.

The repudiation of Penn's charter and *Frame of Government* and the loss of British citizenship forced the Revolutionary leaders of Pennsylvania to grapple with the relationship of republicanism, morality, the church, and government. Benjamin Rush, a signer of the Declaration of Independence, and James Wilson, a member of the Pennsylvania delegation to the Federal Constitutional Convention in 1787 and the primary author of the state's 1790 constitution, justified religious liberty with the new American political language of equal rights, inherent truths, and natural law. They argued that reason and an innate moral sense reinforced the virtues commanded in Scripture. Government and religion worked together because, under God, reason and revelation harmonized but in their institutional embodiment – state and church – remained distinct with different ends. Separating church and state facilitated spiritual devotion and civil order; merging them brought superstition, persecution, and tyranny.

In 1776 and 1790 Pennsylvania created new constitutions that guaranteed religious liberty. Yet the legislature also passed new laws that showed no more leniency toward moral deviation than the statutes of 1700. And these new laws remained unrepealed for over a century. In fact, before the Civil War the legislature enacted stricter laws on alcohol, dueling, and lotteries.

In the early republic the advocates of religious liberty echoed themes first enunciated in colonial Pennsylvania.[6] Ignoring the tax support for an established Congregational church in New England, they wrote as if the Pennsylvania pattern were normative for the entire country. The debates on republican religious liberty in Pennsylvania after 1790 showed that while virtually everyone approved the general policy there was disagreement on details. All agreed that the church must be free of state interference and that the state and the institutional church must be separate. Most thought that fragile democratic governments required officials and citizens to have a moral character that only the churches could create. So the state had to exercise benevolent neutrality toward religious institutions.

Politicians, clergymen, and judges, the three professions most influential in defining and maintaining the Pennsylvania traditions of religious liberty in the nineteenth century, are treated in Chapters 6, 7, and 8. Politicians and clergymen normally shrouded their discussions of the American pattern of church and state with platitudes, but on occasion sharp differences emerged. For example, in the election of 1800 the Democratic-Republicans compared Thomas Jefferson to William Penn and portrayed both as suffering from clerical opposition because they sought religious freedom. Federalists and Republicans portrayed themselves as defenders of religious liberty against opponents who either attempted to create an established church or to overthrow revealed religion and bring the wrath of God on America. But, once in power, the Pennsylvania Republicans did not modify the state's attitude of benevolent neutrality to organized religion.

The Pennsylvania constitutional convention of 1837 featured two debates – one on paying the clergy for praying at the convention and the other on religious tests for office–in which legislators offered contrasting interpretations of the role of religion and the state. Other moral-political-religious issues involved Sabbath legislation, temperance, and anti-Catholicism. Although each of these could be viewed as a religious issue in which the demands of the evangelical Christians jeopardized the separation of church and state, those Pennsylvanians agitating for change saw themselves as preserving morality and protecting liberty.

In the 1750s Covenanting Presbyterian clergymen began a debate over constitutional principles, which lasted one hundred years within the Presbyterian community. Arguing that the Solemn League and Covenant was still in effect, the Reformed Presbyterians insisted that Christians were obliged to oppose any system of government that tolerated Roman Catholics and slavery and did not acknowledge God as sovereign. In response the clergy and laity of the Presbyterian Church in the U.S.A., reiterating natural law principles of John Calvin and the Founding Fathers, distinguished the sacred covenant of the church from the political covenant of the state. America's tradition of religious freedom preserved the church and fostered the morality of her people. In the 1830s the power of the moral reform societies generated by the Second Great Awakening occasioned acrimony over the power and alleged political meddling by the Presbyterian Church, U.S.A. The legislature's refusal to charter the American Sunday School Union was a direct rebuke of the evangelical alliance. The Pennsylvania assembly wished the clergy to instill morality in the people, but not to instruct them in politics.

Because churches owned property and had disputes involving the civil peace, the state created a jurisprudence to settle differences. It had to determine whether it had any legal responsibility when churches divided over theology. The legislature decided that religious institutions helped unify the state and thus should be encouraged. So the state decided not to tax church buildings, to exempt ministers from the militia, to forbid all unnecessary labor on the Sabbath, and to require state officials to believe in the existence of a future state of rewards and punishments. Like the oaths and affirmations used in courts, such beliefs would protect the Commonwealth against atheists, who could not be trusted to act responsibly. The courts, the politicians, and the clergy advocated both a strict separation of church and state and a pattern of accommodation. Although their lack of consistency occasioned little comment, religious liberty remained a potentially politically divisive issue because the citizens did not agree on what constituted correct moral behavior.

Chapter 9 shows how a sizeable number of Roman Catholic immigrants and the creation of a public school system forced Pennsylvanians to redefine the relationship of the Protestant churches to public institutions. The result was a major riot that showed how misleading was the claim that Pennsylvania enjoyed perfect religious liberty. The Catholics then created a parochial school system that allowed them to teach what they saw as the only true Christianity. The Protestants continued to use the public schools to promote what they defined as a nondenominational Christianity designed to foster morality.

With the exception of liabilities for pacifists and legality for the theater, William Penn could have felt comfortable with Pennsylvania's patterns of religious liberty in 1860. The Commonwealth before the Civil War bore little resemblance to the holy experiment initiated by Penn and the Quakers. Presbyterians, Roman Catholics, Lutherans, German Reformed, and Methodists each outnumbered the sectarians. Pluralism, two Great

Awakenings, and denominationalism reduced Penn to a monument and Friends to an anachronism. The politics of factions and trade and agricultural patterns of the colony before 1776 had virtually no similarity to the parties and factories of the state. Independence, republicanism, and democracy created a new political vocabulary just as antislavery, temperance, and penitentiaries transformed the moral world. There might have been a corresponding metamorphosis in religious liberty. Yet, judging by institutions and ideology, there was extraordinary continuity in ideal and practice.

In 1860, as in 1700, Pennsylvania remained committed to the legal equality of all denominations, minimal religious tests to hold office, separation of church and state, freedom of belief, and autonomy for the institutional churches. There was no tithe, no establishment, no persecution for religious practice so long as the peace was not disturbed. Pennsylvanians still expected their legislators to be religious men and to use the law to discourage vice and encourage morality. The courts assumed that natural law as reflected in Christianity undergirded the law of the land. Blasphemy, profane swearing, drunkenness, and desecrating the Sabbath were illegal acts.

Before 1850 the rest of the nation caught up to Pennsylvania on religious freedom; or, perhaps it would be more accurate to say, Pennsylvania stood still while the other states continued to evolve. The result was that before 1770 the colony's religious liberty was famous; in 1900 the state's blue laws were famous. Even when the Commonwealth's courts cited its distinctive heritage, the resulting decision was the same as in New York or Massachusetts. Except for its law denying Catholic bishops the right to own church property, there was little singularity to Pennsylvania's treatment of legal disputes within or between denominations. All states had some kind of Sunday law, though Pennsylvania's was more stringent. Americans everywhere opposed persecution for religious belief, tax support for churches, government involvement in purely religious matters, and direct exercise of political power by churches or clergy. Their consensus on religious liberty left room for debate on the many moral issues at the intersection of religion and politics: alcohol, divorce, the family, aid for parochial schools, prayer in public schools, the Sabbath.

The Pennsylvania patterns of mutual support and separation of church and state created before the Civil War endured until the mid-twentieth century. After World War II the United States Supreme Court declared that the traditional Pennsylvania understanding of religious liberty violated the First Amendment. The Court applied rigorously the part of the definition of freedom of conscience that requires separation of government from religion as both an institution and system of belief. The inconsistencies in the practices of Pennsylvanians are no longer legal. Both supporters and opponents of the Court's decisions need to understand that accommodation and separation are firmly rooted in the past. Even then, controversy over whatever pattern prevailed in the state was endemic, and political power, rather than abstract ideology, normally determined actions. Pennsylvanians thought Christian values so important that they were willing to ignore or coerce the nonreligious minority. In the 1990s, as in the 1680s, whatever stance a state takes or does not take on religious-moral issues will be offensive to many. The dilemma of guaranteeing freedom for religious practice and liberty from religious persecution is perennial.

CHAPTER I

The Creation of Religious Liberty
in Early Pennsylvania

William Penn is commonly ranked among the heroes of American history
for his contribution to religious freedom. Such an emphasis is eminently
justified, for, as one historian recently argued, a consistent political theme
in Penn's life was his opposition to persecution for religion and attempts
to gain toleration.[1] The story of Pennsylvania begins with the early Quakers' struggle against persecution in England. In the 1670s Penn's efforts to
transform that struggle politically and intellectually bore fruit in the
Frame of Government and early laws of Pennsylvania. Penn only began
the process, for the initial history of religious freedom in the colony is a
convoluted story, which involved the proprietor, the English government, Quaker settlers, and adherents of other faiths.

The experiment in Pennsylvania shows that implementing religious
liberty required complicated adjustments in ideas and institutions: the
rights of a religious majority and minorities, the limits of moral legislation, the property rights of churches, the privileges of the clergy, and the
relations among denominations. The theme of this chapter is that while
Penn initiated the move toward religious freedom, circumstances as well
as ideology created the final pattern.

In England before 1660 the Quaker demand for an end to persecution
rested upon the belief that the focus or seat of religion came from the
conscience. True religion was very much an inward, though not a subjective, matter. God only was Lord of conscience and to erect any external
authority in this sphere would be to subject God to a lesser entity. For
early Friends the spiritual return of Christ meant that any physical element in religion was a nonessential; therefore, any organic or corporal
control of religious impulses by the state (or church) was of the devil.[2]
Spiritual impulses are governed only by spiritual means.

A crucial question from outsiders looking at early Friends was: What
did they mean by spiritual matters? The example of the Ranters was at

hand, a group who started with essentially the same principles as Quakers, and ended by repudiating marriage, the moral law, and property because all actions were permitted to the elect under the governance of the spirit of God.[3] From the beginnings of their movement, Friends rejected the conclusions of Ranterism and insisted upon the necessity of moral actions and rights of property, but the Quaker critique of injustices in contemporary English society made conservatives suspicious.[4] Even without the radicalism, Quaker ideas could gain acceptance only in a narrow range of sectarian thought. Arguments for toleration resting upon the purely spiritual nature of religion could not attract Anglicans or Presbyterians, whose traditional doctrines included the necessity of outward means of grace such as preaching, sacraments, the authority of the visible church, and the linkage between church and commonwealth. If Quakers were to obtain the right to exist legally after 1660, they would have to find arguments for religious liberty not based upon inward spiritual authority.

Penn and other second-generation Friends did not have to look far for wide-ranging discussions of religion and the state. Since the breakdown of royal authority and continuing through the entire period of the English Commonwealth, religious and political leaders had conducted a debate on liberty of conscience.[5] William Penn's contribution to the continuing debate was to combine several ideas, whose sources cannot be isolated with any precision, and to express them vigorously in the pamphlet warfare.[6] For our purpose the origins of his ideas are not as important as the result of his blending of theological, political, historical, and utilitarian arguments.

Like earlier Quakers, Penn found the source of religion in direct revelations of God within the conscience, but he also saw conscience as the seat of intellect and reason. The result was a blurring of the distinction between the divine light *in* conscience, and natural reason and thought, which were products *of* conscience. The shift was subtle but crucial, for beliefs became not spiritual but mental products and toleration could be based upon intellectual freedom. Conscience cannot be coerced, because reason and intellect cannot be. "A Christian implies a Man, and a Man implies conscience and understanding."[7] Persecuting a person for reading and believing the Scriptures was destructive of reason and Protestantism. By making spirit less theocentric, Penn linked toleration to an emerging rationalism.

Before 1660 Friends had sought to emphasize their distinctive beliefs, but now Penn attempted to minimize differences with other Protestants in an effort to gain toleration. His goal required defining what was essential in religion and necessitated leaving out a great many beliefs and practices to arrive finally at a stripped down faith in the interest of peace.

After the Restoration of Charles II, unity among Anglicans and Presbyterians in a comprehensive body appeared a realizable goal to many in each tradition, but neither church dreamed of accepting that Quakers were actually Christian.[8] Penn's strategy was to list certain beliefs on which all Christians agreed, and to ignore sacraments, church government, and ritual upon which there could be no unity. For Penn, the essence of religion was reverence for Scripture, faith in God and Christ, and virtuous or moral living.[9] Proof for his reductionist model of religion came from scriptural citations and postulates of reason and natural law, using the implicit assumption that dictates of God, nature, and intellect must agree.

At first Penn was not inclined to grant the right of religious freedom to Roman Catholics, because he believed that religion was based upon persecution, superstition, and popery, and that such practices were incompatible with true Christianity. Penn did not mellow in his view of the perverted nature of Catholicism, but in the belief that peaceful adherents of that religion should have the right to worship. In 1678, before Parliament, when defending himself against the charge of being Catholic, Penn showed how broad his viewpoint of civil rights had become:

I would not be mistaken, I am far from thinking it fit that *Papists* should be whipped for their consciences, because I exclaim against the injustice of whipping *Quakers* for *Papists:* No, for though the hand, pretended to be lifted up against them, hath ... lit heavy upon us, and we complain; yet we do not mean, that any should take a fresh aim at them, or that they must come in our room; for we must give the liberty we ask, and cannot be false to our principles ... for we ... would have none suffer for a truly sober and conscientious dissent on any hand.[10]

Citizenship was not only the birthright of all Englishmen, but a natural right for all who supported the government, lived peacefully, strengthened the realm by hard work, and agreed on fundamental Christian truths.[11] Government originated to protect property, and persecution for religion, which included fines and imprisonment, subverted the foundation of government by attacking property. Property and liberty of conscience were natural rights, and, by a selective reading of English history and law, Penn proved the inseparable linkage of these two rights.[12]

If the historical, scriptural, theological, and natural rights arguments failed to persuade, Penn's utilitarian argument offered a different approach. It was based upon two experiences. One was that all the turmoil over religion and persecution of Quakers had not worked. The realm was still not united religiously and the Society of Friends continued to gain members. The other utilitarian argument looked at the contribution of dissenters to the wealth and prosperity of England. These people by their

hard work and moral living strengthened the kingdom; persecution reduced their families to want and weakened the nation.[13]

Penn designed his tracts on toleration for immediate problems of persecution of his fellow Quakers and did not settle or address the long-range
issue of the role of religion in the state. He did not grapple, as had early
Friends, with the possibility of granting civil rights to the heathen or
doing away completely with an established church linked to the state,
because such conditions did not appear to be realistic possibilities. He
advocated toleration, not separation of church and state or complete
religious liberty, and undergirding his argument was the assumption – a
commonplace in Reformed theology – that God instituted government
and that the church and the state must foster piety and virtue. Consequently, when confronted with the issues of Quaker meeting and state in
his new colony, Penn had never considered the implications stemming
from his ideas.

Penn took account of the wishes of various groups in providing for
religion in Pennsylvania. The charter stipulated that the colony's laws
must be "consonant with reason" and "neare as conveniently" to the laws
of England. It also required that when twenty people petitioned the
bishop of London, an Anglican church could be founded.[14] More important than the charter in determining policies on religion were the comments of a number of leading citizens, mostly Friends, about the contents
of the *Frame of Government* and *Laws Agreed Upon in England*. We do
not know everyone consulted or how thoughtfully their advice was considered, but in answering a critique Penn listed prominent Quakers like
George Fox, George Whitehead, James Claypoole, Christopher Taylor as
the *Frame*'s supporters, and added that more than one hundred Friends
had approved of it.[15] The final products – the *Frame of Government*,
Laws Agreed Upon in England, and the Great Law drawn up in Chester in
December, 1682 – all had Penn's imprint, but also expressed the wishes
of many Friends.

An analysis of these three documents will show the expectations and
inconsistencies in the ideas of religious toleration. Buried in Article 35 of
the *Laws Agreed Upon in England*, but prominently displayed as Chapter
1 in the Great Law decided at Chester, was a provision for liberty of
conscience.[16] The law begins with a series of theological postulates: God
is the "only Lord of conscience" and "Author as well as Object of all
divine Knowledge Faith and Worship," who alone can "Enlighten the
Mind and perswade and Convince the Understanding of People." The
assumption here, clearly drawn from Quaker beliefs, is that all religious
knowledge is centered in the mind, which only God can control. This
language, however, could be interpreted in several ways. A Quaker could
understand enlightening the mind and convincing the understanding as

referring to the experience of the Inward Light of Christ. Here "all divine Knowledge" would refer to the entire Christian faith. An Anglican might see in the wording a series of clichés referring to rational religion or orthodox Christian doctrine. After all, God was in one sense "Author" of Scripture. Or, the "all" might refer only to the doctrines of God derived from a study of nature. Whatever the exact meaning, the conclusion is clear that the state cannot define religious faith.

After first insisting that all knowledge of God is from conscience and cannot be coerced, the law now required a confession of the being and attributes of God. Any individual living in the province who shall "Confess and acknowledge one Almighty God to be the Creatour and Upholder and Ruler of the World" and who "Professeth him or herselfe Obliged in conscience to live Peaceably and Justly under the Civil Government" shall not be molested for "his or her Conscientious Perswasion or Practice" or obliged to support a place of worship or minister against his persuasion. Penn might mitigate a seeming contradiction by insisting that the law here is requiring a confession based upon postulates of reason with which all right-thinking individuals could agree. The disparity between the first use of conscience and acknowledging God's governance of the world is not resolved.

The law then proceeds to use conscience, which earlier could not be coerced but whose results have just been announced, in two different, and perhaps incompatible, ways. The person is to oblige himself "in Conscience to Live Peaceably and Justly under the Civil Government." Here conscience means an unconditional and perpetual mental assent, or promise. The law finally guarantees that no one shall be molested "for his or her Conscientious Perswasion or Practice," which might limit permissible religious observances and customs to include only those sincerely held and/or divinely inspired, but could more likely include any religious belief or custom.

In England Penn had hoped that granting religious toleration would enable all Protestants to live peacefully together. His desire for religious harmony may have influenced the next clause in the law: that each person shall "freely and fully Enjoy his or her Christian Liberty without any Interuption or reflection and if any Person shall abuse or deride any Other for his or her Diferent Perswasion and Practice in Matters of Religion Such shall be Lookt upon as a disturber of the Peace and be punished accordingly." What exactly does this mean? Could it mean that no controversial writing on religion would be allowed in Pennsylvania? Or that the generally Quaker population was not to be disturbed by other religious groups? Or that each religious group could worship in peace? Considering the Friends had used the right of conscience to criticize other religions, the phrase is a curious example of potential censorship in the law designed to deny anyone such a right. When Pennsylvania Quakers did experience an acrimonious schism is the 1690s, this phrase might have been used to imprison the dissenters. The phrase was at best vaguely worded, and Penn's later revisions of the law omitted it entirely. Still, the proprietor continued to insist that one function of government was to preserve peace among various religious groups, although his instructions to Lieutenant Governors John Blackwell and John Evans did not specify how this was to be done.[17]

An unusual feature of the law is the emphasis upon the religious rights of both men and women. In several places the "his and her Conscientious Perswasion" emphasis is explicit. Quakers insisted on the religious equality of women, who had the same spiritual gifts as men. Singling out women for special mention is probably an echo of the fact that women could be ministers, and Penn wanted to guarantee their equality under the law.

In the preamble to the first *Frame of Government,* Penn argued that government had a sacred function, not to bring men salvation, but to stop evil actions and to foster good habits. Government not only exercised a check on sin but could legislate acts of compassion and charity to aid virtuous men and women. "Christian and Civil Liberty" were juxtaposed against licentiousness and "Unjust Practices."[18] The law on toleration concluded with an exhortation that liberty was not to be used as a cloak for "Looseness Irreligion and Atheism," and the means for preventing such were keeping the Sabbath (because of the example of the early church and need for rest but not because it was a holy day), through refraining from toil, engaging in worship, and reading Scriptures. The connection between Sunday observance and religious liberty was tenuous and in both the *Laws Agreed Upon in England* and the 1705 statute on toleration such provisions were kept separate.[19]

The 1681 statute of toleration did not say that there could be no religious establishment, but only provided for liberty in worship and not paying taxes or tithes to a form of worship one did not profess. Did Penn believe that a voluntary religious establishment was compatible with freedom of conscience? It would be surprising if he did not. English Friends and other dissenters after 1688 aimed at modifying the tithe law, but not disestablishing the Church of England.[20] Penn's controversies with the Crown over the legislative standing of Quaker practices before 1712 give no indication that he ever understood the distinctiveness of Pennsylvania's religious pattern enough to create a new theory of the relationship of religion to the state. During negotiations with the Crown over selling the right to government of the colony, the Board of Trade asked Penn what "Liberty of Conscience" meant. Penn's answer was, "I mean, not only that relating to worship, but education, or Schools, a

Coercive Ministeriall maintainance the Militia."[21] In other documents, he added the right of Friends to "any Civill employment but Governor," "To Marry according to our way and method," "To be exempted from Militia Services and charges thereof So as well watch and Ward in times of trouble," and the use of affirmations rather than oaths. Penn admitted that the assembly could pass a law for voluntary support of ministers and churches but that "no person or persons shall be bound by the Act or Acts, Vote or Votes of any Majority but only by his her or their own free consent."[22] Here Penn seems to be arguing that a noncoercive establishment of the Church of England in Pennsylvania was not incompatible with religious liberty. Penn never discussed the far-reaching implications required by the legal equality of all churches.

Friends in England, when complaining that the government persecuted innocent Friends while ignoring guilty evil-doers, had postulated maxims for the foundation of laws. Robert Barclay insisted that no man pleading the right of conscience should be allowed to "do anything contrary to the moral and perpetual statutes generally acknowledged by all Christians."[23] Penn argued that certain crimes — murder, adultery, theft, and perjury — were against the ends of both government and religion. The magistrate could foster "general and practical religion" or the "ten commandments, or moral law, and Christ's sermon on the mount", and his actions would make men "fitter for government."[24] On other occasions, in enumerating a series of "crimes," Penn argued that the state's responsibility encompassed not opinions but actions. "To be drunk, to whore, to be voluptuous, to game, swear, curse, blaspheme and profane ... These are sins against nature; and against government, as well as against the written laws of God."[25]

Only the concept of sin against government requires explanation. Penn argued that government was strengthened by hard work, the good health of subjects, and the wealth produced by such industrious and healthy citizens. Debauchery, however, led to idleness, improvidence, and poverty requiring eventually charity and weakening the strength of the nation. It was in the "interest" of government to suppress vices.[26]

In the *Laws Agreed Upon in England*, Penn had listed a number of moral offenses that would be punished. The Great Law drawn up in Chester in 1682 expanded this moral code. Commentators have often noticed the puritanical nature of early Pennsylvania laws; indeed, one of the sources for these statutes was the laws of New York, which had drawn upon the statutes of New England.[27] The Great Law had strong statements against drinking, swearing, defamation, fighting, "rude and Riotus" sports including stage plays, bullbaits and cockfights, and illegal pernicious games including "Cards, Dice Lotterys."[28]

Neither Penn nor the colonists saw these laws as infringing upon freedom of conscience. Evidently, these laws were popular at least among the assemblymen, for they were passed again with only minor changes in 1700. When many were vetoed by the Crown in 1705, the assembly made the necessary adjustments and passed them again. After some further modifications in language, the Crown accepted most of them.

There were certain laws, however, whose consistency with religious toleration is more dubious. These laws had no analogue in the Duke of York's code, but grew out of Quaker testimonies. No oaths of any kind were permitted in the colony. English statutes forbade oaths in common speech, but Quakers had also refused to swear in court and in Pennsylvania made all testimony in trials and qualifications for citizenship and office-holding by a solemn declaration.[29] In England, Quakers had borne a testimony against the pagan names of the days of the week and months, and in Pennsylvania legislated that a scriptural or numerical listing would be used, although no penalty was given for nonobservance. Quakers had a testimony against drinking in the health of, because it led to drunkenness and false praise, and such toasts were made illegal. The Quaker marriage procedure was made standard practice. In a marriage ceremony a couple, in the presence of witnesses, took solemn vows. No provision for a minister was included.[30]

Early Pennsylvania laws also ignored normal English practices. No statutes allowed churches corporate existence; that is, the right to hold property. None of the criminal laws made any mention of benefit of clergy, a medieval right that allowed those who could read and write certain alleviations from punishment. Most significant, the early laws mention nothing about fortifications or defense. A comparison with the 1683 laws of East Jersey shows the difference.

In the 1680s the proprietors of East Jersey included Quakers like Penn, Robert Barclay, Thomas Rudyard, Edward Billing, Robert Turner, and Ambrose Rigge, and also a substantial number of non-Quakers. This religious diversity showed in the pattern of settlement. The Fundamental Constitutions of 1683 attempted to allow pacifist Quakers and those who believed in military force to exist together without the denial of rights to either group. Those who objected to bearing arms would not have to do so and would provide substitutes, but those who supported defense could do so in a legal manner.[31] The government would form a committee of six proprietors and three freemen who believed in defense. This committee was to propose to the Great Council measures for keeping internal peace and external defense. Because the pacifists on the Great Council might obstruct all military matters, such proprietors could agree on defense issues by divorcing themselves from their Quakerism and "to speak after the manner of men, and abstractly from a man's perswasion in matters of religion." Operating in this fashion they would decide whether it was "convenient" and "suitable" for the inhabitants to build forts, and whether such defense was necessary. Two-thirds of the council and twelve of the proprietors had to agree. If they did, then the conduct of the military measures or war would be entrusted to the original committee who believed in defense. The pacifists would have no responsibility for the actual conduct of the war. The colonists who believed in military force would pay all its costs; those who were pacifists would then "bear so much in other charges, as may make up that portion in the general charge of the Province." The law was a fascinating attempt, however unworkable in practice, to guarantee the civil and religious liberties of two groups.

The contrast between East and West Jersey is striking. The West Jersey Concessions and Agreements ignore the subject of war and contain detailed instructions on conciliation of grievances. In 1676 a statement by Penn and two other proprietors clarified any ambiguity on the possibility of using force to guarantee "liberty of conscience." Although the proprietors would "never consent to any the least violence on conscience; yet it was never designed to encourage any to expect by force of arms to have liberty of conscience fenced against invaders thereof."[32] People with scruples against war founded and settled West Jersey, and no provisions would be made for defense. The *Frame of Government* and early laws of Pennsylvania on this subject conform to the West Jersey, not the East Jersey, pattern of government. Pennsylvania would have no militia, no fortifications, and no war; inhabitants who thought otherwise would have to acquiesce to Quaker domination.

Clearly, the case can be made that Quakers wanted to transport the English church pattern to America, with major modifications. In Pennsylvania, there would be no legal church establishment, no tithes or forced maintenance of any minister, and no military appropriations, but the Society of Friends would occupy a position comparable to that of the Church of England. Friends would determine the laws and government and the tone of the society. Others would be welcome, but they would have to be governed by Quaker principles. The unwillingness of the inhabitants of Delaware to accede to such Quaker domination was a factor in the separation of the two colonies.

The *Frame* and early laws provided for religious liberty, but the settlers had to define in practice the relation between the meeting and the state. Toleration would be tested and modified by the virtual Quaker monopoly of political power in the 1680s, a schism in the 1690s, Penn's temporary loss of the right to govern, the opposition by members of the Church of England, and the scrutiny of the English government.

In Pennsylvania important governmental officials were often influential

Friends, and Quakers saw no incongruity in a minister serving as assemblyman or justice of the peace. Because Friends had no conception of a paid clergy, a member who was a minister – whose gift for speaking in meeting was recognized as fostering God's presence – could engage in business or hold any position in government. Penn moved easily between his responsibilities as proprietor and minister. His first deputy governor, Thomas Lloyd, was a minister as were several members of the council, including Samuel Jennings and Griffith Owen. Every early assembly included at least one recognized Quaker minister. Ministers and influential Friends played a disproportionate role in controlling the Society of Friends and the local government of Pennsylvania. The colony in its formative period was controlled by members of the religious group who had the only organized worship[33] and the overwhelming preponderance of the colonists as members. Those who were not Quakers had no choice but to follow Friends' practices. That the council would even entertain the suggestion that all men be limited to two sorts of clothing, one kind for winter and another for summer wear, shows the presumption that the Quaker testimony on plain dress could be made universal.

During the first years of the colony, the Society of Friends appeared to have made the transition from England to America relatively easily. A structure of monthly, quarterly, and yearly meetings for men and women, a special meeting for ministers, and contacts with other meetings in England and America were institutionalized. The local meetings had mechanisms for preventing deviance by Quakers from a set of norms, some of which were also mandated by law.

In this period a schism erupted among Quakers, which severely tested the concept of religious liberty and the relationship between the meetings and the magistrates. The disagreement began over a theological disagreement between George Keith, a well-educated and prominent Quaker minister, and other less sophisticated Friends. Before it ended, a substantial minority of Friends in New Jersey and Pennsylvania declared disunity, a vigorous pamphlet war exposed several Quaker theological tenets and political practices to close scrutiny, and the bitter dispute shattered the religious unity of the colony.

The issue of religious liberty emerged when the magistrates arrested George Keith, his supporter John McComb, and Andrew Bradford, the only printer in the colony. The Society of Friends had contributed to the purchase of Bradford's type and guaranteed the purchase of copies of tracts. Now Bradford was printing in opposition and there was no law of religious censorship in Pennsylvania. The council had, however, previously warned Bradford against printing materials designed to cause religious controversy and had suppressed an almanac that referred to the proprietor as "Lord Penn."[34] There were laws against belittling magistrates, and so the magistrates seized Bradford's type (an effective method of silencing him) and charged Keith and McComb with seditious libel. The magistrates supposedly libeled were prominent ministers (also important politically) who had been active in opposing Keith; the spoken "libels" had occurred in a Friends' meeting, the printed one in religious pamphlets.[35]

In the trial Keith claimed liberty of conscience, insisting that not only were the supposed libels true statements, but they were spoken against ministers in a religious dispute. According to Pennsylvania laws, the state had no jurisdiction in such a controversy. The prosecution cited a passage in a pamphlet in which Samuel Jennings, a member of the council but also a minister and clerk of both Philadelphia Monthly Meeting and the Meeting for Ministers, was accused of prideful insolence in his capacity as a judge.[36] Keith's strictures about the incompatibility of Quaker ministers acting as magistrates, notably in trying to seize a smuggler named Babbitt and in administering capital punishment, seemed to the prosecution to be destructive of the foundation of government. Whether or not Samuel Jennings actually served as one of the judges, he was present and consulted with the other judges, who insisted that the three men were not being tried for their religious views but for their political attacks on magistrates.[37] Resurrecting a statute of Charles II ignored by Quakers in England and never used before or since in America, the magistrates indicted Bradford, the printer, because his pamphlet did not contain the name of its producer.[38] The judges, jury, and prosecution contained Quakers, and Keith's attempts to challenge jurors who were Friends were overruled. Keith's account of the trial reminds one of the Penn-Mead trial in England, only this time the Quakers came close to playing the role of religious persecutors.[39] Keith and McComb were convicted and fined £5, which they do not appear to have paid; Bradford's jury, in spite of some attempts at coercion, could reach no verdict. Still, the government kept the press until Governor Benjamin Fletcher had it returned.

Keith soon returned to England and Bradford moved to New York. The Crown's appointment of Fletcher as governor in 1692 ended any further moves against the Keithians by magistrates. Friends in England rebuked Pennsylvania Quakers for their heavy-handed actions in civil court against religious opponents. The adherents of Keith went diverse ways. Some followed Keith eventually into the Church of England; others became Baptists; a few remained separatist or Christian Quakers; most eventually rejoined the Friends. From this time on, the colony of Pennsylvania was no longer a Quaker enclave, but contained a wide variety of religious persuasions who claimed the rights of liberty of conscience.

In the *Laws Agreed Upon in Chester,* all officeholders had to profess belief in the divinity of Christ and the authority of the Old and New

Testaments.[40] Although Jews were thereby excluded, all Christians were eligible, including Roman Catholics. After the Glorious Revolution of 1688 drove out the Catholic James II, France and England began a long war and the temper in England became rabidly anti-Catholic. Parliament's Act of Toleration (1689) applied only to orthodox Protestants. The Crown's instructions to Governor Fletcher required that members of the Pennsylvania Assembly and Council declare their allegiance to the Protestant monarchs and abjure Roman Catholicism. In 1693 Fletcher allowed Quakers to affirm rather than to swear – not, he insisted, as a right but an act of grace.[41]

In 1696 the colonists drew up another *Frame of Government* that limited service in government to Protestants.[42] The law code of 1700–1 omitted the 1681 statute on religious qualifications for officeholding. The law on attests specified the kinds of affirmations necessary for a wide variety of positions, but did not specify what kinds of oaths or affirmations were necessary for members of the council and assembly. Penn did not end the custom of requiring some kinds of tests of assemblymen and members of the council, and he was present in Pennsylvania in 1701, when they were administered.[43] Charles Stillé argued that only declarations of loyalty to Penn and the Crown were required, and that theoretically, therefore, a Roman Catholic was still eligible for office.[44] But Penn bitterly protested in 1703, when, after the death of Governor Andrew Hamilton, Colonel Robert Quary persuaded or compelled members of the government to obey an Order in Council to abjure Roman Catholicism and extended the English loyalty oaths to Pennsylvania. Penn's complaints did not mention the disqualification of Catholics from holding office (there were few Catholics in Pennsylvania at the time), but focused on the violation of charter rights.[45] Extending the stipulation on oaths contained in an act of Parliament not mentioning America and requiring more rigorous declarations of colonists than were required in England were dubious interpretations of English prerogatives. The colonists did not object and passed a law in 1705 requiring a renunciation of Roman Catholicism and a declaration of loyalty to the monarch that, with modification, remained in effect throughout the rest of the colonial period.[46]

The power of the English government to shape the pattern of Pennsylvania's religious and moral customs was most vividly demonstrated in the reaction to the Pennsylvania laws of 1700–1. Penn's grant of a new *Frame of Government* in 1701 necessitated passing again a complete system of laws and most of the 1682 Great Law of Chester was repassed. This time the newly formed Board of Trade insisted upon exercising the charter provision that all of the colony's laws be reviewed within five years. In 1705 the Board acted and of the 114 laws passed (of which 105 were submitted), only 50 survived. Many of those accepted concerned only local affairs such as the statutes on boats and canoes and the sale of lands to Indians.

The Board's objections were various: Some statutes deviated too far from the laws of England, some were poorly worded, some were too strict, some were too liberal, some did not conform to Anglican religious standards. The Pennsylvania statute allowing divorce was disallowed because it did not conform to the ecclesiastical law of England. Requiring single persons guilty of fornication to marry "may be unreasonable, where young men may be drawn in by lewd women."[47] Specific Quaker customs like outlawing drinking to the health of and use of the plain style of calendar were "insignificant and not fit to be laid before the Crown." The acts against riotous sports, plays, and games, were too vaguely drawn and prohibited "some innocent sports" without reason.[48]

Penn's Act of Toleration, which he declared in 1700–1 a fundamental law that could not be revised, did not survive. The attorney general complained that the law had "no regard" for the "Christian religion," did not specify the limits of allowable "conscientious practices" and ignored the English law requiring Quakers "to profess faith in God and in Jesus Christ his Eternal Son, the True God and in the Holy Spirit one God blessed for evermore, and to acknowledge the scriptures of Old and New Testament."[49] The provision against blasphemy was one of the few laws approved by the English government.

Penn and his appointed deputy governors advised remodeling the laws to take cognizance of the English objections. If the colony was to have any legal code, drastic changes were a necessity. Even when the English attorney-general overstepped his boundaries, the colonists now acquiesced. For example, the new statute of religious toleration incorporated the phrases insisted upon by the attorney-general. The preamble to the bill was the same as in the 1701 act, but only those willing to make the orthodox declaration of Christian faith were guaranteed religious liberty and freedom from compulsory tithes.[50] In England Quaker ministers had to accept such a test, but in Pennsylvania the statute applied to all persons. Quakers in England and America were too busy trying to prove that they were orthodox enough to qualify under the Act of Toleration to protest against the English impositions upon the liberal declarations of William Penn.[51] Still, the 1705 act, which allowed all Christians freedom to worship, meant that Roman Catholics were included and that mass could be publicly celebrated in Pennsylvania.

The stringent moral code was refined, toned down slightly, and repassed without distinctive Quaker emphases. Castration for rape and forcing marriage for fornication, neither of which had been enforced in Pennsylvania, disappeared from the code. The English government was willing to accept most of the new laws, and the "puritanical" basis of the moral code was more important to the assembly than liberal statutes that applied to Jews, Socinians, and freethinkers, none of whom probably lived in Pennsylvania anyway.

A bitter and protracted controversy over religious toleration centered on Friends' refusal to swear. Quaker opposition to oaths influenced legislation on qualifications for office, naturalization, and courts.[52] Under the initial laws no one was even allowed to take an oath, and in any instance in which an oath might otherwise be required, the person had only to solemnly affirm or declare. In 1683 the law specified that if anyone was willing to "Solemnly Testifye as in the Sight of an All-seeing God" that he had been threatened with bodily harm, the person threatening could be bound to the peace. The same formula was used in the 1693 Petition of Right given to Governor Fletcher, but a 1693 law on giving evidence did not mention the name of the deity.[53] Pamphlets written in England stated, however, that witnesses in Pennsylvania were required to affirm "in the presence of God."[54] In the law passed during Penn's second visit, those who desired could take an oath if a person willing to administer it was available.

In England in the aftermath of the Glorious Revolution, Friends persuaded a reluctant Parliament, in 1696, to permit an affirmation in courts of chancery and exchequer, but such affirmations were not accepted for jury duty, in criminal cases, or as a qualification for public office. The wording of the affirmation, requiring a declaration "in the presence of God, the witness to the truth of what I say" was offensive to some Friends.[55] The provisions of the act did not, of course, extend to the colonies.

In Pennsylvania the dispute over the use of affirmations became complicated by the battles between the governors and assemblies over establishing courts, and Anglicans and Quakers over the control of the colony. Pennsylvania Anglicans remained few in number but had the backing of the bishop of London, a revitalized Church of England, and of royal officials in the colony and in London who sought tighter control of American governments. The resulting battle occasioned twenty-five years of intricate political maneuverings and threatened the existence of the unofficial Quaker establishment in Pennsylvania.[56]

The conflict involved the meaning of religious liberty to two groups with diametrically opposed views on the necessity of oaths. The Quaker position was that courts could and should function without oaths. No Friend should be forced to take an oath, and, equally important, no Quaker justice should be required to tender an oath. Yet Quakers, because they established the colony and were the most numerous religious group, had the right to serve on juries and to be justices. Because county courts operated with a minimum quota of three judges and most magis-

trates were Friends, particularly in Chester and Bucks counties, the Anglicans felt that justice could not be achieved because criminals could
escape testifying under oath.

The opposition's stance was complicated because in addition to feeling
dissatisfied with the quality of justice obtained in Quaker courts, some
wished to use oaths to force Penn to surrender the government and to
bar Quakers completely from government. Petitions against affirmations
came from the clergy and vestries of Anglican churches in Pennsylvania
and, in one case, from Burlington, New Jersey. Anglicans saw the growth
and prosperity of their church as requiring an establishment. They witnessed the disqualification of Friends from holding office in Maryland and
the Carolinas by requiring an oath of office, and saw the close relationship between the loss of Quaker political power and laws establishing the
Church of England in these colonies. When Maryland (briefly) and New
Jersey became royal colonies it seemed that Pennsylvania might be
next.[57]

Anglicans did not wish to establish the church in Pennsylvania just for
political purposes. Both Anglican clergy and laity, a few of whom were
former Keithians or converted by Keith on his return in 1702, thought
that Friends were really not Christians. If Quakers were not papists (a
persistent rumor in England that occasionally surfaced in Pennsylvania),
perhaps they were Socinians or deists. None of these groups qualified for
the benefits of the English Act of Toleration. Pennsylvania Anglicans believed in religious toleration equal to practices in England. There Quakers could worship, but not hold political office, and the government
distrained property from dissenters to pay tithes.

Pennsylvania Quakers and Anglicans accused each other of aiming at a
religious establishment and attempting to bar the other from serving in
government. Penn attempted to recruit a few Anglicans so there would
be one non-Quaker justice in each county court, but this did not alleviate
the opposition.[58] Quakers relied upon Penn's proven abilities as a lobby-
ist and repassed laws similar to those vetoed in England. Because there
was a time interval of up to five years before laws had to be submitted to
the Privy Council, Quaker justices could function, at least during these
intervals. Anglicans who refused to accept an oath before one justice
rather than the entire court attempted, successfully at times, to shut
down the entire court system, and then complained to England about the
anarchy in the colony.[59]

In 1711 the assembly yielded enough to guarantee that all who wished
an oath should be allowed to take one. In 1714 the assembly passed two
different affirmations, one using the name of God and one not, and the
king did not disallow the law using the name of God. Queen Anne in an
Order in Council had permitted affirmations to be substituted for oaths in

1702. Now a new difficulty emerged. The English Quaker affirmation act had to be renewed periodically. In 1715, when the act was made perpetual, the House of Lords passed an amendment extending provisions to all plantations, and the Commons accepted it.[60] If the English standards had been enforced in Pennsylvania, no Quaker could have held office, served on a jury, or witnessed in a criminal case. In spite of attempts by Anglicans in England and Pennsylvania to apply the 1715 law, the Privy Council ignored its provisions.[61]

With the accession of Robert Walpole to power and the loss of strength in England of the Tories, English Quakers obtained in 1722 an affirmation act requiring no naming of God and not extending to the colonies. In 1724 the Pennsylvania Assembly passed a statute using the same wording that, in spite of a token protest by churchmen, was accepted. In practice, Quakers obtained their right to conduct justice by affirmations; Anglicans obtained the right to have their oaths and the oaths of those who were not Friends required. County courts would be composed of representatives from several religious traditions. Even before 1724, neither side talked of miscarriages of justice by the custom of accepting affirmations.[62] The affirmation controversy eased because the British government was not willing to force Friends out of office in Pennsylvania, and experience in the colony showed that few inconveniences resulted from the Quaker testimony.

A colony accepting religious toleration needed to define the legal status of churches and clergy. The *Frames* and early laws ignored the subject. Official recognition that liberty of conscience had resulted in more than one religious group came slowly. In 1690 and 1701 the assembly provided that the records of "any Religious Society" (notice the avoidance of the word church) could serve as a legal record of birth, marriage, and death.[63] In 1693 Governor Fletcher objected to a statute regulating clandestine marriages as discriminating against Anglicans (there was at this date no organized Anglican church in Pennsylvania or Delaware). The revised marriage law required the posting of notice or banns, and specifically allowed a duly authorized Anglican "person" (not minister) to follow English rather than Pennsylvania statutes aimed at controlling secret marriages.[64] In 1697 this exemption was reworded to permit duly registered members of every religious society to marry, if the intended wedding received due publicity. A redrafted law in 1701 continued the exemption, but provided for a one-month notification of parents, etc., before the ceremony.[65] In spite of Anglican objections, the Privy Council accepted this law.

In neither the 1681 or 1701 codes of laws was any provision made for the ownership of church property. Members built meeting houses and churches and trustees acting on behalf of religious groups controlled lands and buildings, but no legal foundation existed for control of the property by the organization. When a special institution like the Quaker school in Philadelphia formed, William Penn granted it a special charter. In 1705 the assembly, worried that the property of dissenters needed the same protection as that of Anglicans, passed a bill empowering religious societies to "hold, buy and sell Lands" but the governor refused his assent because of adverse comment by local Anglicans, though he may have sent the proposal to England for comment. The assembly repeatedly requested the governor to approve the bill. In 1712 the assembly framed another law that attempted to meet previous objections. It applied only to religious societies and left out earlier clauses giving power to sell and alter title. Until 1714 the assembly and governor could not agree, and when a law did pass in Pennsylvania it was disallowed in England as potentially interfering with the rights of property. When the assembly drew up another bill, the governor returned it, saying that the previous act was vetoed in England and he could not approve it here.[66]

For fifteen years after 1715 there was no discussion of a bill entitling religious societies to own land. In 1730 the issue again became important, and involved Anglican and dissenters' property rights, only this time the conflict was with the Baptists. Originally, in 1695, Baptists and Presbyterians worshiped together in Philadelphia but, growing in strength, the Presbyterians managed to gain control of the building and insisted on using it alone. The Baptists at first had to be content with renting Anthony Morris' brew house, but in 1707 were invited to use the structure originally built for the Keithian, or Christian, Quakers. Title to this meetinghouse was vested in four of the Keithians, but there were no longer enough Christian Quakers to meet separately. The Baptists used the building for over twenty years and made no effort to clarify their title. All of the original trustees but one died, and he had become a member of Christ Church. Upon his death, it was discovered that his will deeded the property to the Anglicans. The Baptists charged that the Anglican rector had influenced the dying trustee to change his will and in 1730 appealed to the assembly for redress, claiming that the original trustees had all wished the Baptists to have the church. Perhaps because the Anglicans recognized that the Quaker-dominated assembly and courts would not be sympathetic and would use the issue against them, or because they wanted to avoid litigation, they offered to give up their claim for £50.[67]

The significance of the affair for religious liberty is this: in 1730–1 the assembly again took up the issue of the property rights of churches. Though the bill did not esentially change the law of 1714, this time it passed in Pennsylvania and England. For the first time, all Protestant religious societies were vested with rights, and, in essence, declared legally equal.[68]

If all churches were legally equal, were clergymen subject to the same jurisdiction as other citizens? The medieval concept of benefit of clergy, which had long lost its clerical content, was taken over from English law and incorporated in the 1718 criminal code. The bishop of London claimed jurisdiction over offenses committed by Anglican clergy in America. The case that raised this issue involved the rector of Christ Church.[69] On a Sunday morning in 1714 the Episcopalians of Philadelphia arrived at church to learn the distressing news that their minister had been imprisoned upon the complaint of two prominent Anglicans who had learned of his boast to two other men that he had seduced a council member's wife, the collector of customs' daughter, and another gentleman's wife. Later the rector denied all charges and claimed that it was not credible that he would have told such a tale to two men he scarcely knew. By statute, the case should have been tried in Pennsylvania by a civil jury, but Lieutenant-Governor Gookin, an Anglican and political opponent of the council member and collector of customs, released the rector from jail, suppressed the trial, and agreed with the clergyman's assertion that ecclesiastical courts had jurisdiction.[70] The Pennsylvania Assembly protested that the Governor had acted improperly.[71] Because no ecclesiastical court had any jurisdiction over a citizen of Pennsylvania in a criminal case, all citizens, including clergy, were equal before the law.

William Penn's experience of persecution prompted him to make religious liberty a salient feature of his new colony. For Penn and the first settlers toleration required the abolition of British practices like tithes, oaths, and church courts. Freedom of conscience also meant that distinctive Quaker customs on oaths, peace, marriage, and morality would receive the sanction of law. Ignoring other churches and any diversity of sentiment by Swedish settlers, the proprietor and his government created a refuge for Quakers. The result was a quasi or noncoercive Quaker establishment.

The Keithian schism, the founding of Anglican churches, and pressures from the Crown toned down the Quaker domination. The English government required restrictions on holding office, limitations on acceptable religion, oaths for those wanting to swear, and revision of stringent moral legislation. The Crown failed to obtain a militia act but resisted local Anglican efforts to force Friends out of office. Quakers in the assembly attempted to defend their distinctive testimonies in a series of statutes protecting the right of diversity and the equality of all Protestant churches. By 1725 the outlines of the Pennsylvania pattern of church and state were clear and accepted as a given by virtually all denominations.

The Pennsylvania pattern began with the theories of William Penn. There remained a Quaker tone to the government, but this rested upon the free election of Friends to the assembly. There were no feast or fast days proclaimed by the assembly (when the governors proclaimed special days, Friends refused to observe them and complained that they infringed on liberty of conscience) and, in contrast to New England, no election sermons discussed the religious or political significance of the colony. The government remained vigilant against a wide variety of moral offenses, because a dissolute people could preserve neither religious nor civil liberties. All denominations had legal equality; all enjoyed property rights; all kept registers of births and deaths and marriages. Because of royal restrictions, only Protestants had full liberty of conscience. Foreign Catholics could not legally become naturalized and hold property, but they could worship openly. Legal discrimination remained at the level of English policy, but in practice in Pennsylvania non-British Catholics owned property.

Why had Pennsylvania become the most tolerant colony in the New World? The Quaker heritage was important. Friends had experienced persecution in England and were determined to found a land in which such sufferings would not be repeated. Penn, more cosmopolitan than most other Quakers, became the founding father and his ideas became the heritage of generations of immigrants. To those who cherished his memory in the mid-eighteenth century, like Isaac Norris I and Christopher Saur, Penn stood for both civil and religious liberty. The Quakers' battles among themselves and with the Church of England also broke down restrictions. Friends learned to accept limitations on their power and Anglicans learned to accept a minority status. By 1725 both denominations learned to live with each other, to cooperate on certain issues, and to assert their differences in the context of a broader agreement on the function of religious values within the society. The British government, paranoid over Roman Catholics but sympathetic to Anglican and Quaker pressures, also helped foster the pattern of Protestant freedoms by balancing the demands of both groups. Finally, least important in the creation of toleration but of great ultimate significance in preserving such liberty, was the bewildering variety of religious sects and churches that populated eighteenth-century Pennsylvania. Attracted by toleration and enthusiastic about freedom, the laity created churches that enforced moral standards, trumpeted distinctive doctrines and practices, and rejoiced in the conditions of civil and religious liberty.

RELIGIOUS LIBERTY.

DEDICATED

TO THE

PEOPLE OF THE UNITED STATES

BY THE

ORDER B'NAI B'RITH

AND

ISRAELITES OF AMERICA.

"Religious Liberty," carved by Sir Moses Ezekiel, an American Jewish sculptor, and placed in Fairmount Park, Philadelphia, in 1876. It was moved to the mall on Independence Hall National Park in 1976. The group of figures represents liberty protecting religious freedom.

CHURCH THIRD AND ARCH:—Built in 1750.

Second Presbyterian Church, Philadelphia, traces its origins to George Whitefield and the Great Awakening. Gilbert Tennent served as pastor. Under its most famous nineteenth-century pastor, Albert Barnes, the church remained pro-revivalist and anti-slavery in the two major Presbyterian schisms.

Old Guinston, formerly Old Muddy Creek, Church, York County, was organized in 1754 as part of the Associate Presbyterian Church.

Merion Friends Meeting House, Lower Merion. The simplicity of Merion Meeting House, which dates from 1695, can be contrasted with the more elaborate city Presbyterian and Anglican churches.

Bethel African Methodist Episcopal Church, Philadelphia. Drawn on stone by W. L. Breton in July 1829. Richard Allen helped organize and became pastor, then bishop, of an independent denomination of African-American Methodists.

"Peaceable Kingdom," by Edward Hicks (1780–1849), a Quaker minister and artist whose many versions of the Peaceable Kingdom join scriptural prophecies of the millennium with a celebration of Penn's treaty with the Indians and a harmonious early Pennsylvania.

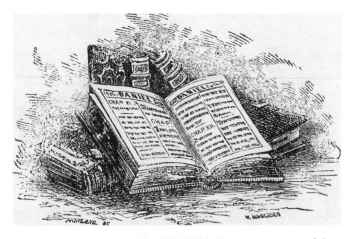

American Bible Society logo. The Bible Society was one of the many Protestant benevolent associations attempting to Christianize American society. By printing and distributing Bibles as economically as possible, it sought to provide a Bible for every citizen.

Burning of St. Michael's Church, on Wednesday afternoon, May 8.

West View, on Second street, with the Residence of the Rev. Mr. Donahue.

The burning of St. Michael's Church, Philadelphia, during a series of anti-Catholic riots that erupted in 1844 over Bible readings, prayers, and religious exercises in schools. Illustration from *A Full and Complete Account of the Late Awful Riots in Philadelphia* (Philadelphia: John Perry, 1844).

Nineteenth-century camp meeting. A Rider print.

Lucretia Mott (1793–1880), Quaker minister, advocate of women's rights, active in anti-slavery movement, critic of evangelical religion, defender of absolutist position on separating church and state.

John Ettwein (1721–1802), bishop of the Moravian Church and defender of pacifists in the American Revolution.

THE
GREAT CASE
OF
Liberty of Conscience
Once more Briefly
Debated & Defended,
BY THE
Authority of *Reason, Scripture,* and
Antiquity:

Which may ferve the Place of a General Reply to
fuch late Difcourfes, as have Oppos'd a
Tolleration.

The Authour *W. P.*

For whatfoever ye would that men fhould do unto you, that do you unto
them, Matth. 7. 22.
Render unto Cæfar, *the things that are* Cæfars; *and to* God, *the*
things that are Gods, Matth. 12. 27.

Printed in the Year, 1670.

Title page of William Penn, *The Great Case of Liberty of Conscience.*

William Smith (1727–1803), Provost of the College of
Philadelphia, Anglican minister, advocate of Proprietary Party
and military preparedness, supporter of having a bishop in
America. Portrait by Edward Dalton Marchant after Gilbert Stuart
original, 1871.

Ezra Stiles Ely (1786–1861),
Presbyterian minister of Old Pine
Street Church in Philadelphia,
supporter of Andrew Jackson,
and advocate in 1827 of a
Christian political party.

Francis Alison (1705–1779), Vice-
Provost of the College of Philadelphia,
"Old Light" Presbyterian minister, and
opponent of the Quaker party.

James Wilson (1742–1798), delegate to the federal and 1790 Pennsylvania constitutional conventions and Supreme Court Justice.

Benjamin Rush (1745–1813), universalist, opponent of religious tests and defender of religious liberty, social reformer, physician, and advocate of adoption of the federal and 1790 Pennsylvania constitutions.

Gilbert Tennent (1703–1764), "New Light" itinerant revivalist, minister of Second Presbyterian Church, Philadelphia, opponent of pacifism, and defender of religious liberty against the Covenanting Presbyterians.

CHAPTER II

Pacifism and Religious Liberty

Pacifists and proponents of the military used their rights to liberty of conscience in debates over the Quaker peace principles. Most of the fighting in the English civil war (though not the invasions of Ireland and Jamaica) ended before the birth of Friends in 1652, and circumstances did not prompt Quakers to arrive at a consistent policy of pacifism before the Restoration. Alan Cole, Wayne Spurrier, and Barry Reay have discovered examples of Friends advocating the use of force or serving in the army during the last years of the Commonwealth, but these should be balanced against the pronouncements by Fox and other leaders of the nonviolent approach of Friends.[1] The Quaker peace testimony became indelible only in 1660, and after the Restoration the policies of nonresistance, support of established authority, and no service in the military prevailed. Friends paid taxes to the government during war as a tribute to Caesar and a few weighty Friends affirmed a state's right to self-defense.[2]

The charter to William Penn gave him responsibility to "Levy muster and traine" men, the rights of a "Captaine-generall of any Army," and the ability "to make warr," but during the first years of the colony these provisions were ignored.[3] After the Glorious Revolution the imperial wars between England and France brought tensions to the New World, particularly to New England and New York. Penn lost his colony from 1692 to 1694 partially because of its defenseless state, and he had to accept responsibility for military preparedness to regain his control of government. Except for Penn, all the colony's governors after 1688 were non-Quaker, and beginning with Lieutenant Governor Blackwell (1688), each executive recommended to the assembly the creation of a militia and appropriations for fortifications. In 1693 the assembly's bill to create a militia passed through a second reading, but was defeated on the third reading.

The assembly in 1696, 1709, and 1711 voted funds only in response to specific commands from the English government, but never as much as was requested and not for direct military expenses. Governor Fletcher promised that the colony's money would not be "dipt in blood," but that kind of promise and the assembly's stipulations of using money to buy grain or aid Indians did not legally bind English authorities.[4] In 1711 the assembly entrusted the £2000 for the "Queen's use" to a committee instructed to make sure that no military expenditures resulted, and the funds had not been spent at the end of the war. The assembly consistently refused to send quotas of men to help invade Canada, to create a militia, or to erect fortifications of any kind. The attempts of Lieutenant Governors Hamilton and Evans to recruit a voluntary militia without statutory authority, based upon the powers granted by the charter, did not succeed.[5] The assembly refused to grant an exemption from participating in the watch as an incentive to volunteer, and few people showed up for drill. Evans' attempts in 1706 to frighten Quakers by spreading a rumor of a French invasion and in 1707 to establish a fort on the river in non-Quaker Delaware and then to tax Philadelphia's shippers to pay for it were total failures.[6]

The assembly's refusal to provide for any kind of defense for Pennsylvania occasioned a vigorous debate on the relationship of religion to government.[7] Thoughtful expositions came from various governors who attempted to persuade the assembly to create a militia. The governors relied upon a variety of arguments, both military and theological. Militarily, they pointed to the aggressiveness of the French, the rumors of French infiltration of neighboring Indian tribes, the numbers of foreigners living in Pennsylvania, the need to help English colonists elsewhere, the ease with which French or pirate ships could sail up the Delaware, the contributions of other colonies, and the lawfulness of the demands of the Crown. Self-defense was a natural right and the first duty of any government, even mentioned in the charter, was to provide for the protection of subjects. No governor objected to the conscientious scruples of Friends, but all insisted that Friends did not have the right to impose their practices and beliefs upon others. Anglicans argued that because Pennsylvania was a mixed colony and Delaware did not even have a Quaker majority, Friends had in essence denied religious freedom to others, and jeopardized human life and rights of property.[8] The assembly's failure to provide for defense was an infringement of an Anglican's liberty of conscience.

Occasionally, a governor would attack the assembly's stubbornness upon theological grounds. There were numerous Old and New Testaments texts that could be cited as justifying war and requiring obedience to governing authorities, in this case the English Crown. The golden rule required helping one's neighbor, but the Quakers, rather than helping their neighbors who lived in exposed frontiers, only left them more vulnerable to Indian attacks.[9] The best way to ensure peace was to have a strong defense. The logical corollary of the governors' positions, not drawn by them but insisted upon by Anglican leaders and agreed to by such Friends as James Logan, was the incompatibility of Quaker principles with the necessities of government.[10]

The assembly, controlled by Quakers throughout the period, answered the contentions of defense-minded opponents but never created a systematic definition of the Quaker peace testimony. First, Friends attempted to refute military arguments. A fort on the Delaware, in addition to being expensive for such a poor colony to build and maintain, would not stop ships from sailing around it. From Cape Henlopen to Philadelphia was a distance of over one hundred miles, and even a series of forts would not protect that area. The Delaware River Valley needed to be defended by sea, and providing ships was the responsibility of the home government. Penn's charter did not give him admiralty jurisdiction and the right to command or outfit ships on the high seas. Militia forces were not needed to protect the colony from hostile Indians, because the Indians in Pennsylvania were friendly and the assembly was willing to provide funds to keep them happy. A volunteer militia could be formed under provisions of the charter, and no legislative authority was necessary. Because few settlers were willing to join, the assembly found no strong desire by the inhabitants for such an institution. Besides, if pirates were to sail up the river, it would be better for the inhabitants to flee to the hinterlands rather than attempt to battle an armed vessel. Quakers in the assembly accepted the necessity of providing money in response to the Queen's commands, but complained on numerous occasions that other colonies that did not provide quotas of men and money seemed little concerned about the terrible scenarios predicted by the governors.[11]

The official response by Friends generally relied upon utilitarian reasons. It is plausible that Quakers knew that their peace testimony irritated the Crown and they deliberately kept it in the background. Still, on occasion, the religious underpinnings were made explicit.[12] Charles II knew when giving Penn the charter, and William and Mary also recognized when restoring the province to Penn, that Quakers had scruples against fighting in wars.[13] Pennsylvania was created as a haven for Quakers, and the first settlers had staked their lives and fortunes upon creating a place where their distinctive principles could be put into practice. The assembly could not authorize the erection of forts nor create a militia without making Quakers dissenters in their own colony.[14]

When William Markham informed Lieutenant Governor Blackwell in 1689 that the colony's constitution forbade defense, he may have been thinking of the provision for liberty of conscience.[15] Blackwell tried to persuade the council to make provisions for defense, but the members first played down the seriousness of the situation, then advocated keeping a low profile, and finally insisted that, if the English government persisted in requiring a militia, the settlers were prepared to "suffer" the consequences.[16] God's providence, not secular arguments, determined war and peace. Prayer and just treatment of the Indians would preserve Pennsylvania's Quakers from war. Outsiders could either accept Quaker principles, form a voluntary militia, or leave.

The assembly's willingness to vote funds for the "Queen's use" and the failure of any immediate threat from French or Indians allowed Friends to preserve the peace testimony within the colony. The coming of peace in 1713 removed the problem until the 1740s. Anglicans and those who believed in the compatibility of Christianity and war never accepted the Quaker understanding of religious freedom on this issue. The affirmation issue could be compromised, because the court system functioned successfully. Neither Quaker nor opponent worked out a satisfactory arrangement for defense like that proposed in the East Jersey constitution of 1683.

During the quarter century of peace following the Treaty of Utrecht in 1713, Quaker pacifism occasioned little comment either in England or Pennsylvania. But from 1739 until 1763 England enjoyed peace only eight of twenty-four years, fighting Spain, then France, and finally France and Spain. In these wars England expected the colonies to contribute men, supplies, and money. To the builders of the British Empire Pennsylvania was an anomaly with no forts, no stockpiled military supplies, and no militia. Of course before 1750 there were no French either, but there was a substantial Indian population and strategic borders on Lake Erie on the north and the Ohio River in the west.

In 1739, at the beginning of the War of Jenkins' Ear, the Pennsylvania Assembly was controlled by the so-called Quaker party, formed during the 1730s, when Quaker political leaders, confronted by an influx of German immigrants, curtailed their feuding and united.[17] This party controlled the assembly until the eve of the Revolution, in spite of the minority situation of the Society of Friends, by attracting the support of English, German and even some Scots-Irish settlers.[18] Members of the Society of Friends composed from half to two-thirds of the assembly. Because the annual sessions of Philadelphia Yearly Meeting of Friends occurred just before election time, opponents of the Quaker party charged with some justification that the leaders decided political strategy and established tickets during that religious gathering.

The Quaker party offered to voters policies based upon low taxes, freedom for religious practices, no tithes, no compulsory military obligation.[19] Most of all, the government left people alone so that they could make a living, worship, and raise their families without interference from the magistrates. To the Quaker party religious liberty brought internal harmony, external peace, and prosperity.

The opposing faction, termed the Proprietary party, gained offices through the patronage of the Penn family, but had to overcome the settlers' antipathy to the policies of the Penns that aimed at extracting the largest possible purchase price and quit rents for land[20]. Thomas Penn, who like William Penn's other surviving children left the Quakers, wished to rebuild the power of the proprietor against the assembly. Because Thomas Penn normally resided in England, it was relatively easy to portray him as an absentee landlord interested in increasing his wealth and power against the welfare of the colonists.

The Proprietary party had one issue that they knew appealed to the British government and that they hoped would prove attractive in Pennsylvania: a policy of military preparedness directed against the apparent French attempt to encircle British America. If the Proprietary faction could convince the non-Quaker majority that the colony's pacifist stance risked a loss of British Protestant freedom, then the Quakers would be voted out of office. Unfortunately for the Propretary party, to many settlers military preparations brought connotations of European traditions of impressment, high taxes for defense, arrogant military officers, and incessant wars. Until 1755 the settlers thought they had more to fear from a military establishment than from nonpreparedness. Still, the debate on the Quakers' peace policies raised basic issues. Our concern is not to delineate either the political infighting or the theological controversy over whether the Friends understood correctly the New Testament. Rather, we will focus on the political implications of this theological dispute to show why the debate involved the definition of religious liberty and the separation of the institutional church from the state.

During the eighteenth century many of the most important clerical and political leaders of Pennsylvania wrote about pacifism. The deist Benjamin Franklin, the Anglican William Smith, the Presbyterian Gilbert Tennent, the Quaker James Logan, the governors, and the leaders of the Proprietary party all opposed the assembly's peace policies.[21] Defending pacifism (the term comes from the late nineteenth century but the concept fits the colonial context) were Samuel Smith (the historian of New Jersey), John Smith, Benjamin Gilbert, John Churchman, John Woolman, Anthony Benezet, and the leaders in the assembly.[22] All these men were Quakers, and their epistles and pamphlets had to be read by a committee of influential Quakers to make sure that the Society of Friends approved the contents. In spite of the various perspectives, the issues debated by Lieutenant Governor Thomas and the Quaker assembly in 1739 were still being discussed on the eve of the Revolution. A general summary of the position of each side is sufficient to delineate the relationship of pacifism to church and state.

The Quakers saw Pennsylvania as an area enjoying God's special protection, not as a backwater in the British Empire. The founding of Pennsylvania and the success of the colony were providential. If the settlers, particularly the members of the Society of Friends, kept their trust in God and maintained the purity of their outward profession of religion, then God would preserve them. Quaker Pennsylvania was God's holy experiment in peace, and the history of the colony should convince all of God's hand in directing events.[23] Quaker relations with the Indians constituted empirical proof for the political soundness of conciliation and justice, rather than military might, in settling grievances. William Penn's policy established the framework for peace and by the 1720s both the Indians and the leaders of the colony used Penn's Treaty as a symbol of enduring friendship. Voltaire probably gained his knowledge of Penn during a visit with a Quaker family in England, and he gave the icon of Penn and the Indians a prominent place in his *Letters to the English Nation* in 1733. Pennsylvania employed the image of William Penn and the Indians as a symbol of peace in a medal cast by Quakers to give to the Indians in 1755, in Benjamin West's 1773 picture of "Penn's Treaty with the Indians" and, in the nineteenth century, in the many versions of Edward Hicks's paintings of the "Peaceable Kingdom."[24]

Closely linked to the providential history of Pennsylvania was a view of the colony as a Quaker "birthright." The biblical story of Jacob and Esau showed how the Lord determined the characteristic of the land based upon a blessing to the first-born. Supposedly, Friends now enjoyed the birthright. Penn established the colony as a refuge for Friends who were being persecuted in England, and the Crown when granting the charter had known that the Quakers opposed military service. Penn and the first Quaker settlers assumed the financial and physical risks in creating the colony as a religious community of toleration and peace. All those who immigrated later knew what the colony stood for. To force Pennsylvanians into a militia would subvert the intentions of the charter and the founders.[25] A legally authorized compulsory militia service would in Pennsylvania constitute religious persecution.

Quakers insisted that pacifism was integral to Penn's definition of rights of conscience, and therefore part of the fundamental law of the colony. It would be illegal or unconstitutional to force military service.[26] A militia was permissible so long as it did not require a law and the service was purely voluntary. Quakers did not believe in coercing to pacifism those who believed in defense and a militia. Such people remained free to form voluntarily a militia, and the governors had the authority to call such a force into being.[27] Benjamin Franklin's 1747 attempt to collect private donations to buy a cannon for a fort on the Delaware River was also protected by liberty of conscience, although Quakers refused to contribute to this "charity." Similarly, a non-Quaker merchant who wished to arm his ship had the right to do so. If the dangers from the French were as apparent as the governors and the Proprietary party claimed, then colonists who approved could form companies and drill. When they did not, this supposedly demonstrated that the Pennsylvanians saw no danger.

The Quakers rested their position on natural rights and freedom. They did not assert that pacifism was part of natural law.[28] But British freedoms included the right to elect assemblymen. Those who elected the assembly's members knew what the Quaker party stood for. The votes showed that the people approved of Quaker policies and disliked a militia. If the Quaker policies were incompatible with government, why did the people not know it? The history of Pennsylvania, its prosperity and peacefulness, proved the soundness of the freemen's votes. To destroy the Quaker government of Pennsylvania by disqualifying Friends from serving through the imposition of an oath, for example, would be to subvert the natural rights of the British colonists.

The final test of the Quaker policy was empirical. Friends did not justify their position as a subjective religious tenet on which men of good will could differ. Rather, they defended their government by looking at past events. Pennsylvania had never been attacked by any enemy.[29] New England and New York constituted a barrier to the north that would stop the French, while the entire South lay between Pennsylvania and the Spanish. The Royal Navy controlled the ocean, and colonies were not responsible for building warships. The Indians were the only conceivable nearby threat, but justice and conciliation had created good relations. In the meantime the Friends had supported the British Empire by voting funds at Crown request in 1696, 1709, and 1711.

The Quaker party espoused a political pacifism as dependent upon historical events as theological justification. It required the Indians to remain friendly, the French to stay away, the Royal Navy to provide protection, and New England and the South to hold off enemies. The rationale might suffice for Pennsylvania, but it could provide no solace for a pacifist Quaker in Rhode Island or North Carolina. The assembly's position also drew upon a distinctive interpretation of the providence of God, the history of Pennsylvania, and the meaning of religious freedom. In essence, when the assembly members decreed their nonmilitia policy for religious reasons, then even while preserving the institutional separation of meeting and state they had made the colony espouse Quakerism.

The Quaker pacifists in the assembly justified their position by using incompatible arguments. Within the Society of Friends there were always a few who wondered whether the compromises required by government service were a betrayal of religious consistency. The critique could come from those like George Keith and William Rakestraw who wanted no part of government, or from politicians like James Logan or Isaac Norris II, who wanted to change the testimony on peace.[30] Making pacifism dependent upon either the French and Indians or elections was also risky. Equally dangerous was making pacifism a policy dependent upon worldly success. The Bible identified the children of Israel as being conquered; Jesus' kingdom according to the New Testament was not of this world. The assembly's peace testimony assumed that prosperity, freedom, and peace stemmed from Penn's policies and God's providence. What if war came to Quaker Pennsylvania?

The nonpacifists denied every argument that Friends put forth. The alleged Quaker birthright was nonexistent. The Swedes and Finns were the first settlers, and Pennsylvania's government stemmed from a charter granted by Charles II, a monarch not known for favoring pacifism. The Crown, not the Society of Friends, established the constitution of the new government, and the charter's naming the proprietor as captain-general of the forces showed that the Crown never saw Pennsylvania as a distinctive nonmilitary land.[31] Even the early Friends had not been consistently pacifist. During the English civil war of the 1650s Quakers served in the parliamentary armies. Robert Barclay, the most famous Quaker theologian, in his *Apology,* a summa theologica of the religion, allowed for the legitimacy of a magistrate's conducting a defensive war in this still imperfect world.[32] Nor had the Quaker settlers in Pennsylvania been consistent. They had on several occasions provided funds for military purposes, the most important being the £2,000 voted for the Queen's use in 1711.[33] If Quakers could provide funds to be spent on war, then they could vote for a militia and make provision for the defense of Pennsylvania.

The assembly's position, according to nonpacifists, denied religious freedom and subverted the English tradition of toleration.[34] A religious tenet of a minority was imposed on the majority. This action denied the equality of all religious denominations and flaunted the dominance of the Quakers.[35] The majority of the colony would experience the brunt of the suffering in case the French sailed up the Delaware, while the wealthier Friends could escape by horse and carriage into the interior.

In addition, proponents of defense thought that the assembly's policies went against natural law. The first element of natural law was the right of self-preservation. All governments had an obligation to defend their citizens' rights and property.[36] An individual might have the right to sacrifice his life to a religious belief, but the state could not cause people to sacrifice their lives and property for a belief that the majority did not accept. Quakers had not been conspicuous followers of the Gospel. They had used the fruits of early arrival, hard work, and speculation to amass wealth. Such wealth tempted foreign powers, because the Friends would not defend it by military means. Friends should either give up the pursuit of riches or governing.[37]

While the assembly assumed that Pennsylvania remained a special land receiving God's special help, its opponents saw the colony as a small segment of England's overseas possessions.[38] That Protestant empire in America was surrounded by French and Spanish Catholics. God had not restrained France from devastating much of Europe during a long series of wars. Why could the Quakers be certain that He would protect Pennsylvania but not Massachusetts or New York? Friends misunderstood the nature of a Christian's obligation. God worked through the good deeds of people. Lieutenant Governor Thomas argued in 1739 that God caused the winds to blow, yet sailors still had to build ships and set sails to take advantage of God's providence in giving winds.[39] The Hebrew Scriptures showed prophets of God summoning his people to war for their political survival and the protection of true religion.

The arguments based upon electoral success and the history of the colony were difficult to counter, because the strategies of defense-minded politicians failed. The Proprietary faction tried to enlist the efforts of sailors to vote the Quakers out in 1742, but the riot that ensued discredited that tactic.[40] The key to electoral success was the German vote. Christopher Saur, who published the only German language newspaper in the colony, was a pacifist who reminded Germans that their security against tithes and a militia rested with Friends.[41] Franklin established another German language newspaper in 1751 in order to counter Saur's influence, but the paper lasted only a short time. Creating a school system for the Germans was a way of educating them to the need for defense. Franklin participated in an attempt during the 1750s to subsidize charity schools for the German-speaking population. An organization to promote the schools received the endorsement and support of the king, the proprietor, and many of the German Reformed and Lutheran ministers in Pennsylvania. Reverend Michael Schlatter of the German Reformed Church solicited funds in Europe and in Pennsylvania, and a few schools began.[42] But even if the schools had indoctrinated German children into supporting a militia and the Proprietary faction, turning that program into electoral victories would have taken years. Christopher Saur opposed the venture from the beginning.[43] The anti-German sentiments expressed by Anglican Reverend William Smith and Benjamin Franklin and the suspicion by the German ministers and people that the sponsors wanted charity schools to force acculturation to English norms doomed the venture. The Germans continued to support the Quaker party. Unable to win elections and apprehensive about the approach of war, Thomas Penn determined that the English government must intervene to require oaths and bar the Friends from serving in the assembly.

Both the political Quakers and their opponents used arguments that could not easily be combined into a coherent framework. They merged historical observations, common sense, biblical exegesis, political theory, and scare tactics. The Quakers pointed to years of peace in Pennsylvania; their opponents to decades of war close by. The Proprietary faction rightly claimed that the majority of Pennsylvanians were not pacifists; the Quaker party enjoyed repeated electoral success. Both sides agreed that a successful military apparatus required compulsion. At this point the issue was focused: Did the Quakers' nonmilitary stance fulfill or negate freedom of conscience and civil liberties?

The events of 1755 that initiated the Seven Years War offered a partial resolution, because the assembly's version of peaceful Pennsylvania proved false. The defeat of the British force led by Major General Edward Braddock and the retreat of the army to Philadelphia in August, 1755, left the frontier unprotected. Indians raids on settlements in northern and western Pennsylvania destroyed the empirical and historical argument that the colony enjoyed a unique destiny of peace.

The assembly Quakers' position, unlike that of the main body of Friends, changed immediately. Prior to 1755 the assembly never initiated an appropriation for war; monies granted, generally begrudgingly, came in response to the Crown's direct request.[44] Even then, the assembly always included some qualification so that the money never went directly for war materials such as munitions, uniforms, or soldier's pay. Such a policy fit into Robert Barclay's formulation allowing magistrates to wage defensive war but forbade Friends direct participation. This rationale also justified British Quakers' payment of war taxes as part of the duty of obeying lawful magistrates. The 1755 assembly tax bill was different. Now, the Friends in the legislature determined the need, specified the ends, and appropriated the money.[45] The assembly also established a militia. The law preserved part of the traditional Pennsylvania definition of religious freedom.[46] All conscientiously opposed to war would receive exemption from militia duty. Coercion would not even apply to men whose religious principles allowed military service. Those who fought would all be volunteers and, as an inducement to enlist, they could elect officers. After the inhabitants signed up and elected officers, the officers would read to the soldiers the regulations of the British army, that would become binding at that juncture.

There was no penalty of any kind attached for those who for religious reasons refused to serve. No one had to furnish a substitute or pay double taxation. Such stipulations protected the Quakers' and other pacifists' freedom of conscience. The law even acknowledged that a majority of those passing the law opposed military service, but that they were unwilling to stop the majority from defending themselves. The leaders of the assembly thought that they had preserved liberty of conscience and provided for the defense of the colony.

The compromise law, drafted by Benjamin Franklin, satisfied neither Philadelphia Yearly Meeting of Friends, the Proprietary party, the Crown, or the frontiersmen threatened by Indians. Even before the events of 1755 reformers within the Society of Friends questioned whether the trimming that political power required from assemblymen came at the expense of religious consistency. John Woolman, John Churchman, Anthony Benezet, and Israel Pemberton, Jr., led a minority among Quakers seeking to purify Quaker meetings by tightening enforcement of the discipline of Friends on marriage to nonmembers, simplicity in dress and speech, and freeing slaves. The war served as an opportunity for these weighty Friends to bring sufficient pressure through the Yearly Meeting on those Quaker assemblymen who voted for the war tax and the militia either to resign or not stand for reelection in 1756.[47] In 1758 the Yearly Meeting publicly rebuked all the political Quakers still within the assembly. So many Quakers heeded the advice of the Yearly Meeting that after 1756 there was never again a Quaker majority in the assembly. Even so, the Proprietary party could not gain control. Non-Quaker sympathizers of the Friends under the leadership of Benjamin Franklin and later Joseph Galloway replaced the Friends.

The reforming Quakers also decided that strict adherence to the peace testimony meant that they could not in clear conscience pay a tax levied for war. During the Seven Years War and after, the war tax resistance was not endorsed by the Yearly Meeting. The reformers used against war taxes the birthright, coercion of conscience, and religious freedom arguments that the assembly had previously used against creation of a militia. The political Quakers and most English Friends not only continued to pay all taxes, but rebuked the reformers for disobeying St. Paul and changing Quaker testimonies. The new policy not only made Quakers unfit to govern, it allegedly made them bad citizens.

Even before 1755 the Proprietary faction determined to use the war issue to force Quakers from power. In 1754 and 1756 the Reverend William Smith, newly arrived from New York and now provost of the College of Philadelphia, published in England tracts detailing the irresponsibility of the Quaker assembly's position on war.[48] Smith distinguished between the main body of Friends who supposedly had little to do with politics and a small group of political Quakers who controlled the assembly.[49] These politicians used the peace testimony as an excuse not to defend the colony either because they were pro-French or because they saw the Scots-Irish frontiersmen as a threat and did not care if they were killed.[50] The Friends monopolized the Indian trade and would do nothing to jeopardize their profits. The Quaker politicians were supported by Germans termed "ignorant, proud, stubborn clowns," who either did not understand the issue or who were sympathizers to Roman Catholicism and willing to betray British liberties.[51] Neither the Friends nor the Germans were willing to stake their lives to defeat Roman Catholic tyranny. The religious liberty extended to Catholics was a device by the pacifist sects and Quaker politicians in the assembly to weaken the colony.

Smith advocated that all officeholders in Pennsylvania be tendered an oath as was the practice in England and that naturalization requirements for the Germans be extended.[52] Smith's two pamphlets managed to ignore the assembly's appropriation for the war. He mentioned the militia law only to dismiss it as unworthy because of provisions to protect religious objectors and to elect officers.[53]

Thomas Penn privately approved of Smith's objectives, but not his means.[54] The English government showed its approval by vetoing the militia act.[55] Because the assembly and the governor deadlocked over another militia law, the colony in essence fought the rest of the French and Indian War with a militia that had no legal standing.[56] Volunteers, recruited on occasion by their ministers, defended the threatened settlements. The militia companies proved unable to defeat the French and Indians, but in 1757 British regulars arrived and took the offensive.

The pamphlets of Smith, lobbying by Penn, and petitions from military-minded citizens of Pennsylvania convinced the British cabinet that the Quakers would not fight. English Friends, in order to forestall the complete loss of Quaker political power in the colony, agreed to an arrangement whereby Friends would not hold a majority in the assembly during wartime. So there was no imposition of an oath. Before the delegation of English Quakers arrived in Pennsylvania to explain the policy, the American assemblymen had withdrawn. Their replacements still opposed the proprietary policies but approved the governor's policy of fighting Indians by declaring war on them and offering a bounty for scalps.[57]

Members of the Society of Friends who had withdrawn from politics pondered the course of events and sought to understand the providence of God. Why had he allowed the war to occur? Why had the Indians risen against their longtime advocates? The Yearly Meeting's answer infuriated the British, the proprietors, and the settlers on the frontier. Injustices to the Indians, said Quakers, caused the war. The sons of William Penn and fur traders consistently defrauded the Indians of the lands and goods. In particular, in 1737, the proprietors staged the Walking Purchase in the Lehigh Valley and changed the terms of a purchase agreement from the amount of land a person could walk around in one and a half days to the acreage a runner on a trail could cover. Having gained a huge area by guile, the proprietors used the Iroquois to coerce the Delaware Indians into acceptance.[58] The Indians had also not been compensated for the lands the Scots-Irish had occupied in the area around Carlisle and Harrisburg. The resolution to the war followed a conference to redress grievances and then to institute a policy of good faith in dealing with Indians over lands and trade. In 1757 and again in 1758 at the Treaty of Easton the Delaware Indians and the governor of Pennsylvania made peace and the next year the Iroquois joined in the peace. The Quaker position that abuses by the proprietors caused the Indians to attack essentially ignored the French role. Those whose relatives had been killed or who were refugees from the frontier thought the Quaker position self-serving. Friends lived in the east and, according to one report, did not care if the Indians killed Presbyterians in the west.[59] But with the capture of Fort Duquesne in 1758 by a British expedition under General John Forbes, the war in Pennsylvania ended.

The war eliminated the French as a threat, but the English now faced the problems of conciliating Indians who had never recognized French suzerainty and were not now prepared to accept British domination. When the English occupied former French forts at Pittsburgh, Detroit, Niagara, and Presque Isle, the Indians attacked in a movement termed Pontiac's conspiracy. Again, Indian raids threatened the settlers in northern and western Pennsylvania. Although members of the Society of Friends did not now control the assembly, the Quaker party did. When the assembly's response did not appear adequate to the frontiersmen, they still blamed the Friends.

The Moravians, who had politically supported the Quakers, had an active program of proselytizing the Indians. They had converted Indians living near the Susquehanna River north of the Wyoming Valley. Fearing that the praying Indians who were pro-English might be attacked by frontiersmen who charged them with supplying and harboring hostile natives, the government of Pennsylvania took these Delaware Indians into protective custody. The Paxton Boys, settlers in the area of modern-day Harrisburg, fearing that the government would also protect the Conestoga Indians struck first, killing many, and not sparing women and children.[60] When the colony confined some Conestoga Indians for their protection in the Lancaster jail, the frontiersmen massacred them. The government tried to send the praying Indians to New York or New Jersey for protection, but neither colony would accept them. They were then brought to Philadelphia. The Paxton Boys then threatened to come to Philadelphia to kill the Indians, and perhaps the Quakers too, whom they saw as more concerned about savages than whites.

Both proprietary officials and the assembly condemned the Paxton massacres and sought to bring the vigilantes to trial. Members of the

Society of Friends took the lead in caring for and defending the Indians. When the Paxton rioters approached Germantown, the government prepared to defend itself but at the same time sent negotiators including Proprietary officials, Lutheran and Presbyterian ministers, and Benjamin Franklin of the assembly.[61] After getting a respectable hearing for their complaints, the Paxton marchers went home. In the meantime, to the surprise of many church people and the dismay of weighty Friends, nearly one hundred young Quakers took up arms to defend the threatened Indians.[62] The relationship of these complex events to religious liberty is this: The pamphlet literature attacking and defending the Paxton rioters oversimplified the issues into a Quaker versus Presbyterian dispute.

For years Philadelphians had lumped together all inhabitants of the frontier as Scots-Irish Presbyterians. They also had not liked the frontiersmen's habits of squatting on Indian lands and being unruly citizens. A recent study of the Paxton area concluded that as many Germans as Presbyterians took part in the disturbances and that there was no effective colony or county government in the area.[63] The most effective pamphleteer for a redressing of the frontiersmen's grievances was the Anglican rector Thomas Barton, who had denounced the massacres.

The frontiersmen, after reaching Germantown, issued a remonstrance setting forth their grievances and blaming the Indian troubles upon the Society of Friends. Quakers were more committed to Indians than to white settlers, and secretly wished the farmers killed as a way of weakening Presbyterian influence.[64] Barton, a close associate of William Smith, argued that the Quakers were incapable of governing because they were pacifists.[65] The Quaker party blamed the dispute not on governmental failures, but on the normal traits of Scots-Irish Presbyterians. Presbyterians were king-killers and rebels who had attempted to destroy the Hanoverian dynasty in 1715 and 1745. These ungovernable people had now arrived in Pennsylvania bringing their gospel of sedition.[66] No member of the Society of Friends wrote any of the pamphlets blaming the Presbyterians, but for the supporters of Benjamin Franklin it made sense to blame the Presbyterians and ignore the German role.[67] The key to the Quaker party's success was the German vote, and blaming the Presbyterians paved the way for conciliating the Germans. Eastern Presbyterians had not sympathized with their western brethren in their political grievances and had condemned the massacre of the Indians. But when the issue was phrased in such a way that all Presbyterians were attacked, the ministers responded.

In both the crisis over war in 1755 and over Indians in 1764, Quaker pacifism became an issue. In 1755 the policies of the Society of Friends were legitimate issues. But in 1764 they were not. When Barton blamed

Israel Pemberton, Jr. for Indian coddling and identified him with the assembly's policies, he should have known that Pemberton had broken with the Quaker politicians before 1750 and had held no government office since.[68] The positions of the Society of Friends in conciliating Indians and in embracing antislavery were not those of the Quaker party of Benjamin Franklin. Similarly, when Franklin and his adherents defended the Quakers, they were borrowing the prestige of a religious society for political purposes.

The attacks upon religious bodies showed a residue of animosity beneath the surface placidity of relations between denominations. That hostility surfaced when religious commitments appeared to mask or fuel political ambitions. The Quaker definition of religious liberty as requiring legal equality among different denominations and no tithe and no governmental intervention in church disputes was accepted by virtually all of the laity, though the clergy had reservations. But the adherents of the Proprietary party rightly saw that the Quaker position of pacifism and the Quaker party's position after 1755 of noncoercion were controversial. The Quaker party still wished to utilize the prestige of Friends, but it distanced itself from religious commitment. In 1764 and 1765 Franklin attempted to change the destiny of Pennsylvania by attacking William Penn and the charter and seeking royal government. The controversy over the charter divided the Society of Friends, and showed that many Presbyterians and Germans wanted to preserve the distinctive heritage of Pennsylvania. Not Quakers, but Lutheran, Reformed, and Presbyterian ministers rose to the defense of the Pennsylvania pattern of religious liberty.

CHAPTER III

The Clergy and Religious Liberty

In September 1756, Reverend Thomas Barton of Carlisle wrote to Reverend William Smith of Philadelphia soliciting letters of endorsement from Reverend Gilbert Tennent and Reverend Francis Alison[1] to be used in selecting candidates for the Proprietary party's electoral ticket. Alison was an Old Light Presbyterian, Tennent a New Light; Barton and Smith were Anglicans. Yet, in the crisis of war these clergymen buried their distrust of each other in order to cooperate in a kind of political maneuvering that all thought appropriate. This ministerial involvement in politics raises the issue of how the clerics understood their role in worldly affairs and what they thought of the relation of church and colony.

Ministers who opposed pacifism for theological reasons – and all of the above did – also disliked the Quaker party. The Quaker political, economic, and social domination of Pennsylvania imparted a sectarian flavor to cultural life. Regularly ordained clergymen with university or college degrees received little respect from denominations that made the term "hireling ministry" seem like one word.[2]

In Europe clergy and magistrates worked together to support the social order and both groups expected and normally received deference. Virtually all the Lutheran, German Reformed, and Anglican clergy, and even many of the Presbyterians immigrated as adults to Pennsylvania from areas with state churches. They then required, according to immigrant Lutheran minister Henry Melchior Muhlenberg, seven years of seasoning to Pennsylvania conditions before becoming effective.[3] They had to learn that many politicians disdained them and that their own congregations could be gently led but would not accept dictation. No longer recipients of salaries set by the state or patrons, ministers became dependent upon free-will gifts and offerings from poor immigrants who were trying to earn a living, perhaps buy a farm, and contribute to a church building fund.[4] The laity had learned from sad experience that a long-term contract to a newly arrived clergymen would have to be paid, even if he turned out to be a scoundrel. They would make no more such calls.[5] Many foreign clerics were not psychologically qualified for life in America, and their moral failures and quarrels with each other and their congregations embarrassed the devout church people, although supposedly greeted with glee by sectarians.[6] A clergyman who faithfully served the church might not receive his salary, but if he asked court intervention he was likely in the future to receive even less.[7] He had to learn to consult with the vestry in disciplining sinners or distributing pews. A minister who censured a layman incorrectly could end up in court charged with libel.[8] The Presbyterian Synod in 1729 complained about the number of "religious lawsuits" and advised ministers to persuade their congregations to use arbitrators for settling differences.[9] If a clergyman married a couple without determining accurately that they were of age, had parental permission, and were not indentured servants, he might have to pay a £50 fine.[10] Under Pennsylvania law a clergyman could perform marriages, but otherwise he had the same rights and obligations as a layman.

The province would not intervene if a clergyman were attacked for theological unsoundness. The state refused to certify whether a new minister was actually ordained or was only a schoolmaster trying to escape manual labor.[11] A German settler became outraged when informed that an individual could openly belittle a tract of Martin Luther.[12] A Lutheran minister who asserted that God would destroy the Moravians was charged by his parishioners with blasphemy. Muhlenberg had no redress when a Quaker said baptismal water had as much efficacy as pouring piss over a head.[13] In theory, but often not in practice, God, Christ, and the Bible received legal protection from blasphemy, but not the ministers, sacraments, and most religious beliefs. Freethinking and scoffing at divine providence were not crimes. Taverns closed on Sunday but not on Christmas and other holy days or fast days.[14]

An immigrant clergyman had to learn that the state had no official religious commitments and recognized no theology, except for toleration, as normative. Disputes within a congregation or denomination had to be settled without state aid. The clergy and the churches had to create, without outside help, synods or ministeriums capable of resolving disagreements among congregations and preachers. These organizations, if they had previously received the congregation's consent to accept the synod's decisions, could control the ministers but had no authority over church property.[15] Synod control over any minister was light because with a chronic shortage of trained clergy any individual who wished could defy a synod or ministerium without penalty. (A minister's threat to leave was his most effective weapon to coerce a church to pay his salary.) The schism between Old Light and New Light Presbyterians in the aftermath of the Great Awakening and the controversies in individual congregations occasioned no discussions or laws in the Pennsylvania Assembly and did not result in precedent-creating lawsuits.[16] After all, the legislature and the courts had no basis for determining which clergy or what beliefs were correctly Presbyterian.

The state's only interest in church squabbles was in keeping the peace and securing rightful ownership of property, and the courts determined these either by considering the intentions of the lay founders or determining what the majority wished.[17] So when the Moravians and Lutherans sought control of a building in Philadelphia, the court polled the members as to their preference. Using the same procedure the courts supported the founders of the Germantown Lutheran Congregation against a faction in favor of an itinerant preacher named Heinrich Rapp.[18] When the Philadelphia Reformed church divided over a minister, both sides after acrimonious wrangling eventually entrusted the decision to outside arbiters – in this case five Quakers and an Anglican, because they were clearly neutral.[19] After one branch built an expensive new building, the congregation experienced financial difficulty and negotiated with Lutherans, Reformed, Presbyterians, and Anglicans over joining that denomination.

There was a great deal of informal cooperation among different churches. Lutherans and Reformed often built Union churches. Presbyterians cooperated with the Reformed; Lutherans debated unity with Anglicans.[20] When Reverend Michael Schlatter went to Europe on a fundraising trip for Reformed churches, he carried testimonials from Anglican, Presbyterian, and Lutheran ministers.[21] In the church community, the most bitter disputes were within a congregation or denomination. The one possible exception was when the Lutheran and Reformed churches resisted what they thought was an attempt by the Moravians during the 1740s to capture their churches.[22] Because Moravians claimed to be Lutheran and/or Reformed as well as Moravian, from their perspective even these disputes were intradenominational.

Immigrant ministers had to learn to face competition from other churches and sects. The church competition was tolerable, because all the ministers believed in infant baptism, communion, an educated ministry, and some pattern of liturgy within the worship service. But the Mennonites and Baptists denied infant baptism and their ministers had no degrees. The Quakers denied all these marks of a true church. And the state seemed indifferent as to whether the denomination's control of members was flexible as in the Church of England or rigid as in the Society of Friends, so long as peace and morality prevailed. The Amish received exemption from jury duty. The state did not intervene when the Moravians or Brethren at Ephrata practiced a kind of communism, or when married women ran away from their husbands to join the celibate sisters at Ephrata.[23] A church censure of an individual for adultery had no legal standing. The churches learned to accept these legal restrictions. The Lutheran ministerium refused in 1750 to discuss the legality of a divorce, because that was a matter for the state.[24] The Presbyterian Synod complained in 1734 that the Pennsylvania law on marriage by licenses favored the Church of England and forbade ministers to conduct marriages under it.[25] The next year the synod softened its opposition because the assembly did change the form of the law.

The Pennsylvania clergy cared about politics because the Quaker vision of what the colony originally was and should remain did not include them. The earliest Reformed ministers in Pennsylvania, Martin Boehm and Michael Schlatter, complained about the lack of government support. Muhlenberg noted that ministers in Pennsylvania had more difficulty than shepherds in Germany, because each peasant wanted to be a patron, and Gottlieb Mittelberger declared that Pennsylvania was heaven for farmers but hell for government officials and ministers.[26] The Anglican missionaries sent by the Society for Propagation of the Gospel bemoaned the anticlericalism and hostility to their ministry among the sectarians.[27] When in 1754 the Charity School organizers debated having a minister as a trustee for each school, Conrad Weiser, the Lutheran father-in-law of Muhlenberg, opposed the proposal because of the hostility of the population to the clergy.[28] Clearly, an immigrant clergyman coming to colonial Pennsylvania faced a loss of authority and status.

The ministers could not expect to improve their position if the leadership of the colony remained with the Quakers. The Proprietary party would not end freedom of religion, but it would be more sympathetic to clerical concerns. The leaders of the party were church people. William Allen was a Presbyterian, the Shippens and Benjamin Chew ex-Quakers turned Anglican, and the provincial secretary after 1737 was an ordained Anglican minister.

Most Pennsylvania ministers approved their necessary civil duties as spokesmen for religion but resisted actual involvement in politics. Those ministers who participated in politics were criticized by others within their denomination who refrained.[29] All the church ministers, unlike their sectarian colleagues, would preach a jeremiad or appropriate call to repent when the governor and council proclaimed fast days. Some denominations regularly scheduled fast and feast days. During wartime the clergy exhorted the people to unite against the Indian enemies and proclaimed the righteousness of the Protestant British cause against the French. A sermon might take place before a newly formed volunteer company of soldiers or before the men left for the battlefield. The pacifist sects ignored all such events.

Henry Melchior Muhlenberg, a Lutheran pietist who served in Pennsylvania from 1742 until the 1780s, exemplifies the secular commitments of the German clergy. Muhlenberg justified his nonparticipation in politics both because his task was to preach an eternal kingdom of God and because of the vulnerability of the German minority to English distrust. When preaching sermons on fast days and on military subjects, he always made the political context subservient to the need of all to repent and seek an inward experience of God. Still, he willingly provided certificates for Germans who partook of communion so that they could prove they were Protestants and become naturalized. The events of the 1760s show the limits of Muhlenberg's nonpolitical stance, because he was in private a strong supporter of the Proprietary party. When the Paxton rioters marched on Philadelphia, Muhlenberg counseled Germans to stay out of the commotions. Although sympathetic to the frontiersmen's grievances against the Quakers, he would not counsel resistance. He feared that the English might desert the march at the last moment, leaving the Germans as the only visible complainers. He told his congregations to obey the powers that be, not to become revolutionary.[30] The Swedish Lutheran Reverend Charles Wrangel, one of the negotiators the government sent out to meet with the marchers, discussed their complaints and later preached a sermon against rebellion to the group. Muhlenberg followed the policy of withdrawal when requested to join the English churches in tolling the bells in mourning the effective beginning of the Stamp Act. He met with vestry and all agreed that the German bells would not ring.[31]

Politicians in Pennsylvania recognized the power of the German vote and attempted to court Muhlenberg, particularly in the controversy over adopting royal government. Muhlenberg did not favor repeal of the charter, seeing in it a guarantee of religious and civil liberty. Opponents of repeal circulated petitions after church services. Muhlenberg resisted Quaker party politicians' overtures to enlist him for their cause, but presented to his deacons and elders a petition favoring proprietary government.[32] A recent biographer speculates that Muhlenberg made a deal with William Smith to provide German support against repeal in exchange for including Germans on the electoral ticket of potential office-holders.[33] Muhlenberg also chided the Quaker party representatives about their neglect of Germans.[34] He showed his political shrewdness in gaining a charter for the Philadelphia Lutheran church. Thomas Penn generally discouraged giving churches legal incorporation, arguing that the legal equality of churches would be undermined by selective incorporation.[35] During the early years of the colony no churches were incorporated and by midcentury not even Christ Church had a charter. Because the Penns now were courting the German interest, both the Lutheran and Reformed churches in Philadelphia asked for charters.[36] They got them.

Richard Peters and William Smith were politician-clergymen, a dual role they could practice more easily because they had not initially served churches. Peters came to the colony in 1737, after a scandal in England over a bigamous marriage, to serve as assistant rector of Christ Church. After a disagreement with the rector, Peters turned to secular employments and Thomas Penn appointed him provincial secretary and member of the council. Peters became an important spokesman for the proprietary interest. His strong advocacy of the Penns caused him not to be elected rector of Christ Church until 1762, and even then he accepted no salary. Because of his secular employment Peters' political expertise remained uncontroversial and, after he became rector, his resignation from the land office and ill health later in life curtailed his nonclerical functions.[37]

William Smith, also an Anglican priest, came to Pennsylvania as a teacher in Benjamin Franklin's experimental academy and helped transform that institution into the College of Philadelphia.[38] Smith's dislike of pacifism and strong support of imperial war, desire to control the Church of England in Pennsylvania, unscrupulous tactics as a pamphleteer, support of the proprietors who helped him by both stipend and office, and his role in the college propelled him against the Quaker party. The Quakers opposed higher education that was literary and theological rather than practical. A Friend who wished to be a doctor could attend Edinburgh University, but the meeting disapproved of would-be gentlemen going to the College of Philadelphia to read classics, compose Latin poetry, participate in theatrical performances, declaim ornate orations, and study theology. The Proprietary party supported the College of Philadelphia and its faculty, which included Anglican, Presbyterian, Baptist, and Lutheran ministers, and trained young men for the cloth or the law.[39] The Quaker party's charity was the Pennsylvania Hospital.[40] Here was a practical institution that cared for the sick, particularly those who were poor, and the mentally ill.

Smith burst into the political scene in 1754 and 1756 with his attacks upon the Quaker party's pacifism. He played a major role in the Charity School movement and became the favorite Philadelphia preacher on ceremonial occasions. His open political involvement and his strong support for a bishop in America – he hoped to be the man – caused animosities. He also worked quietly to make the College of Philadelphia an Anglican-controlled institution and succeeded in easing out Franklin as president and making Anglicans trustees while undermining the Presbyterians on the faculty, most notably Francis Alison.[41] Seeing the slow growth of the Anglican Church as a liability, Smith sought to unify the Lutherans and Anglicans into a single denomination.[42] Though he cooperated with Presbyterians in the Proprietary party, he feared the rapid growth of their church.

In 1755, after the defeat of Braddock's army, William Smith sent a circular letter to Pennsylvania's Anglican clergy, which was published as a foreword to Thomas Barton's *Unanimity and Public Spirit.* Smith's preface spelled out the minister's obligation to speak out on public issues. Religion, argued Smith, was as basic to civilized existence as government and rested "on the same foundation as society." True virtue fostered by Protestant religion required a "sense of liberty." Religion formed "minds of people to the knowledge of both law and duty." Because God in his commandments joined social and religious duties, the minister had an obligation to discuss both spheres. Jesus' weeping about the future destruction of Jerusalem showed his concern for politics. Eighteenth-century Protestant clergy had the same obligation to preach on anything that could hurt or make men afraid in our "civil or religious capacity."[43]

The colonists had to fear both the French military threat and Catholicism. All ministers should oppose a system of religion that led to slavery. "The subject of papacy can never be exhausted, while the danger of it remains." Sermons on political topics should not be delivered frequently because their focus was secondary to a cleric's primary responsibility of preaching the gospel of peace. But Eden was a past and future existence, and wars in this time were the result of "public sin." The minister bewailed sin and summoned his listeners to repentance, but he exhorted them to be prepared to fight and even to die in the service of Protestant liberty.[44]

Smith's advice, which could cover many of his political activities only with some stretching, might have been echoed by the Presbyterian clergy of Pennsylvania. The Presbyterians could look to Scotland or New England for models of moral and political activities. They could see in Ireland or Virginia the disabilities their co-religionists suffered at the hands of the Church of England. In New York the animosity between Presbyterians and Anglicans over the control of King's College became so important an issue that the two major political factions became identified with different churches.[45] Pennsylvania Presbyterians opposed an Anglican establishment, but had difficulty understanding that Quakers and Anglicans feared the creation of Presbyterian-Congregational establishments extending from New England to Maryland.

The migration of Scots-Irish to Pennsylvania brought a rapid increase in the number of Presbyterians.[46] New churches flourished because the Great Awakening furnished a supply of native-born men whose conversion experience fired them to endure the rigors of the ministry. The New Light Log College, which later metamorphosed into the College of New Jersey at Princeton, turned out an ample number of ministers.[47] The few new Old Light ministers came either from Europe or studied at the Newark Academy or the College of Philadelphia under Francis Alison.

The Presbyterian numerical growth failed to translate into political power because of the incessant wrangling and splits that stemmed from the Great Awakening. For example, in the area around present-day Harrisburg, the feuding between Presbyterian churches broke up any sense of community and contributed to the Paxton disturbances. The main concentration of Presbyterian settlers was in the west, an area underrepresented in the assembly, and before the 1750s the farmers voted for the Quaker party because of their dislike of the land policies of the proprietors. The war, the alleged Indian coddling by Quakers, the toleration of Roman Catholics, and the pacifism of some in the assembly gave the Proprietary party a chance. Presbyterian ministers denounced Roman Catholic France and called for vigorous prosecution of the French and Indian War.[48] The frontiersmen showed little patience with the constitutional battle between the assembly and Thomas Penn over the taxation of proprietary lands.

The Presbyterian clergy focused the resentment of the frontier settlers on the Quaker party and its pacifism and favoritism of Indians in both 1755 and 1764. The ministerial leaders were Gilbert Tennent and Francis Alison. Tennent, in 1747, published his first attack on Quaker pacifism. Quaker John Smith responded with a withering rejoinder that prompted Tennent into writing a ponderous tome justifying defensive war. Both of Tennent's tracts on war were primarily theological and his volume of published sermons generally ignored politics although defending a minister's speaking of God's natural and moral law as reflected in the social order.[49] In 1755 Tennent was primed to defend British liberties against Roman Catholic France on behalf of the Presbyterians on the frontier. As the religious and intellectual leader of the New Lights and minister of the Second Presbyterian Church in Philadelphia, Tennent would play an important role in mobilizing the frontiersmen for the Proprietary party.

Francis Alison played no role in politics during his first twenty years in Pennsylvania, devoting his energies to mending the division between Old Lights and New Lights. In 1747 and 1755 he supported Franklin's voluntary militia and when war began, criticized the Quakers, the assembly, and the frontiersmen. His January, 1756 sermon on "Love of Country" marks his politization. The sermon parallels Smith's "Preface" to Barton's tract in many ways. Like Smith, Alison called for unity against an enemy in order to protect religious and civil liberty. The assembly, the proprietor, the churches, and the people must subordinate their differences to the common good. All citizens who enjoyed "equal" privileges of liberty must sacrifice to preserve their rights and no one sect or party should monopolize power and privilege, particularly if its members refused to fight. "All . . . should have a free use of their religion, but so as not on that score to burden or oppress others." Alison's negative references here to the

Quakers and the Quaker party would be grasped by his audiences. The clergy's role was to join with officials by speech and example in leading the populace in defending against a common enemy. All must recognize that God would determine the victor and that virtue remained the basic foundation of the country.[50]

The government recognized the influence of the clergy in mobilizing the population. Two frontier pastors, the Anglican Thomas Barton and the Presbyterian John Elder, served as conduits of information to and from officials in Philadelphia. Barton and Elder helped organize the militia in 1755 and again in 1764.[51] Proprietary officials attempted to use the ministers to defuse the tensions on the frontier after the clergy had alerted the government to the danger. His biographer believes that Francis Alison accompanied the colony's officals to Germantown to negotiate with the Paxton marchers. He may have been responsible for taking the frontiersmen's declaration of grievances and changing the anti-Quaker and anti-Indian focus into a demand for reapportionment of the legislature and an end to pacifism.[52] The attacks upon the Quakers and the Presbyterians served to embitter relations between the two denominations and to ease the conflicts between Old Light and New Light Presbyterians.

The Paxton riot was followed by another divisive action: the attempt in 1764 by the Franklin-led faction in the Quaker party to repeal the charter and make Pennsylvania a royal colony. The Presbyterians saw charter repeal as a Quaker plot to keep control of the colony. The Presbyterian clergy took the lead in opposing the change. Francis Alison, Gilbert Tennent, and John Ewing wrote a letter to their fellow ministers advocating keeping the charter. Presbyterian ministers in the city and country preached against and circulated petitions against the change to their congregations.[53] When the Quaker party tried to gain petitions supporting a royal colony, the church clergy and the Proprietary party politicians joined forces and more than twice as many signatures opposed as favored the change. The churches had several reasons to oppose change. One was that the British government did not look more benevolent than the proprietors in the aftermath of the French and Indian War. A second factor was whether the traditional religious freedom of the colony could be maintained under royal government. Anglican, Lutheran, Presbyterian, and Reformed joined some Quakers in opposing royal government. The sectarians did not approve of Thomas Penn but they did not trust Benjamin Franklin. In rural districts Quaker party politicians repudiated repeal of the charter and in the city the Quaker party lost the election of 1764.[54] Repeal was as unpopular in England as in Pennsylvania, and the effort was soon ended.

In 1759 Gilbert Tennent preached two sermons on peacemaking to the newly reunited Philadelphia synod of the Presbyterian church. The sermons were not immediately printed, perhaps because Tennent's emphasis upon mutual forbearance, an irenic spirit, and a willingness to tolerate diversity on minor points seemed out of keeping with the prosecution of the war against France. The sermons were printed in 1765, a time when pamphleteers trumpeted the political dangers of Presbyterian ascendancy and warned of the example of Scottish Covenanters in the Puritan revolution. The reassertion of the validity of the 1643 Solemn League and Covenant by a group of dissident Presbyterians added credibility to the fears of those who saw all Calvinists as potential persecutors.[55] Tennent's sermons attempted to reassure all Pennsylvanians that Presbyterians wanted religious liberty for all. The sermon provides the clearest definition of the Presbyterians' acceptance and understanding of the Pennsylvania pattern of separation of church and state.

Tennent sought to demonstrate that Scripture and reason supported religious liberty. The Bible witnessed that the kingdom of God did not interfere "with the prerogatives of princes, or the properties of their subjects."[56] Any contrary precedent derived from ancient Israel no longer had validity, because the Hebrews enjoyed a unique status with God serving as their king.[57] Christianity dealt only with spiritual matters which could be decided by reason, argument, and love. "The use of *Force* tends to CONFOUND the KINGDOM OF CHRIST with the kingdom of this world, to change its spiritual NATURE, and make it carnal and political." So long as religion did not "directly affect the peace and safety of the state," no temporal penalties should be used even for false belief.[58]

Persecution on religious matters was also "contrary to REASON, seeing *Religion is a reasonable* service . . . founded on argument, a matter of choice . . . proceeding from *love* as its *principle.*" Though Tennent had earlier in his career appeared as the most enthusiastic of Presbyterians, before the synod he stressed that man was a reasonable creature whose constitution required him to "examine and judge" truth for himself.[59] Such examination was a constant process requiring education and self-examination, and Roman Catholicism showed the dangers of a religion claiming infallibility. In keeping with the original wartime setting of his sermon, Tennent then rehearsed the standard anti-Catholicism charges that infallibility led to "IMPLICIT FAITH," "IGNORANCE," and "blind obedience."[60] Tennent made clear that his attack upon Catholicism did not include an end of freedom of worship for Catholics in Pennsylvania.

Instead, Tennent's anti-Catholicism made stronger his claim for religious freedom. In the past both Catholics and Protestants had been guilty of religious persecution. Both sides asserted correctly that religious practice was the most important human activity. If religious principle allowed any degree of persecution, then the practice of the Spanish Inquisition would be defensible. "The lowest degree of punishment on a religious account, includes the highest." Persecution was wrong, whether inflicted by "Papist or Protestant, Jew, Turk, or Pagan, whether by church or state, or by both in conjunction." All persons have an equal right to religious liberty and "it is [as] bad for us to *persecute* others, of a different *denomination,* as for them to persecute us."[61]

Tennent's strong libertarian stance did not result in a relativism. He denounced antinomians, Moravians, and the "polished Paganism" of the latitudinarians. Still, in the sermon there were omissions and contradictions. Tennent justified Pennsylvania religious liberty as deriving from the British monarchy, not William Penn and the Quakers.[62] He argued that "the *religion* of *Jesus* rightly understood, is a real, a valuable friend to the *law* of *nature,* to liberty, and society, and has explained and enforced them with greater *clearness, argument,* and *pathos,* than ever any other institution did."[63] Tennent provided no reconciliation of how the purely spiritual kingdom of God which never attacked property and government could also support them. During the French and Indian War the Presbyterian clergy, Tennent included, preached in support of the British position and against Quaker pacifism. After 1765 they would preach opposition to British taxation. Tennent's sermon exemplifies the inconsistencies in the colonial Presbyterians' defense of religious liberty. After 1765 the Anglicans' proposal to create an American bishop was defended by them as required by religious liberty and denounced by Presbyterians as against religious liberty.

In 1765 the Anglican missionaries of New York and New Jersey, meeting in convention, decided to petition for the appointment of a bishop. Such an appointment would have to gain the approval of Church of England officials in Britain as well as an act of Parliament. A favorable response from the archbishop of Canterbury and some sympathy within the government led the clergy to renew their request in 1767. The convention unanimously approved publishing a pamphlet by Reverend Thomas Bradbury Chandler setting forth the reasons why the Church of England in America needed a resident bishop.[64]

Chandler hoped that by wording the proposal modestly he could forestall opposition from vestries in the South and from other denominations in New England and the Middle Colonies. The leader of the Anglicans in Pennsylvania, William Smith, was not consulted, and disapproved when he learned of the proposal.

The Anglican missionaries of New York picked a singularly inauspicious time to raise the issue of a bishop. The Sugar Act, Stamp Act, enforcement of the Navigation Acts, and the Townshend Acts had already made the colonists suspicious of British designs on their liberty. Was the campaign for a bishop another of the cabinet's efforts to make the Americans subordinate? Although there was already an established Church of England in all colonies south of the Mason-Dixon line, was the proposal an attempt to create a tax-funded Church of England in New Jersey and Pennsylvania? Outside of Philadelphia all Anglican clerics in Pennsylvania relied upon a subsidy from the Society for the Propagation of the Gospel for part of their salaries. A tax to maintain a bishop might be the first step in a more general assessment for local priests.

Chandler tried to reassure the suspicious non-Anglicans that the proposal would in no way diminish religious liberty. Episcopal government was a defining characteristic of the Church of England and the apostolic succession guaranteed the authority of the faith.[65] Just as other churches practiced their distinctive polities, so the Church of England should have the same right. Because there was no American bishop, all candidates for ordination had to journey to England for consecration.[66] The journey was dangerous, expensive, and time-consuming. In addition, the "Church" needed resident authority over clergy. Chandler reassured the "Dissenters" that the bishop in America would have no civil jurisdiction, no ecclesiastical courts, no authority over laymen.[67] There would be no tax to support him; rather his revenues would come from an already existing fund set up to support an American bishop.[68] Chandler's *Appeal* was permeated with a pro-England view. The Anglican clergy were loyal, never preached sedition from the pulpit, (unlike Presbyterians), and supported the "National Civil Establishment." "Some Religion has been ever thought by the wisest Legislatures to be necessary for the Security of Civil Government, and accordingly has always been interwoven into the Constitution." Anglican bishops kept the necessary "alliance" between church and state. Neither episcopacy nor monarchy could thrive in a republican polity.[69]

Chandler's pamphlet provided a tempting target because of a certain carelessness in terminology. He offered no guarantee that the safeguards on the bishop's power were more than an interim arrangement, and claimed a share of any tithe that might be paid. He even speculated that, should the endowments prove inadequate, Anglicans might be willing to pay a special fee or tax for the support of the bishop.[70] He complained about the state of discipline in the church and implied that both clergy and laity needed to be supervised. Yet he sought to improve discipline with a bishop who had no authority over laity. Such supervision was bound to conflict with the powers traditionally exercised by Anglican vestries in America.

In 1768 a series of articles signed by "The Centinel" in the *Pennsylvania Journal and Weekly Advertiser* focused the opposition and provided insights into the ongoing debate on the meaning of religious liberty.[71] John Dickinson, member of the Pennsylvania assembly, delegate to the

Stamp Act Congress, author of the *Letters of a Pennsylvania Farmer,* wrote at least three of the Centinel letters. Dickinson's argument was narrowly political, a corollary to his view of the British constitution.

Pennsylvania was part of the Empire, Dickinson reasoned, owing allegiance and obedience to the Crown. Legislative authority rested in the assembly, which was the representative of the people. When the colonists settled America, they had not given up their rights as Englishmen or their God-given natural rights. The regulation of the religious character of each colony belonged to each assembly, which had the right to consider a complex, simple, or no religious establishment.[72] Dickinson's argument considered religious liberty as a subordinate question to the issue of parliamentary power. He was the only Centinel author who mentioned William Penn and his policy of toleration.[73]

The other authors were Reverend Francis Alison and George Bryan, a New Light Presbyterian, merchant and judge and a supporter of the Proprietary party and then the Presbyterian party. Both Bryan and Alison had grown up in Ireland and experienced the disabilities of belonging to the dissenters. Alison had later attended Glasgow University and so had been a part of the established Church of Scotland. The similarity in tone and content of their essays allows us to treat their positions as identical.

Alison and Bryan needed to proceed deftly. A theological attack upon episcopacy would alienate Church of England adherents in Pennsylvania and the South who might not wish, for political reasons, to have a resident bishop. An attack upon any tax support for the ministry would likely repel New Englanders like Yale President Ezra Stiles with whom Alison had been corresponding. Yet, too strong a support for a New England establishment would make suspicious the Quakers and other sectaries who thought that Presbyterians aimed at an establishment in the Middle Colonies like the Congregationalists had in New England. Only once did the Centinel announce a general theory of church and state: "Religion and Government are certainly very different Things, instituted for different ends; the Design of the one, being to promote our Temporal Happiness, and thereby the Salvation of our Souls. While these are kept distinct and apart, the Peace and Welfare of Society is preserved, and the Ends of both answered."[74] The logical corollaries from this declaration should have been that only Pennsylvania, New Jersey, and Delaware practiced that "Liberty wherewith Christ has made us free," and that Roman Catholics deserved equal rights. Instead, the Centinel contrasted the "middle" and "eastern colonies" from the South, where church and state were not separated. Governments had the right to pass laws against Catholics because of Rome's political ideals and practices. Even so, the Centinel admitted that the freedom Pennsylvania's Catholics enjoyed brought no inconveniences. He did not address the issue whether the war-rousing sermons and political activities of Presbyterian ministers like Alison and Tennent contributed to the "Salvation of our Souls."

The Centinel letters never mentioned the Presbyterian establishment in Scotland. New England was praised as having a "lax" system where all churches received tax support of their members. There separation of the institutional church from the state meant that the clergy constituted no threat to the state. The South had not solved the issue so well, since non-Anglicans suffered various disabilities and had to pay taxes which went to the Church of England.[75]

The main strategy of the Centinel was to focus on England. English "Dissenters" faced a test act that barred them from most political offices and attendance at the universities.[76] All had to pay support to the Church of England, and its hierarchy was deeply involved in politics. The supposed apostolic succession, the calling the Church of England the "Church,"[77] showed that the Anglicans claimed a monopoly on truth. The Society for the Propagation of the Gospel did not recognize the Congregational, Lutheran, Reformed, Quaker, and Baptist churches as true churches. Therefore, it was bound to persecute.[78]

Religious persecution from Anglicans remained a possibility even when that denomination constituted a minority, because of the designs of the clergy for religious and political power.[79] The Centinel showed a distrust of all clergy which was remarkable considering that Alison was a minister, but anticlericalism was a persistent feature of eighteenth-century Philadelphia. The Centinel's articles made the quest for power an inevitable trait of all men. The only difference with the Anglican clergy was that a bishopric would provide an institutional framework for subverting liberty.[80] The newspaper provided a graphic account of the history of religious persecution and the role that Roman Catholic and Anglican bishops had played. The only safe policy was to keep the clergy out of politics.

Provost William Smith, writing under the pseudonym Anatomist, dissected the Centinel in a series of letters to the *Pennsylvania Chronicle.* Leaving the defense of the need for a bishop to Chandler, Smith sought to establish the right of the Anglican Church to self-government as a part of religious liberty. Like Chandler, Smith defended the legitimacy of bishops over presbyters and the Protestant nature of the Church of England, but he insisted that the central issue was the discrimination against the Anglicans.[81] In America all churches should have equal rights in their internal government.

An American bishop would receive no tax support and have no civil jurisdiction. He would have no power over the laity, even of his own church. By neither common nor statute law could a bishop gain civil power in the colonies, and, unlike Chandler, Smith did not argue that even parliamentary action could grant this. Each colony already had its own laws and had established civil jurisdiction over wills, adultery, blasphemy, etc. The Centinel's fears of bishops corrupting politics were mere "ghosts and hobgoblins."[82] There was more to fear from Presbyterian ministers than Anglican bishops, because history proved that the most intolerant and persecuting church was the Presbyterian. The Centinel's opposition to bishops stemmed from Presbyterian ministers' fears that a strong Church of England would foil their plans for expansion and domination in America.[83]

The English government had so many difficulties controlling Americans after 1767 that it had no wish to inflame passions by becoming embroiled in a religious dispute over bishops. In Pennsylvania both Anglicans and Presbyterians demonstrated their support for religious toleration by opposing tithes, ecclesiastical courts, and clerical political power. The only real issue was whether a resident bishop would upset the status quo. Bishops in England had political and legal as well as spiritual authority and, given the distrust of Parliament, the Pennsylvanians did not feel confidence in any guarantees from Britain. In 1773 the Philadelphian Robert Bell published an edition of Blackstone's *Commentaries on the Laws of England.* The final volume contained Joseph Priestly's debate with Blackstone over whether dissent in Great Britain was still a crime for which Parliament had suspended the penalties.[84] Pennsylvanians did not want on this shore any part of a British ecclesiastical establishment in which the equality of all churches was still debated.

Long before the Revolution the settlers in Pennsylvania agreed that religious freedom was a precious natural right. The colony's policies of civil and religious liberty contributed to prosperity, peace, and happiness. On ceremonial occasions governmental and religious officials praised William Penn and his constitutions; in 1751 they created a Liberty Bell to commemorate the 1701 *Frame of Government.* When Pennsylvania's Baptists and Presbyterians complained about religious intolerance, they referred to Virginia and New England, not Pennsylvania. All denominations had learned that churches should be free of the state in order to manage their internal affairs. Legal equality improved relations among different churches and created a positive attitude toward religion.

It was easy to approve of an abstract freedom of religion, but in practice there was considerable friction. The Presbyterian and Anglican tracts in favor of religious liberty did not convince the adherents of either denomination that the other could be trusted.[85] Smith and Tennent argued that in Pennsylvania no church should be established, not that establishments in New England, the South, and Great Britain were wrong.

So their opponents said that they favored separation of church and state only because of the existing safeguards in Pennsylvania, but that given the opportunity the Presbyterians and Anglican clergy would still seek monopoly power. The failure of the church clergy – Anglican, Presbyterian, Lutheran, Reformed – to criticize their coreligionists elsewhere meant that their theories remained unpersuasive.[86] Pennsylvanians would advocate religious freedom as a universal standard only after the Revolution.

The Quakers and the sects were a numerical minority, and their pacifism and toleration of Roman Catholics were more popular in peace than in wartime. The discriminatory practices against Roman Catholics in Pennsylvania originated in England.[87] When the governor wondered in 1734 whether Roman Catholic worship was legal, the council assured him that Penn's charter and 1701 *Frame of Government* took precedence over English law. St. Joseph's Church, built in 1733, was the only legally functioning Catholic church in the British Empire. The proprietor of Lancaster gave land for both Catholic and Protestant churches, and Catholic priests, like Protestant clergy, received licenses for marriages.[88] In 1740 and 1755, when a mob formed outside the church, the Quaker magistrates dispersed them before any harm was done.[89] Yet, in spite of the assembly's efforts, throughout the colonial period a foreign-born Catholic could not become a citizen and, therefore, could not legally transmit property to heirs.[90] Such restrictions could be ignored, but not repealed.

Religious freedom allowed open competition among denominations. In spite of bitter competition within and among churches, no one suggested imposing civil liabilities on religious opponents. Instead, there was a great deal of ecumenical exploration between the German Reformed and Presbyterians, the Reformed and the Lutherans, the Lutherans and Anglicans. The Moravians' early success came because they held up a model of nondenominational Christian unity. Leaders in all the major religious traditions – Zinzendorf, Duché, Peters, Muhlenberg, Wrangel, Tennent, Alison, Saur, Woolman, Benezet – stressed the internal spiritual harmony of true Christians that transcended denominational differences. Those less sympathetic to the mystical nature of Christianity, like Franklin, found in religion a common morality conducive to civic virtue.[91]

The blending of politics and religion brought power but also hostility and distrust. Clerics resented sectarian power and laymen opposed political ministers. Still, the conditions of religious freedom gave to ministers opportunity to criticize governmental policy. The colonists expected the ministers to weld them together against a common danger in wartime. Religion was the source for moral values, which remained an essential requisite for human society. The colony assumed that all sects and churches would work together to foster moral living.

CHAPTER IV

Religious Liberty in the Revolution

In the decade prior to the Revolution the surface signs of Pennsylvania's commitment to religious liberty and the equality of denominations seemed little changed. The Quaker party remained the dominant power in the assembly and Friends constituted, between 1761 and 1774, from 42 to 50 percent of the representatives.[1] Ministers in the meeting continued to complain about the corruptions of politics, but the political Friends insisted that the protection of the liberties of the colonists and the preservation of the traditions of William Penn demanded their continuance in office.[2] Those active in the Quaker party as justices of the peace and assemblymen were not important figures in the Yearly Meeting. Joseph Galloway, leader of the Quaker party since Franklin was in England, was at best a nominal Friend who did not use the plain style of dress and speech and did not believe in pacifism. He catered to the desires of Friends because his electoral majority depended upon the support of Quaker-dominated Chester and Bucks counties.[3] John Dickinson, leader of the opposition, married a Quaker and attended meetings but was not a member nor a pacifist.[4] Political leadership remained largely in the hands of the English-Americans with few Germans or Scots-Irish holding office.

Originally, the Proprietary party had been an alliance of Presbyterians and Anglicans, the Quaker party a blending of sectarians, Germans, and those English and Scots-Irish who approved of the assembly's policies. During the agitation and approach of the American Revolution these coalitions tended to break down. Several of the leaders of the popular, Presbyterian party, left the Quaker party either over pacifism, charter revision, or the temporizing course followed by Galloway and Franklin in dealing with British taxation. In the controversies with England the Quaker and Proprietary parties discovered they had much in common. Both opposed what they saw as unconstitutional taxation by Great Britain, but they wanted the protests against the stamp, Townshend, and tea taxes to be carried on in a peaceful manner.

The slow growth of cooperation between the leaders of the Quaker and Proprietary parties paralleled closely the relations among Anglicans and Friends. Their rapproachment occurred because both churches came from positions of numerical weakness. The Church of England, unsuccessful in her campaign to obtain a bishop, by the Revolution still only had ten clergy and twenty churches in all of Pennsylvania. Only the Philadelphia parishes were strong enough or willing to support a minister without a subsidy from England. Neither Friends, Moravians, Mennonites, Amish, or German Baptists experienced rapid growth. Many Quakers moved to the south or west, and the revival of discipline among Friends in the 1750s resulted in a large number of disownments for violation of the peace testimony or marriage out of unity; that is, marriage not endogamous or performed by a priest. No immigration, revivals, or proselytizing by the sectarian churches caused rapid growth. The Church of England clergy might not like the sectarians, but they had little to fear from them. The Presbyterians were the powerful rival.

Pennsylvania's Presbyterians had papered over the Old Light – New Light schism and reunited in 1758 in the Synod of Philadelphia and New York,[5] but the New Lights now had numerical dominance. The College of New Jersey, under the presidency of John Witherspoon, seemed less radically prorevivalist though still strongly evangelical. The Scottish-born and educated Witherspoon combined Calvinist orthodoxy with common-sense philosophy. His tact and abilities helped solidify the Presbyterian church and gave him a prominent position in New Jersey politics, where he served as an advocate of colonial rights, delegate to the Continental Congress, and signer of the Declaration of Independence.[6]

The relationship between the Presbyterian church and the opposition or Presbyterian party in Pennsylvania was even more tangential than that between Friends and the Quaker party. If the Presbyterians had a political leader, it would have been John Dickinson, who was not a Presbyterian. William Allen and his sons were more closely allied with the proprietors than the emerging popular, radical, Presbyterian party. Radical leaders like Charles Thomson and George Bryan, who were Presbyterians, emerged, but they were no more influential than Thomas Wharton and Thomas Mifflin, who had once been Quakers.[7] The Presbyterian party – the name was used as early as 1764 – owed its name to the habit of Pennsylvanians of lumping ethnicity, religion, and politics. The party gained support from the settlers in the west who were disenchanted with both the Quaker peace and the proprietor's land policies. The frontiersmen allied themselves with the artisans and tradesmen in Philadelphia who favored strong resistance to parliamentary taxation, including total boycotts of British goods after the stamp, Townshend, and tea acts.[8] In New England and in Pennsylvania the English Calvinist clergy became identified with popular opposition to the English government. Because the Presbyterians and Congregationalists had begun negotiating some form of union, their combined strength made Anglicans and Quakers even more fearful. Both denominations looked to their brethren in England to preserve them from Presbyterian domination.

The German Lutheran and Reformed churches increased in number and membership as much as the Presbyterians.[9] A shortage of clergy, difficulties with the English language, a conservatism brought from Europe, and ties with religious leaders in Holland and England prompted the German clergy to play little role in politics. The ministerial organizations of Lutheran and Reformed did not officially mention any of the difficulties occurring in America between 1766 and 1775, except for endorsing participation in fast days.[10]

The Quaker party served as spokesmen for the sectarian cause, and Joseph Galloway's attempted compromise or negotiated settlement proposed at the First Continental Congress in 1774 expressed the conservative and Quaker belief that without some solution there would be a war between Britain and the colonies. The defeat of Galloway's plan of union led to his charge that the radicals aimed at independence. The Society of Friends now suggested that members withdraw from politics and officeholding.[11]

The battles of Lexington and Concord in April 1775, forced the colonists to decide whether to arm themselves. Congress asked the states to create militias. In Pennsylvania the issues that had been debated since the 1690s again were rehashed. Was Pennsylvania founded as a pacifist colony? Did the liberty of conscience guarantees in the *Frames of Government* require no coercive military service? Could any government that did not protect property and liberties be legitimate? Did the Quaker position sacrifice colonial liberties? Were the pacifists undermining the liberties of their fellow citizens by seeking favors from the Crown, which would bring material rewards when the taxation problems ended?[12]

The Quakers announced their position in a memorial to the assembly; the Mennonites and German Baptists sent a petition as well.[13] The opposition this time did not originate with the Proprietary party, but in the volunteer companies of militia that were already in existence and drilling.[14] The Quaker party survived until 1776 only by repudiating the goals of the Society of Friends. The assembly's authority was threatened by the existence of nonlegal committees and associators, who enforced a boycott of British goods and corresponded with men in other colonies. So the assembly not only authorized a militia, but made service a duty of all male citizens between sixteen and fifty (later fifty-three).[15] Those whose religious principles did not allow them to fight were exempted, but they had to pay an equivalent service tax of 2s.6p. per day of drill, or about the amount of a laborer's day wage. The militia law exempted from service all indentured servants who did not have their master's permission to enlist (but fined the master 3s.6p.), schoolmasters, and clergymen. Since Augustine's time clergymen had been exempted from military service because of their religious vocation. Quakers had insisted that all men had a religious vocation, but the assembly was now unwilling to accept that tenet of faith.

In the winter and spring of 1775 the religious leaders of Pennsylvania provided their congregations with conflicting advice on the war with Great Britain. The Lutheran and Reformed ministers refused to issue a declaration.[16] The Presbyterian Synod, meeting in New York in May, broke what it claimed was silence on political affairs to proclaim loyalty to the king, endorse the colonists' defense of liberties, and give advice on winning the war. Insisting that magistrates must defend liberty of conscience, the synod's clergy called upon all churches to cease criticizing each other and to unite in enforcing moral discipline on their congregations so that God would favor the Americans. "There is no soldier so undaunted as the pious man, no army so formidable as those who are superior to the fear of death."[17] In January the Philadelphia Yearly Meeting of Friends issued a declaration supporting pacifism and requiring members to withdraw from a rebellion against rulers ordained by God. Local meetings began disowning those who enlisted in the militia or who too vigorously supported the resistance against Britain.[18] The Mennonites, Moravians, and German Baptists supported the Quaker positions, even though all the sectarian churches were now labeled by the patriots as Tories or loyalists. There was no mention of independence by the churches in 1775, because that treasonous subject was not openly advocated until after Thomas Paine's *Common Sense* appeared in January 1776.

Adherents of the Church of England in Pennsylvania were in a delicate position. Provost William Smith had preached in support of colonial resistance to British encroachments, and Jacob Duché, rector of Christ Church, was chaplain to and preached a sermon justifying the colonists' defense of liberties before the members of the Continental Congress.[19] But when defense of English liberties gave way to rebellion and independence, many clergy drew back. The liturgy required prayers for the royal family and ordination vows had included pledges to the Protestant succession. Without a tie to Great Britain, there could be no ordination and no funds from the Society for the Propagation of the Gospel. After independence was declared, William Smith, having lost his position at the College of Philadelphia in 1777, moved to Maryland, William White, assistant rector at Christ Church, omitted the prayers, and Thomas Barton joined the English in New York. Jacob Duché first seemed to support the patriots but later, after the British imprisoned him, wrote to General George Washington advocating ending the war.[20] He finally returned to England.

Henry Melchior Muhlenberg, the most influential Lutheran clergyman in America, confided to his diary his mixed feelings about the course of events. British arrogance had brought the disastrous policies, and God was punishing their sins.[21] Virtue among the Americans was also a rare commodity, and the influence of freethinkers and skeptics among the patriot leaders could bring God's wrath on America.[22] Muhlenberg did not favor independence, even after two of his sons left the pulpit to become military leaders.[23] He also had no sympathy for Quakers, whose pacifism and political posturing had led to their just fall from power.[24] When the Lutheran ministerium agreed to omit the prayers for the royal family after independence, Muhlenberg concurred.[25] He opposed the new loyalty oath and did not take it until the final deadline for compliance approached.[26] He preached sermons at the request of military companies and expressed dismay that some British thought him a patriot and some Americans charged that he was a loyalist.[27] He found the war destructive of piety and awaited with prayerful seeking the Almighty's determination of which side would prevail. His conclusion was that clergy should preach the gospel, not politics.[28]

The Revolution in Pennsylvania was clearly a civil war and in early 1776 the population remained divided, disliking independence but distrusting the British and unable to foresee a workable compromise. The Quaker party continued to control the assembly and had instructed the delegates to the Second Continental Congress to oppose independence. The elections of May 1, 1776 served as a referendum on independence and, even with the nonparticipation of Quakers, showed a nearly equal balance between the Quaker party, which favored negotiation while fighting, and the Presbyterian party, which sought independence. Fifteen days later Congress suggested that any government deriving power from a charter be replaced. By June Pennsylvania's radicals had subverted the colonial government and the first task for the new state was to draw up a new constitution.

Their repudiation of the charter government in 1776 permitted Pennsylvania's revolutionaries to hold a constitutional convention in July to rethink traditional policies, including those on religious liberty. The new constitution built on but also modified Pennsylvania's heritage of separation of church and state. Even though virtually all the members of the convention opposed the colony's Quaker political heritage, the religious provisions of the new constitution showed marked similarities with past practices and demonstrated that Pennsylvanians accepted the inherited pattern of liberty of conscience.

The preamble to the 1776 constitution used two euphemisms for God. He was the "Author of existence" who bestowed "natural rights and other blessings" and the "great Governor of the Universe" whose "goodness" was confessed, and which was demonstrated by his allowing the people to form peacefully a new government that might enable the inhabitants to reach hitherto undreamed heights of happiness. The bill of rights, which began the constitution, defined religious freedom as the "natural and unalienable right to worship Almighty God" according to each man's conscience and understanding. No "power" (such as, government) will compel any person to attend, erect, and support any church or interfere with or "in any manner control" either the right of conscience or the free exercise of religious worship.[29]

Still, the freedom of religion was not absolute. No person who acknowledged the "being of God" could be "justly deprived" of any civil right. Obviously an atheist was not entitled to full legal equality. Officeholders before 1776 had been required to affirm or swear to stringent tests imposed by the British government in defense of Protestant Christianity and against Roman Catholicism. The antipapal portion of the loyalty oaths now disappeared. The convention's first proposal, which was published in the newspapers but never submitted to popular vote, asked that all officeholders acknowledge the being of God who punished the wicked and rewarded the good. The clergy of Philadelphia who read of the proposed oath objected, insisting that it would not bar Jews, deists, or even Muslims from holding office. The convention, already estranged from the sectarian members of the Commonwealth, could not risk a rupture with the important churches. The clergy drew up the language they wanted and brought it to Franklin, the president of the convention. The convention then adopted the clergy's stipulation requiring officeholders to acknowledge the divine inspiration for the Old and New Testaments.[30] Even so, conservatives like the Lutheran Muhlenberg and Moravian Bishop John Ettwein disliked the influence that freethinkers allegedly had on the new constitution and complained that the convention had not defined the meaning of divine inspiration, so that a deist, Jew, or Muslim remained eligible for office.[31]

The right of conscientious objection, understood by Friends as implicit in Penn's *Frames of Government* but not endorsed by non-Quakers, was now modified. Those who for religious conviction could not conscientiously bear arms were excused from military service, but they would have to pay a special tax, the equivalent of a substitution fee.[32] Provost William Smith wanted to guarantee the independence of the College of Philadelphia, particularly because many of the trustees and a few of the faculty inclined to loyalism and Smith's patriotism was suspect. So under Smith's guidance the clergy proposed and the convention accepted an article confirming all religious bodies and chartered charitable and educational institutions in their property rights. Smith's safety net was efficacious for the chartered churches, Presbyterian insurance company for ministers, Pennsylvania Hospital, and Penn Charter School, but not the College of Philadelphia. In 1779 the state revoked the college's charter citing the number of Tories on the board, the previous subversion of the nondenominational nature of the school, and the importance to the Commonwealth of republican education of its children.[33] William Smith was dropped as provost. The new governing body included as ex officio members the senior clergy from the major denominations: Lutheran, Reformed, Episcopal, Baptist, Presbyterian, and Roman Catholic.[34] The revolutionaries in Pennsylvania believed in ecumenical republicanism.

William Penn and the colonial assemblies insisted that governmental divorce from the institutions of religion would not weaken the state's commitment to fostering moral goodness. The 1776 constitution shared this belief declaring that laws for the encouragement of virtue and the prevention of vice and immorality should be made and constantly kept in force.

After promulgating a constitution the Pennsylvania government faced the difficult task of winning a war while gaining the allegiance of a substantial minority of the population.[35] To the revolutionaries there could be no bystanders when the fundamental liberties of a people were at stake. Pluralism and toleration in religion were good, but a religious dissent that threatened the war effort would not be acceptable. Being pro-British was now treason, and pacifists who did not contribute money or men were disloyal. At the very least, all citizens should support the government by declaring allegiance, paying taxes, using the new paper money issued to finance the war, and either serving in the militia or paying for a substitute.

In the fall of 1776, delegates from all the Quaker Yearly Meetings in America met at Philadelphia to define Friends' position on independence and the war. Their announcement asserted the primacy of religion over all political commitments and grounded their dissent upon religious freedom. Quakers would be neutral in the war and provide aid to neither side. Neutrality meant that Quakers would not fight, would make no declarations of allegiance to anyone, would pay no taxes to governments of uncertain legitimacy, and would not vote.[36] Quakers now would occupy the sidelines while God worked His own purposes in the pulling down of the old order and the establishment of new governments. Friends in 1776 repudiated what they had done since the 1680s – seek power and assume responsibility for government.

The patriots in the new government saw the Quaker position as a cover for loyalism. Quaker merchants who refused to accept paper money were undermining the value of the currency. Friends had no right to opt out of society when they continued to occupy prominent positions and would enjoy the fruits of an American victory.[37] The patriots were sacrificing for the benefits of the entire community; justice required that the Quakers should do the same, whether willingly or not. The new assembly attempted to increase the penalties for noncompliance for the wealthy, prominent Friends, who were only waiting for the British to conquer before reassuming their political roles. Those who refused to serve in the militia were subject to fines and double taxation. In June 1777, as the danger from British invasion increased, the assembly passed a test act giving only three weeks to pledge allegiance. As the British forces approached Philadelphia, the government seized several prominent Quaker leaders and exiled them to western Virginia without benefit of trial or even formal charges.[38] The next spring, while the British still occupied Philadelphia, the assembly repassed a test act, gave until June 1 for affirming allegiance, and increased the penalties for noncompliance. All who refused to take the test lost their citizenship and voting rights and the protection of law for their property, which could be confiscated. In addition, they could be fined. Teachers who refused the oath could not hold school.[39] Under the law the Penn Charter School in Philadelphia stopped functioning. The meeting held firm, and disowned Quakers who paid war taxes, joined the military, or took the test oath. Friends compiled an account of property seized by the military for supplies, but refused to accept payment. They also recorded the amount of fines and distraints upon property.[40] A few Quakers who dissented from the meetings' position and were disowned formed the Society of Free Quakers to support the Revolution.[41] Most Quakers still would not take the test, even after peace came in 1783, and did not regain their voting rights until Pennsylvania repealed the test act in 1786.

The issue for Friends and other sectarians was not just an unnecessary loyalty oath, but the contents of that declaration. The act required the following oath or affirmation:

I . . . do swear (or affirm) that I renounce and refuse all allegiance to George the Third, King of Great Britain . . . and that I will be faithful and bear true allegiance to the commonwealth of Pennsylvania as a free and independent state, and that I will not at any time do or cause to be done any matter or thing that will be prejudicial or injurious to the freedom and independence thereof, as declared by Congress; and also that I will discover and make known to some one justice of the peace of the said state all treasons or traitorous conspiracies which I now know or hereafter shall know to be formed against that or any of the United States of America.[42]

The diary of John Ettwein, Moravian bishop of Bethlehem, provided a vivid picture of the effects of the test act upon sectarian religious groups. The Moravians remained sympathetic to Great Britain. Parliament in 1749 had granted them the right of affirmation and exemption from military service and the Church of England recognized the spiritual authority and apostolic succession of Moravian bishops.[43] In Pennsylvania the Moravians, allied with the Quaker party, enjoyed virtual self-government in communities at Bethlehem, Nazareth, and Lititz.[44] A justice of the peace and an assemblyman from Northampton County until 1776 were normally Moravians. The Moravians in Pennsylvania conducted an extensive missionary program in the West Indies and to the American Indians and wanted to do nothing to jeopardize their ties with their brethren in England and Germany and their evangelical activities in the British Empire.

Most Moravians refused to take the new loyalty oath. Unlike the Quakers, the Moravians left the matter to individual conscience, and a few members of the dispersed country congregations did subscribe. The main body informed the assembly of their willingness to obey peacefully the new government and to pay taxes. But they would not pledge allegiance for all future time to governments still awaiting God's verdict on their survival.[45] A vow had lasting religious significance that could not be abrogated, and many Moravians had earlier affirmed loyalty to the British government when they became naturalized citizens. In addition, pacifism required that they not engage in warlike acts but should withdraw from worldly activities like fighting, which were the product of sin.[46] Finally, the test act required the person to sign a statement that he voluntarily took the pledge. This requirement was incongruous considering that refusal meant the loss of a right to vote, serve on juries, collect debts, hold important political office, be guaranteed the rights of citizenship. The liability to double taxation, confiscation of estate, and banishment accentuated the coercive elements in the law.[47]

The Moravians grounded their refusal upon liberty of conscience and the guarantees in the 1776 Pennsylvania constitution.[48] Theoretically, the new government established freedom of religion upon the autonomy of conscience that could not be forced by outside authority. Now the revolutionary authorities sought to rule conscience. The authorities in Northampton County threatened, fined, distrained, and imprisoned Moravians. They confiscated property.[49] They charged exorbitant fees for substitutes for the militia. The Moravians thought the government intended these punitive measures to drive them away so that the patriots could obtain their lands. Even the Moravian service to wounded American soldiers after the government established a hospital at Bethlehem brought no respite. The Schwenkfelders joined with Moravians in petitions to the Pennsylvania assembly asking relief.[50] Ettwein visited sympathetic congressmen and assemblymen, but the requirements for a test were not changed, even after the Peace of Paris in 1783.

During the French and Indian War the Mennonites had refused to fight, but they had furnished wagons and supplies to the British army and paid taxes without question. After 1775 the Mennonite position was similar to the Quakers. Although the Mennonites supported colonial rights, they looked upon the charter government as a guarantee of religious liberty. Their claim of neutrality after independence seemed to outsiders as loyalism. Christopher Funk, a minister, supported the Revolution, took the affirmation, and paid taxes, though he did not serve in the militia. The Mennonites shunned him. They refused to take the test oath because it required an affirmation of enmity and Christ called for loving one's enemies. Mennonites declared that they would obey any government in power as ordained by God. They would provide relief to war sufferers but would not furnish substitutes or pay taxes levied on pacifists.[51]

Eventually the test act became a political issue between those who defended the 1776 Pennsylvania constitution and those who wanted revision, but the test act remained in effect until 1786. Arthur Young estimated that between 14 and 24 percent of those covered by the test acts refused to take the oath of allegiance.[52]

In colonial Pennsylvania the church people, sectaries, and freethinkers agreed that the creation and preservation of good government depended upon virtuous citizens and honest officials. The legislature's task included passing laws to discourage vice and encourage morality. There was some disagreement on what constituted morality, or at least just what immorality the state could or should deal with legally. Sunday, lotteries, and the theater had all occasioned controversy before the Revolution. An examination of the policies of Pennsylvania on these three areas before and during the Revolution will show the effects of replacing the sectarians with members of churches as elected officials.

Before 1776 Quakers had to contend with the ideals of the Church of England in moral legislation. Friends normally did not consider Sunday a holy day, but still wanted all labor to cease. They wished to outlaw sports, games, and diversions on Sunday because they did not approve of such idle time-wasters at any time. The Presbyterians wanted all labor and all recreations to cease on a day they viewed as holy. Anglicans agreed that the day was holy and that all labor should cease, but not innocent recreations and sports. Pietists supported the Calvinist view of the Sabbath and the Baptists and most of the Lutheran clergy in Pennsylvania were pietists.[53] The Seventh-Day Baptists wanted a strict observance of Saturday and freedom to labor on Sunday, but their wishes were ignored. Soon after their arrival in Bethlehem the Moravians began to observe Saturday as the Sabbath, but after their neighbors complained the elders decided to observe both Saturday and Sunday.[54] In 1683 and 1700 the Quakers tried to legislate their vision of the Sabbath, but the Crown interposed. So Pennsylvania's statutes did not define Sunday as a holy day and prohibited labor, not recreation.

Friends also opposed lotteries as a form of gambling. The Crown vetoed laws prohibiting sports, games of chance and lotteries until the assembly passed an act only regulating lotteries in 1730. The fines in the 1730 act could be remitted and the assembly could authorize lotteries, although it did not do so. In 1747 the Philadelphia Council authorized a lottery, organized by Franklin, to provide cannon for the city. The governor did not enforce the 1730 act, and many private lotteries occurred until the assembly in 1758 outlawed all Pennsylvania lotteries (except those authorized by Parliament) and all plays.[55] All fines from the lottery statute were to go to the Pennsylvania Hospital. The Crown vetoed the statute, seeing it as a method of reducing the financing of the Academy and College of Philadelphia, which sponsored lotteries. Still, the Crown would have accepted the act if it had not also outlawed plays.[56] So the assembly in 1762 passed a second antilottery act. The preamble gives the rationale for opposing lotteries:

Whereas many mischievous and unlawful games called lotteries have been set up in this province which tend to the manifest corruption of youth and the ruin and impoverishment of many poor families. And whereas such pernicious practices may not only give opportunities to evil-disposed persons to cheat and defraud the honest inhabitants of this province, but prove introductive of vice, idleness and immorality, injurious to trade, commerce and industry and against the common good, welfare and peace of the province....[57]

The act did not forbid lotteries licensed by the assembly. Churches took advantage of the act to gain lotteries for buildings. Anglicans, Presbyterians, Lutherans, and Reformed all received permission from the assembly for lotteries.[58] As a fund-raising device the lotteries were often not successful. The assembly had to extend the time on occasion because too many tickets remained unsold. Even if not all tickets were sold, the prizes had to be distributed. There were also problems with the honesty of managers. After 1770 there was a period when few lotteries occurred.

The 1758 act against lotteries was also designed to suppress plays.[59] Early Pennsylvania laws against plays did not survive royal review, but the issue did not seem crucial until a theatrical troop came to Philadelphia. The assembly was deluged with petitions from Quakers, Lutherans, Baptists, and Presbyterians.[60] There was none from the Anglicans. The assembly responded by outlawing plays, but the Crown vetoed the law arguing that plays could be regulated but not outlawed. When a playhouse was built in 1766 the assembly received several petitions, but the governor refused to take action and plays continued to be produced in Philadelphia.

The approach of the Revolution quickened the impulse of Pennsylvania's leaders for moral legislation. Virtue might abort tragedy by inducing the Almighty to favor the Americans as well as discouraging the consumption of luxuries and thereby make the boycott of British goods successful. In 1774 the assembly passed a law against "every species of extravagance and dissipation," which included many of the offenses in Penn's first law code, such as "gaming, cock fighting, exhibition of plays."[61] When the assembly created a militia in 1775 Article 1 of the "Rules and Articles" stated: "It is earnestly recommended to all officers and soldiers diligently to attend Divine service; and all officers and soldiers, who shall behave indecently or irreverently at any place of Divine worship, shall, if commissioned officers, be brought before a court martial." Officers received reprimands and noncommissioned and soldiers could be fined for profane swearing.[62] The soldiers' religious life would be aided by having chaplains. In 1780 the assembly stipulated that army chaplains would receive half pay for life with a rank of captain.[63]

In 1779 the assembly passed a stringent Act for the Suppression of Vice and Immorality. It accepted the Presbyterian version of the Sabbath by protecting the "Lord's Day" from any labor as well as "any game, play, sport or diversion."[64] The populace learned that any profane swearing or cursing that named God, Christ, or the Holy Spirit, overheard either by one witness or by a justice of the peace, brought a fine of 10s. A public housekeeper or retailer of strong liquors who promoted horse racing or sold liquor to people attending a race forfeited his license and was fined £20. The same penalty came if the tavernkeeper allowed cards, dice, billiards, bowls, and shuffleboard. In colonial days the assembly had complained that the governors licensed taverns and were more interested in fees than cutting down the number of tippling houses. After 1779 the assembly delegated the power to grant licenses to the president, required those who had not obtained licenses earlier to pay several years' back fees, and raised the cost because during the war the profits had been considerable.[65] In 1778 the legislature forbade using wheat for producing grain-based alcoholic beverages, and in 1779 restricted the quantity of whiskey made from rye, barley, and malt. These laws were repealed in 1780. The laws clearly stated that their purpose was to reserve grain for the army and civilians.[66]

The assembly also attempted to outlaw gambling. Gambling debts were made not collectable. If a person paid such a debt, he could later sue and receive both the money and cost of the litigation. Cockfighting and horse racing brought £500 fines. A duel cost the same amount plus imprisonment for twelve months. Previous attempts at restricting theaters in Philadelphia had proved ineffectual. The British during the occupation of the city had performed numerous plays. So the state now outlawed all theater and stage plays in "any city, town, or place."

The Pennsylvania blue laws were not just a wartime measure. In 1786 and 1794 the assembly repassed the laws against vice. The provisions of the three laws were virtually identical, with one exception. In 1779 and 1786 all theatrical observances had been outlawed. When one theatrical director defied the ban in 1782, the magistrates stopped the plays. But under various subterfuges plays were performed until 1788, when Quakers and others petitioned the assembly. After a vigorous debate in the newspapers, petitions to the assembly showed that about 4,000 opposed the theater and 6,000 were in favor. In spite of the fact that most of the clergymen in Philadelphia opposed, including Anglican William White, the assembly legalized the performance of moral plays. George Washington and other members of the new Federal government frequently attended Philadelphia theaters.[67]

The Revolution marked the end of the Quaker or sectarian definition of religious liberty. The Quaker politicians who insisted that their continuance in office was necessary for the preservation of minority rights were correct. The revolutionary struggle, which began as an effort to preserve the rights of the majority of Pennsylvanians, resulted in the disenfranchisement of a substanital minority. Historians examining the religious-ethnic composition of the state legislature and county and local officeholders describe the displacing of Quakers and Anglicans by Presbyterians and Germans who were either Lutheran or Reformed.[68] After 1776 the sectarians no longer could determine Pennsylvania's policies on religious liberty, because church people were the decisive factor. The revolutionary governments repudiated pacifism and made military service to the nation or state an obligation that could not be evaded, although it was possible to pay a tax for a substitute. The assembly imposed stringent loyalty oaths. Previously the British government insisted that officeholders and all naturalized citizens take anti-Catholic oaths, but most people need never have made such a declaration. In 1776 the revolutionary government in Pennsylvania was unsure of its mandate, and requiring some kind of declaration of support seemed logical. The radicals almost designed the form of the pledge to alienate the sectaries, and their refusing to change the oath long after the British threat disappeared was clearly punitive, an act of political and religious persecution.

The revolutionary Pennsylvania government was less tolerant than the colonial assembly in the definition of restraints on the Sabbath and equally puritanical in the restriction of so-called moral evils. The only areas in which 1776 marked an easing of colonial restrictions was in dropping the disabilities against incorporation of churches that the proprietors had imposed, and in ending discrimination against Roman Catholics that the English had required. Pennsylvania throughout the period of Quaker domination remained the most tolerant of all the American colonies. The takeover by the churches after 1776 resulted in a situation in which some Pennsylvanians became less free. The Revolution marked a transition from sectarian liberty to creating a Christian commonwealth. The heritage of the revolutionaries of 1776 was Pennsylvania's nineteenth-century blue laws.

CHAPTER V

Religious Liberty and the Republic

Historians have often complained about the lack of direct evidence of the thoughts about the meaning of the First Amendment religion clauses by the delegates of the ratification conventions of the Federal Constitution, the members of the First Congress, and state legislatures. In Pennsylvania politicians, clergymen, and ordinary citizens provided evidence of their beliefs about religious liberty and the relation of God to the state, but they did not discuss the meaning of the First Amendment. Rather, only rarely did they differentiate between the religious responsibilities of the Federal government and Pennsylvania. They also generally ignored the tax-supported churches in New England and wrote as if the Pennsylvania pattern were normative for all levels of government. Virtually all Pennsylvanians believed that Americans enjoyed a religious liberty that was essential for the purity of the church and the prosperity of the state. The separation of the state from the institutional church did not mean official neutrality toward religion. Religious belief was a private decision with public consequences. However, in the midst of Pennsylvania's generally self-congratulatory prose, there emerged tensions over different interpretations of separation of church and state, which continue to this day.

Many of the Pennsylvanians involved in Congress's preparation and the state legislature's ratification of the Bill of Rights in late 1789–90 were also active in writing and the struggle over the adoption of the Pennsylvania constitution of 1790. In the absence of direct evidence of the meaning of the religion clause in the First Amendment, the constitution of 1790 provides a valuable indication of what Pennsylvanians believed about religious establishments and the separation of the institutional church from government. The 1790 Pennsylvania constitution repudiated so many features of the 1776 document that historians have termed the political changeover a "counter-revolution."[1] In religious matters, the new constitution was more radical. The small Jewish community in Phila-

74

delphia had protested that the test for office of a belief in the divine authority of Old and New Testaments discriminated against them.[2] The test also might bar some of the deists or freethinkers, such as Tom Paine, who played a prominent role in the Revolution. Consequently, the preamble, no longer needed to gather support for a war, was one sentence and contained no mention of God. Although the convention voted forty-seven to thirteen against striking the entire test for officeholding, the omission of the explicit references to the Scriptures occasioned no controversy, and the convention restored the reading of the first draft of the 1776 constitution. That test, requiring all officeholders to "acknowledge the being of God, and a future state of rewards and punishments," is part of Pennsylvania's present-day constitution.[3]

Furthermore, in the 1790 constitution full enjoyment of civil rights was no longer contingent upon belief in God, and the convention discussed, though it does not appear in the final document, how a non-Christian could bear a testimony in a court. Also omitted was the declaration that laws should be made for the prevention of vice and the encouragement of virtue, perhaps because the members saw no need to reiterate such an obvious duty. The convention rejected (twenty-three to thirty-nine) an attempt to repeal a special tax on conscientious objectors and ignored a petition from the Pennsylvania Society for the Abolition of Slavery.[4] By these two actions the convention continued to repudiate the Quaker-sectarian definition of religious liberty.

Neither Article VII, which confirmed all rights given to religious bodies previously, nor Article VIII, on freedom of worship, occasioned much debate; at least no divisions were recorded in the minutes. Article VIII proclaimed that, among natural rights, all men had a "natural and indefeasible right to worship God" ("Almighty" had disappeared) "according to conscience, and that no one could be compelled to attend, erect, or support any place of worship." Thus far the language closely parallels the 1776 document. A new clause, whose meaning was not debated in the convention, declared that "no preference shall ever be given, by law, to any religious establishments or modes of worship."[5]

Because this language was reiterated without change in Pennsylvania's constitutions of 1838, 1873, and 1911 and is in force today, some discussion of its original meaning is called for.[6] The statement that no preference be given "by law" left the door open for nonlegal support such as prayers on public occasions, proclamation of fast days, swearing on the Bible in courts, and declarations by government officials in favor of religion. Throughout the nineteenth century most of the religious observances in the militia, common schools, and courts were founded on customary usage.

The language of Article VIII in the 1790 Pennsylvania constitution also differs from the First Amendment in the Federal Bill of Rights. There, Congress is "to make no law respecting an establishment of religion, or prohibiting the free exercise thereof." "Establishment" here refers to a church supported by law; in the Pennsylvania constitution the word is plural and refers to all churches.[7] New York before the Revolution had a plural establishment and New England allowed each individual's religious tax to be applied to his or her church. The Pennsylvania constitution outlawed both the New York and the New England patterns. The additional phrase "modes of worship" is even more inclusive. The Federal Congress was denied the right to make laws either "respecting" or "prohibiting" religion. In fact, given the prevailing assumptions about reserving areas of jurisdiction to the states, it is tempting to believe that those who ratified the First Amendment could see no reason for any Federal legislation on religion. The Antifederalist minority at the Pennsylvania convention to ratify the Federal Constitution proposed an amendment: "The right of conscience shall be held inviolable, and neither the legislative, executive, nor judicial powers of the United States shall have authority to alter, abrogate, or infringe any part of the Constitutions of the several States, which provide for the preservation of liberty in matters of conscience."[8]

The amendment can be interpreted in several ways. If Pennsylvanians thought they had arrived at the apogee of religious liberty, the Federal government could have no say on any religious matters. If, on the other hand, New England's religious freedom was not sufficient, the amendment would not forbid the national government's intervention to extend religious liberty. The most plausible reading of the available evidence is that the Antifederalists thought that because Pennsylvania had already guaranteed the "inviolable" "right of conscience," the Federal government could not interfere in any way in the state's authority over religious matters. There is nothing in the Pennsylvania debates over the Federal Constitution that would indicate that the Federalists and Antifederalists disagreed over the national government's lack of authority in religious matters.

Pennsylvania's constitution was not based on the same degree of self-denial, because the state had to deal with each denomination's property rights. The state had granted charters of incorporation, sponsored lotteries to fund church building programs, and recognized the religious implications of legislation on moral issues and the regulation of marriage. The Pennsylvania constitution of 1790 assumes that there will be legislation on religion and guarantees that it will be nonpreferential; that is, neutral. All religious bodies under the law are to be treated alike, to be equal. Note also that the state constitution refers to "establishments" and "modes of worship," not religion as a system of beliefs. The United States

Constitution refers to "modes" of ratification; the meaning in Pennsylvania's Article VIII is the manner of doing a particular activity.

Unlike the 1776 and 1873 constitutions of Pennsylvania,[9] those of 1790 and of 1838 did not ground the existence of natural rights nor the validity of a republican form of government in the being or providence of God. Indeed, the 1790 constitution provided no statement as to the origins of life and liberty; the constitution was established by "We, the people" and the bill of rights listed "general, great, and essential principles of liberty and free government" which were "inherent," "indefeasible," and "natural." How they had gotten to be that way was not addressed. There were two mentions of the deity. Those who were guaranteed the right to worship were to be serving "Almighty God" – neither devil worship nor non-God worship was protected. Those citizens who refused to acknowledge the being of God and a "future state of rewards and punishment" were not trustworthy and were not to hold office. The same theory underlay oaths taken in the courts.

For all its secularity as compared with the 1776 constitution, the 1790 document still assumed that republican government required a virtuous citizenry, and a virtuous citizenry required moral instruction. The only sound ground for morality was religious observance. This interpretation gains credence from the statutes the Commonwealth passed in 1779, 1786, and 1794. The state really did not need to pass three laws against vice and gaming, because it had already reconfirmed the statutes existing from colonial days. The reason for the new laws of 1786 and 1794 was financial; inflation had so eroded the currency by 1786 that the punishments for profanity, etc., seemed too mild, and the assembly increased the penalties. The 1794 law converted the fines from shillings into dollars.[10] The 1794 act established regulations for the observances of Sunday, placed fines on profane swearing (sixty-seven cents for each invoking of God, Jesus Christ, and the Holy Ghost; forty cents for cursing by any other name), regulated tavern licenses and fined those intoxicated, outlawed all betting on races, games of chance, and cockfights, disallowed the collection of gambling debts, and forbade dueling or issuing a challenge or serving as a second.[11] The practices outlawed were not criminal, though failure to pay fines could land one in jail. These laws for "the prevention of vice and immorality, and of unlawful gaming, and to restrain disorderly sports and dissipation" showed an additional meaning of the separation of church and state. Issues that the churches viewed as religious the state officially recognized only as moral. The legislature knew that there was a linkage between religious and moral language, even assumed that such a linkage was desirable, but the official rationale for legal actions would always be the need for morality to keep the civil peace.

At the same time the state would foster the observance of religion, by favoring all rather than any distinct church. The legislature followed the constitutional provision in not fostering *a* mode of worship, but it did encourage *all* modes of worship. In 1798 an act to prevent disturbances of religious societies allowed the Philadelphia churches to stretch chains across the street during Sunday worship services. The law was extended to the Northern Liberties in 1816 and not repealed until 1831.[12] One statute deputized special people to keep order and outlawed the selling of liquor near camp meetings. The legislature passed special acts declaring the property of certain churches and charities tax exempt, until in 1838 a general policy made all churches' property (with certain limitations) tax exempt.[13]

Although the clauses dealing with religion in the Pennsylvania constitution of 1790 occasioned little debate, prominent politicians and ministers in the state before and after 1790 often wrote about religious liberty. They were generally too busy writing self-congratulatory panegyrics to freedom of religion to focus on different meanings of separation of church and state. The next section focuses on the themes of republican religious liberty in the writings of James Wilson, Benjamin Rush, William White, Samuel Stanhope Smith, Tench Coxe, and Thomas Paine. Except for Paine, these men's diverse religious beliefs, politics, and assumptions did not result in divergent conclusions about religious liberty. They all saw religion as unifying the community against disorder and welcomed the beneficial results for both church and state of a healthy competition among denominations that agreed on a common morality.

   James Wilson was an important member of the Pennsylvania delegation to the Federal Constitutional Convention and the most influential person in the convention that drew up the Pennsylvania constitution of 1790. In 1790–1 Wilson presented a series of public "Lectures on Law" at the College of Philadelphia. The audience included students, many prominent citizens of Philadelphia, and members of the new Federal government. Wilson, speaking as professor, successful lawyer, and associate justice of the United States Supreme Court, in his initial lecture dealt with the origins and authority of all law – divine, natural, and human – and the citizen's obligation to obey. Wilson did not see himself as a theologian, but his views of government and law show a close relationship between religious belief and political theory.

   All legitimate law originated in God, Wilson argued. Humans discovered revealed law through reading the Scriptures. Natural law, another form of human law, could be learned from reason or from conscience, and the faculty in the conscience, which determined law, was an innate "moral sense." The contents of the moral sense, the divine law and natural law were the same because all originated in God, whose "paternal command" could be summarized as "Let man pursue his own perfection and happiness."[14] God used law because it was the "fittest means" to use for "such ends only as promote our felicity." Philosophers disagreed on the source of obligation to obey the law citing utility or the promoting of happiness, sociability or the "care of maintaining society properly," and an innate moral sense. Rather than investigating these alternatives, Wilson opted for innate moral sense. Ultimately a person came to "feel" intuitively the difference between right and wrong. Such feelings were not subjective. "Morality, like mathematics, has its intuitive truth," and the "power of moral perception is . . . a most important power of our constitution."[15] Wilson's choice of the word constitution was hardly accidental, because there was a congruence between man's moral nature, the Federal and state constitutions, and law. All civilized arts – history, poetry, music, eloquence – rested upon a universal agreement on what was right and wrong.

The truths of morality were either "self-evident" or "deduced by reasoning." Those unable to reason could use their innate moral sense to arrive at truth. The moral sense enabled magistrates and the populace to determine the ends of government. The "means" to obtain those ends, because left to the products of human reason and varying with the circumstances, rendered any "single instance" of justice of uncertain widespread application.[16] The innate moral sense was crucial in discovering and obeying the moral law of God. Although the sense was innate, it was more perfectly realized in adults than in children or barbarians because it was both "intellectual and active," and came to "maturity by insensible degrees."[17] In essence, Wilson placed the presumed secularity of the "means" in the *Federalist Papers* and debates over the ratification of the Federal and Pennsylvania constitutions into a theological context. Whether or not these documents contained an explicit reference to God (and normally they did not), religion still provided the ultimate foundation of government.

Those in whom the moral sense never was fully developed were still responsible, because God in his wisdom had provided them an easier source for truth: the Bible. The Scriptures' judgments on morality were "most explicit and most certain." A "public minister" – note the ambiguous connotations as to whether public official or clergyman – based his pronouncements and actions on certain knowledge derived from reason, the moral sense, and Scriptures.[18] If the minister was still unsure, he should deduce his duty by reason from known moral principles.

Wilson's lectures appealed because his audience learned that divisive and complex theological, philosophical, and political issues need not concern them. Scriptures, reason, nature, the moral sense, God, and Americans already agreed on what was truth. The divergent religious beliefs of Pennsylvanians constituted no threat to the harmony of the state because all churches believed the same about right and wrong. Neither toleration nor separation of the institutional church from the state would bring disorder. God's will still guaranteed the sacred obligation to be moral citizens.

James Wilson's premises and conclusions were not idiosyncratic musings. Some of the most prominent men in the Middle Colonies addressed the same themes, and their agreements on fundamentals are more striking than the divergencies. Though no blacks, no women, and no workers left their opinions on religious liberty, the men who wrote exemplify the distribution of religious and political power in Pennsylvania. William White, rector of Christ Church and after 1787 first bishop of Pennsylvania, served as a spokesman for the Anglican community and a leader in many interdenominational charitable activities. White sought to reassure those who feared that a bishop would seek political authority. White counted in his congregation many members of Congress and officials of the Washington Administration, including the President. Samuel Stanhope Smith, first a professor and after 1795 president of the College of New Jersey at Princeton, was the most important Middle Colony Presbyterian. Smith adopted a nonpartisan tone in his writings and criticized both Federalists and Republicans, but he served as a Federalist elector for John Adams.[19] No one could accuse Tench Coxe of being nonpartisan. Suspected of loyalism during the Revolution, Coxe became a supporter of the Federal Constitution, a Federalist, and an official in the Adams Administration. Breaking with the Federalists, Coxe joined the Republicans, became a frequent contributor to the *Aurora,* and an important member and advisor in the Jefferson Administration.[20] Coxe sought to justify the American system of religious liberty in a portrait of the new nation drawn up for a European encyclopedia and first printed in a Philadelphia newspaper. Benjamin Rush, a leading physician of Philadelphia, supported the Revolution, but opposed the Pennsylvania constitution of 1776. He approved of the Federal Constitution and also corresponded with Jefferson before and after the election of 1800. Unlike the other writers, Rush was unorthodox in theology, repudiating Calvinism and sectarianism and embracing Universalism. However, he made no attempt to found a Universalist church in Philadelphia.[21] Finally, Tom Paine was the most radical of these men in theology and, most of the time, in politics as well. Paine lived in Pennsylvania during the Revolution, but then returned to England and France.[22] His *Age of Reason,* an attack upon orthodox Christianity and defense of deism, written in 1794, became a cause célèbre in Philadelphia. Paine did not specifically address conditions in Pennsylvania, but his ideas were widely discussed there and he dealt with themes of religious freedom. In the 1830s the workingmen of Philadelphia would invoke the memory of Tom Paine in their battle against the evangelical alliance. The continuing impact of Paine's ideas showed that there were some people in Philadelphia who did not believe that revolutionary and Federalist Pennsylvania had already attained perfection in religious liberty.[23]

All these men agreed with Wilson that religion was the foundation of government. William White argued that the social compact originating the American form of government rested upon God's prior act of creating man as a social being in need of order. So as its first duty the government should openly acknowledge "religion to be the basis of its existence" and God's will as the source of the reciprocal duties of magistrates and people.[24] Like Wilson, Samuel Stanhope Smith espoused the common-sense philosophy that he merged with evangelical Calvinism. Smith argued that Americans enjoyed a general agreement on the truths of religion. Because of the consensus on the essentials, differences in interpretation did not threaten the overall unity of the country.[25] Benjamin Rush, unlike Wilson, refused to ground religion and ethics upon rationalism or on innate common moral sense, because such notions ignored the scriptural record of the life and death of the Son of God. The spiritual equality of all persons under God served for Rush as the derivation of that republican equality of people proclaimed in the Declaration of Independence.[26] Tench Coxe echoed Wilson by proclaiming that "There can be no honor, or private morals, or public morality which is not found in the system of religion." God's eternal command was "Do justice" and because "eternal justice" had been institutionalized in the various constitutions, they had become "the piety of our politics – the true religion of our constitution."[27]

Even though the state was founded upon religion, the church had no direct political role in the government. William White insisted that the holy spirit did not determine the form of government: "The holy scriptures have founded no temporal dominion on the dispensation of grace; nor created any ecclesiastical authority that is to dictate to the civil. On the contrary, they beautifully harmonize with all the righteous views of government; and support the sanctions of law, with the more powerful sanctions of religion."[28]

In 1799 in a sermon on a presidential fast day, occasioned by the rupture with France, White gave a third version of the sermon he had first preached in 1775 and again on a July 4th celebration. White argued that there should be no preaching on political subjects, but a minister should "adapt his discourse to the civil conduct of his hearers" by explaining and clarifying applicable "precepts of scripture," particularly those often misinterpreted. Christianity's realm was a future world, but the clergy preached "sentiments" which affected "future life, thru' their intermediate influence on the civil interests of the present." True religion would oppose both "arbitrary power" and a "mal democracy." "Faction," "sedition," and "treason" came from resistance to the ordinance of God.[29]

The government had a few limited obligations to religious bodies. Samuel Stanhope Smith argued that the magistrate should secure the "sacred right of religious opinion" and the rights of every denomination over their own members, but did not spell out the implications of these assertions. Clearly the duty did not involve any civil domination of the church, a condition Smith defined as tyranny.[30] White wanted the government to acknowledge openly religion as the "basis of its existence" and God's will as the source of the reciprocal duties of magistrates and people. Public officials should demonstrate their moral integrity by actions and by public profession of religion. The government should pass laws strong enough to suppress "immoral conduct," but not to intrude upon the sacred rights of "conscience." Government also should encourage men to join organizations "for purposes of devotion and charity" and should maintain the "rights and property" of these organizations.[31]

Religious pluralism helped both the church and the state. Competition, said Benjamin Rush, fostered a healthy relationship between churches. Emulation of each other would bring out the best of religion in each denomination.[32] Smith argued that the rivalry among the churches prevented the development of an ecclesiastical tyranny. The laity were able to judge how well the church fulfilled its primary obligation of instilling faithfulness to God.[33] Tench Coxe boasted that American freedom of religion had allowed a society to so develop that small pacifist sects and large denominations believing in the legitimacy of defensive war coexisted in harmony as they worked alone and together to resist "slavery of the soul." Religious liberty preserved the American state from theological controversy and guaranteed, said Coxe, that the churches were a "theocracy."[34]

For all the writers discussed here freedom of religion meant no tax support for churches, no religious tests for government office, no ecclesiastical courts, no established church, and the inviolability of the rights of conscience. Such conditions created the American contribution to religion. Christianity contained the "purest system of virtue that was taught on earth" and provided a "moral discipline" that assured the survival of a "free state."[35] Benjamin Rush proclaimed that "Republican forms of government are the best repositories of the Gospel." Joining Christianity to republicanism combined two life-giving forces that together would inaugurate the millenium. "A Christian . . . cannot fail of being a republican, for every precept of the Gospel inculcates those degrees of humility, self-denial, and brotherly kindness, which are directly opposed to the pride of monarchy."[36]

Religious liberty by preserving the autonomy of the institutional church from the state meant that the nation was free to allow Christianity to permeate government policies. Benjamin Rush hoped that just as the Quaker antislavery protest had spread throughout the nation, so might their peace testimony. War was the hallmark of savages, peace of civilized republicans.[37] In America, proclaimed Tench Coxe, the "law of nations," or international law became the "law of the land" because it was the "*law of morals*" and "guided foreign policy."[38] Religious impulses lay behind the humanitarian fervor, which led to prison reform, questioning capital punishment, and erecting a merciful system of justice. Coxe painted a religious utopia in which the government determined Indian policy on William Penn's principles and where peace churches sent missionaries to civilize the natives. A critique of slavery, the granting of property rights to widows, and the "political morality" of officials reflected the "motions of conscience" responding to the judgments of God.[39]

Unlike the other writings considered here, Paine's *Age of Reason* was not a paean to the Pennsylvania pattern of religious liberty as inaugurating the best of all possible worlds. Paine ridiculed the agencies the others defined as the guarantors of religious liberty: the church, the clergy, and the Bible. Christianity had become the tool of avaricious priests who sought support from "despotic" governments, thereby contributing to the corruption of both church and state.[40] Because of the absurdity of the beliefs of traditional Christianity, its priests attempted to mix their authority with the state. For Paine, the Bible subverted moral law by advocating mystery, idolatry, sacrifice, vengeance, and love of enemies. The Ten Commandments did not summarize the moral law and were contrary to reason and common sense. The *Age of Reason* singled out the Calvinist Sabbath and Connecticut's "stupid blue laws" for attack.[41] The issue — whether or not restrictions on Sabbath labor and recreation were a part of God's eternal moral law – would be extensively debated in nineteenth-century Pennsylvania. Paine did not question the American consensus that a government had a duty legislatively to support God's moral law. He distinguished between the moral function of religion, which had public consequences, and the theological foundations. The intellectual part of religion is between "every man and his Maker, and in which no third party has any right to intervene."[42]

The essence of religion was morality, but Paine's definition of morality threatened the beliefs on which Republican religious liberty rested. If people relying on innate ideas, natural law, the Bible, and reason could not agree on the content of morality, then the intellectual underpinning of republican religious liberty was flimsy. Not even Paine was willing to embrace such potential anarchy. Instead, like Wilson and Rush, Paine saw God as a benevolent being and defined man's duty as "practical imitation of the moral goodness of God" through acting "benignly toward all." True religion consisted of a belief in one God derived from a person's study and appreciation of the created world and his consequent practice of morality and lawfulness. "Jesus Christ founded no new system. He called men to the practice of moral virtues and belief in one God. The great trait in his character is philanthropy."[43]

Wilson, Paine, Rush, Smith, and White divorced the social functions of religion from theology. Such a separation allowed the churches autonomy as a grace-dispensing institution and kept the state from infringing the rights of conscience. Yet the separation did not preclude the state from drawing support from the churches and from relying upon them as founts of morality.

All the Pennsylvania thinkers discussed in this chapter defined morality as a necessary element for a free state, but none defined exactly what morality meant or provided a description of how religion fostered it. All except Paine desired flourishing churches as a method of fostering morality. All, including Paine, envisioned God as the fountainhead and guarantor of morality and held up Jesus as the prime exemplar. None of them favored a tax supported church; none saw the clergy as political actors. All appeared satisfied with the status quo in Pennsylvania. Sovereignty was divided, but the Federal government and Pennsylvania composed one state whose origins stemmed from the will of God. So the theorists had no reason to distinguish between the obligations of different levels of government. Responsibilities were divided, but all worked in harmony.

Like colonial Pennsylvanians, these men divorced religion from its institutional grounding and simplified it into matters of individual belief. Like Penn, they assumed that people of reason discussing Scripture together could agree on fundamentals. They accepted institutional pluralism because they thought that reading the Bible, thinking, and utilizing a moral sense led to one truth. That one truth was a Christian republican liberty, and it was a rather Protestant notion of Christianity. No single element in their thought was original, but together their ideal society resembled federal Pennsylvania far more than New England or Virginia.

Republican religious liberty received powerful support from George Washington's Farewell Address. Washington warned against the assumption that "morality can be maintained without religion." "Religion and morality are indispensable supports" of political life and there could be no security in property without them. All free governments rested upon "virtue and morality" and "Reason and experience both forbid us to expect that National morality can prevail in exclusion of religious principle."[44]

Prerevolutionary clerical advocates of religious liberty often contrasted British Protestant freedoms with Catholic tyranny. After 1776 anti-Catholicism and pro-Church of England sentiments disappeared as did charges that Quakers and their sectarian allies misappropriated religious freedom for political advantage. The suspicions by Quakers, Presbyterians, and Anglicans of each others' ambitions were muted, although the election of 1800 showed that the distrust of New England's Congregational clergy remained. Earlier writings had a defensive or apologetic quality as if the authors' knowledge of and fear of established churches in New England, the South, and Great Britain made the survival of Pennsylvania's distinctive freedom problematic. Ministers and laymen after the Revolution boasted about religious liberty, contrasted it with European intolerance, and made Pennsylvania's heritage and practices normative for American life.

CHAPTER VI

Politicians Debate Religious Liberty

Religious liberty became a political issue in the election of 1800. The question, posed quietly by the Federalists in 1796,[1] but loudly in 1799 was whether the religion of Thomas Jefferson – he was alleged to be an atheist or deist – was a danger to the United States. Because the Federal Constitution contained no religious test, the Federalists had to persuade the voters that Jefferson constituted a threat to their civil and religious liberties. The election of a governor in Pennsylvania in 1799 was a test case for the coming presidential vote. Governor Thomas Mifflin was retiring and his successor would be either Republican Thomas McKean, currently the state's chief justice, or Federalist James Ross, a member of the House of Representatives. Both parties used the religious issue in 1799. The Republicans claimed that James Ross was a deist who did not believe in original sin. McKean, by contrast, was a Christian and member of the Presbyterian church. Deists like Ross could not be trusted because they might become corrupted by power. The Federalists could not say McKean was a deist, but they could link the entire Republican party with the infidelities of France and assert that all Republicans were irreligious.[2] McKean and the Republicans captured the governorship and the house, but Federalists still controlled the senate.

In retrospect the Federalist attack upon Jefferson's religion in 1800 appears disingenuous. Rational religion had already garnered many adherents in Massachusetts, including some clergy. Even John Adams as a young lawyer had deserted strict Calvinism.[3] President John Adams was a model of rectitude, but Alexander Hamilton, the leader of the high Federalists, had recently published an admission of his adultery with Mrs. Reynolds, a confession that had not cost him his influence in the party. Federalist leaders knew that many revolutionary leaders, including Benjamin Franklin, Thomas Paine, Ethan Allen, and George Washington, were at least on the fringes of orthodox Protestantism. The main religious

86

difference between some Federalist political leaders and Jefferson was that the latter was not a member of a church and did not attend Sunday worship. His contemporaries did not know precisely Jefferson's religious beliefs but he had lived in France, sympathized with the French revolutionaries, and corresponded with philosophes. Most important, the ministers and magistrates in New England knew that Jefferson had led the battle for disestablishment of the Church of England in Virginia. The close relationship between church and state that Jefferson fought in Virginia resembled the continuing Congregational establishment in Massachusetts, Connecticut, and New Hampshire. Jefferson was already a symbol of opposition to the New England way; the Federalists now sought to make him a symbol of infidelity.

The Federalist task was to prove that Jefferson was an atheist, even though he had never written openly about his religious beliefs. He was so reticent that he even refused to discuss religion with his family for fear that he would unduly influence them.[4] The only book Jefferson ever wrote, *Notes on Virginia,* was a description of his native state and contained no theology, but the Federalists attempted to make it an irreligious tract. In the *Notes* Jefferson speculated whether all races, including blacks, were of the same species and created at one time. He provided several explanations why fossil remains of sea creatures could be found on Virginia mountains. He defended Virginia's statute on religious liberty and the disestablishment of the Church of England, asserting that "it does me no injury for my neighbor to say there are twenty gods, or no God. It neither picks my pocket nor breaks my leg." Consequently, the state should not interfere with his neighbor's religious beliefs. Religion for Jefferson was a private mental judgment that should not have political consequences.[5]

These passages proved, said Federalists, Jefferson's atheism and deism and constituted an attack upon the veracity of Scripture. The Bible states that God created all people at once. The flood story showing how waters covered the whole earth was a sufficient explanation of how fossil remains came to the mountains of Virginia. Jefferson's statement about twenty or no gods was "nothing less than representing civil society as founded in atheism. For there can be no religion without God. And if it does me or neighbor no injury, to subvert the very foundation of religion by denying the being of God, then religion is not one of the constituent principles"[6]

The Federalists and their clerical allies insisted that character more than interests determined actions. "Exclusion of a Supreme Being and of a superintending Providence tends directly to the destruction of moral taste." Skepticism, as the history of France showed, led to deism, atheism, and sensuality, and such gross tastes destroyed the moral nature of the family, thereby creating a generation of corrupt children.[7]

The clerical and political critics of Jefferson faced several dilemmas. They could be portrayed as creating a religious test, as intolerant and bigoted, and as profaning religion by politics. The ministers insisted that they were not making political utterances, but were fulfilling their traditional roles of proclaiming the gospel. They insisted that Christianity became involved with politics because the gospel regulated all conduct. God ordained the office of the civil magistrate, whose duties included guarding the Sabbath and proclaiming fast and thanksgiving days.[8] Believers prayed for God to guide the policies of the President, but electing an infidel might provoke God's wrath. Even if Jefferson did not openly promote deism, his election would set a bad example. One pamphlet warned that because the United States Constitution did not directly mention God, Americans should demonstrate their faith by electing a Christian. If Jefferson were a Christian, let him publicly endorse the first sections of the Apostles' Creed.[9]

The Pennsylvania Republicans' response to the Federalist charges was hampered because they also did not know Jefferson's religion and the candidate refused to respond in any way.[10] They could easily disprove that Jefferson was an atheist because in the Declaration of Independence, *Notes on Virginia,* and other writings Jefferson had referred to God. Republicans knew the difference between deism and atheism and charged the Federalists with obfuscating. One writer declared that atheism was so absurd that there was not an atheist in the entire United States; at least, neither he nor anyone he knew had ever met one.[11] Disproving deism was more difficult, and so the Republicans just denied it and offered no proof. They generally did not assert that Jefferson was a churchgoer, but his respect for ministers was shown by his voluntary contributions to his local Anglican clergyman.[12]

The passages in the *Notes on Virginia* showed that Jefferson in response to puzzling data engaged in scientific speculation, not that he in any way doubted the truth of Scriptures. Jefferson's comment on no gods or twenty proved nothing about his beliefs upon the origin of the state or the role of morality.[13] Instead, the passage asserted that religious belief was a private matter not affecting economic interest. Most important, said the Republicans, religious belief was a product of the mind and conscience, and the populace could use morality as the only public standard useful for judging a politician. Jefferson was a moral man. His service as governor of Virginia, minister to France, secretary of state, and vice-president showed that he could be trusted. His virtue and patriotism passed the test of Christian character.[14]

What the Republicans in Pennsylvania omitted saying is also revealing. They did not maintain that religious commitments were irrelevant to morality. They did not agree that Jefferson was either atheist or deist, as if

such beliefs were irrelevant. They wanted their candidate to be for organized religion. No one argued that the state was formed from a secular
covenant and that the existence or nonexistence of God was of no political consequence.

The Republicans were clearly on the defensive on Jefferson's religion,
so they attempted to shift the debate from infidelity to religious freedom.
Almost none of the pamphlets attacking Jefferson's religious beliefs originated in Pennsylvania. Only one Pennsylvania clergyman made an utterance sufficiently hostile to Jefferson for the *Aurora* to comment upon it.[15]
The evangelical Protestants in New York and New England who attacked
Jefferson's fidelity claimed they were not meddling in politics; they wrote
as if they were nondenominational and had no state allegiance. By contrast, the literature that defended Jefferson was regional and directed at
specific religious groups. The best way to defend Jefferson was to attack
New England Congregationalists and praise Pennsylvania.

Jefferson was a disciple of William Penn. Penn had suffered from the
unjust attack of seventeenth-century clergy; now Jefferson was meeting
the same fate.[16] Penn and Jefferson had fought for freedom of religion
and opposed tithes. Jefferson obtained for Virginia what Penn had given
to Pennsylvania. Both men feared involving the church with the state
because the resulting mixture led to false time-serving religion and
intolerance in the state. Religious freedom, on the other hand, brought
healthy churches and a prosperous citizenry.[17] The Republican identifica-
tion of Jefferson with Penn marked Penn's rehabilitation as a national
hero. In the 1770s Penn had suffered eclipse because he was invoked by
the Quakers as a defender of the charter and pacifism.[18] Those who
created the Pennsylvania constitutions of 1776 and 1790 never cited
Penn. But after 1800 William Penn would become a Republican, not just
a Quaker, hero.

The *Aurora*, the leading pro-Jeffersonian newspaper in Philadelphia,
charged that the Federalist party promoted religious intolerance and
church establishments. New England's clergy and magistrates feared that
under Jefferson Pennsylvania's religious freedom would spread north.
John Adams had supported the Massachusetts constitution, which taxed
religious dissenters. He had not opposed an alleged Congregationalist
persecution in New England against Baptists, Methodists, Quakers, and
Roman Catholics.[19] Adams had been minister to Great Britain in 1784,
when the nonjuring Church of England bishops consecrated Samuel
Seabury, formerly a loyalist clergyman for Connecticut, as an American
Episcopal bishop. Adams made no protest, and upon his return associ-
ated with Seabury.[20] In his writings about the constitution of Great
Britain, Adams never criticized the union of church and state there. The
Republicans already believed that the Federalists were promonarchists.

They feared that Adams and the Federalists would create a church establishment everywhere in America as a check against republican freedom.

The Pennsylvania Republicans became vague when discussing just what church Adams wanted to establish. It would be difficult to establish a Congregational church in the Middle Atlantic States and the South, because there were virtually no Congregationalists there. The easiest strategy would have been to postulate a Presbyterian–Congregational alliance, but there were many Pennsylvania Presbyterian Republicans, including Governor McKean.[21] Samuel Stanhope Smith, the Presbyterian president of Princeton had supposedly made promonarchist remarks.[22] Another possibility was the Episcopalians, but their churches could form an alliance with the Congregationalists with difficulty because the latter were supposedly discriminating against the Anglicans in New England.[23] The Methodists were another possibility, because a Methodist conference held in Delaware had purportedly had a pro-Adams slant.[24] But they were obscure, few in number, and also being discriminated against in New England. The various peace churches opposed religious establishments. Republicans were already courting Quakers, Moravians, Mennonites, and Dunkers by claiming to be pro-peace against Federalist warmongering.[25]

Fortunately for the Republicans, at the climax of the campaign they received a target. James Abercrombie, associate rector of Christ Church, who had previously been criticized by the Republicans for a fast-day sermon, delivered from the pulpit an impassioned attack upon Jefferson that was printed in the *United States Gazette*, the leading Federalist paper. The sermon did not name Jefferson, but the minister referred negatively to philosophy as a qualification for office and exhorted the "Christian Community" not to make "an acknowledged Unbeliever" and "Enemy to their Faith" "their Ruler and Guide." Conceding that the clergy should not normally mix in politics, Abercrombie claimed a duty as a member of the community and as a minister "professionally" to declare opinions on the "interests of Religion and Morality" "on very extraordinary occasions."[26] The *Aurora* responded with glee. Abercrombie was a failed merchant who attended theater and had attempted to invest in a theater company. He now was guilty of prostrating religion to political ends.[27] The clergy of the Church of England had a tradition of support for the monarchy, and taxing for the tithe had not been repudiated after the Revolution. The Episcopalians wished to join the New England Illuminati in establishing a church.[28]

The fear of the New England Illuminati allowed the Pennsylvania Republicans to focus on New England's established Congregational churches. The Illuminati were a secret society centered in Connecticut.[29] Yale's President Timothy Dwight was the "pope" and his minions included the Yale Corporation, Jedediah Morse, and the presidents of the colleges at

Cambridge, Massachusetts, Princeton, New Jersey, Schenectady, New York, and Carlisle, Pennsylvania, and the Congregationalist clergy.[30] These men wanted to extend their influence through the use of Bible and missionary societies. Princeton bestowed honorary doctor of laws degrees upon Timothy Pickering and Oliver Wolcott, a phenomenon that might make "honest people ... avoid degrees associated with disgrace."[31] A professor of the University of Pennsylvania refused to allow the Declaration of Independence to be read on July 4th. Christ Church refused to toll its bells on July 4, 1800.[32]

The election of 1800 featured several conspiracy theories: the Republicans were controlled by the French, the Federalists run by the British. The New England Illuminati were a strange political and religious issue that made little sense, but it was extremely useful. For Pennsylvania Republicans the Illuminati diverted attention from Jefferson's religious beliefs, focused on New England's clerical power and established church, allowed a critique of political pretensions of all clergy without mentioning any local minister except Abercrombie, and permitted a subtle attack upon colleges as elitist and pro-Federalist. The debate over religion in the election of 1800 does not show whether the Pennsylvania Republicans held a distinctive position on relations between church and state. What one can surmise is that the colonial tradition of anticlericalism survived and found a home within some factions of the Republicans.

The Philadelphia *Aurora* for several weeks after July 4, 1800 printed the toasts drunk at various celebrations in Pennsylvania, New Jersey, and Delaware, and elsewhere. One hopes the celebrants wrote down their toasts in advance because after numerous drinks the participants' recall might be cloudy, but the anticlericalism remained clear. "The American Clergy – May their study be to guide the souls of mortals to a safe haven, and not their money to their purses." (Mifflintown) "The Clergy – May those who have forsaken the first duty of their calling, hereafter remember that the vital principle of our religion is peace and good will toward men; and be no longer the heralds of war and division." (Portsmouth, N.H.)[33] Resolutions in Sunbury and in Philadelphia praised Joseph Priestly for his love of science and liberty, and ignored his Unitarian theology. Toasts in Montgomery County picked up all the Republican themes:

13. The New England Iluminati – Desolation to such clerical political institutions, which shackle a free people with the tyrannies of priestcraft and autocracy.

14. May bigotry and intolerance be driven to the haunts of wild beasts, no longer to disturb our country and government.

15. Our schools and seminaries of learning – May they be the nurseries of science and virtue, and not the engines of tyranny to deprive us of our rights and happiness.[34]

The election of 1800 brought to power a man whose metaphor of a "wall" of separation has come to symbolize an absolute divorce between the Federal government and organized religion. James Madison, Jefferson's secretary of state and successor as President, also opposed an accommodationist, or flexible, relation between church and state.[35] The Jeffersonian party dominated Pennsylvania politics from 1799 until the rise of a second party system in the late 1820s, when the Jacksonian Democrats began winning elections. An examination of the policies of the Democratic-Republicans of Pennsylvania will show whether or not they shared the absolutist views of Jefferson. After briefly summarizing the views of Jefferson and Madison on separation of church and state, this section will focus on the response of politicians to three religious liberty issues: the anticlerical Working Men's party's request for no religious legislation, the quest by the American Sunday School Union for incorporation, and the debates in the 1837 constitutional convention on paying clergymen for praying and on repealing the tests in the 1790 constitution.

James Madison and Thomas Jefferson during the Revolution had striven for the disestablishment of the Church of England in Virginia, and in 1784 worked to defeat a plan for a general assessment on taxpayers with the proceeds to be used to pay the clergy of all denominations, with exceptions granted for Mennonites and Quakers. As President, Jefferson refused to declare public fast days and thanksgiving days, but he did approve of use of Federal money to supply missionaries to Indians.[36] Madison also approved of this negative policy, though at the beginning and end of the War of 1812 he found it politically prudent to declare a day of fasting and one of thanksgiving. In a private letter Madison disapproved of having a paid chaplain to the Congress. Although unwilling to exert himself to end the custom, he thought the safest policy would be to allow no additional encroachments of church on state.[37]

Jefferson and Madison remained constant advocates of the absolutist position. Madison maintained that man was a creature of God before he entered into a state; therefore, his religious obligations originated before civil duties and remained separate from them and took priority over them. Madison defined religious opinions as belonging intrinsically to each individual and, therefore, a special kind of property. Like other property rights it was not subject to governmental authority.[38] The seat of religious beliefs was the mind and conscience, areas in which the state had no ability to intervene. Because freedom of conscience was an undeniable right that could be delegated to no government, any state's attempt to define religious truth debased religion and created opposition, thereby weakening the government. Madison in a 1792 treatise spelled out a wide range of evil consequences of accommodating and merging church and state: civil disorder, persecution, and hypocrisy.[39] Both government and religion flourished best in their separate spheres in which each could perform services that benefited the community. Jefferson and Madison insisted that their views were neither hostile to religion nor irreligious. But even before he became President there was a strain of anticlericalism in Jefferson, and he did not regard the Methodists and Baptists who supported him more favorably than the Congregationalists who wrote diatribes against him.[40]

Absolutists like Madison and Jefferson stressed the diversity of religious views in America, even on fundamentals. They insisted that all sects, churches, and religions receive equal treatment. Jews and Seventh-Day Baptists should not be penalized because they celebrated a different Sabbath, Quakers and Mennonites because they had no paid clergy. All – Hindu, Muslims, pagans, infidels – whose customs did not infringe upon the public peace had equal rights.[41] Having witnessed the factionalism and extreme partisanship in the election of 1800, Jefferson concluded that pagan-classical natural-law morality was insufficient to bind the union, and he sought for a moralistic nonsupernatural form of Christian ethics on which all could agree. Jefferson read and approved of Joseph Priestly's demythologized Christianity and sought to persuade the noted scientist and Unitarian minister, now residing in Pennsylvania, to publish a Christian morality. When Priestly did not do so, Jefferson in 1804 did his own cut-and-paste job on the Gospels in order to create a "Philosophy of Jesus." Jefferson then discussed his "philosophy" and religious views with a few close friends, but he never published his extracts from the Gospels.[42] Jefferson wanted agreement on moral fundamentals from thinking people, but no governmental involvement in this process.

Like the Presbyterians, Jefferson and Madison linked to government the laws of God, the laws of nature, and natural law. Jefferson's best-known writing, the Declaration of Independence, grounded the existence of unalienable rights, the equality of humankind, and the purposes of government in the Creator. But when the Presbyterian defenders of natural rights in the 1780s and the 1830s assumed that a government based on God must follow the Ten Commandments and pass laws favoring worship and prosecuting blasphemy, Jefferson concluded just the opposite. For him God's nature and method of communication meant that no one could claim belief as binding on anyone else. Religious truth was individual and subjective.

In a marvelous paradox, Jefferson's understanding of the nature of American government coincided with that of Covenanting Presbyterians (see Chapter 7). Both grounded government in God's moral law and concluded that the Federal Constitution had no special place for Christianity. The Covenanters said this absence of God and Christianity meant idolatry; Jefferson proclaimed the separation of Christianity from the state a palladium of liberty.

Jefferson and Madison restricted the role of religion at the Federal level and advocated a strict separation of church and state. Did either they or their followers take the logical step of criticizing the fostering of religious observances in Pennsylvania?

Neither Madison nor Jefferson held any office at the state level after 1787. Jefferson's letter opposing thanksgiving proclamations carefully restricted the prohibition to the Federal level. Both men pointed to Pennsylvania as having the ideal relationship of church and state.[43] At a time when the Democratic-Republicans championed the limitations of power of the Federal government and states' rights, Jefferson and Madison certainly did not wish to extend the constitutional prohibitions from the Federal to the state government and, even if they thought the continuation of established churches in New England was unwise, never said it was unconstitutional.[44] Even so, the ideal of absolute separation of the institutional church and state blended well with Pennsylvania's traditions, and radicals might have demanded changes. The Quakers could be expected to be sympathetic with the absolutist position associated with Jefferson.[45] Even so, areas with a predominance of Quakers tended to vote Federalist. In addition, Thomas Paine, whose anticlerical and anti-Christian ideas scandalized conservatives, had lived and worked in Philadelphia.[46] The Pennsylvania Jeffersonians in the aftermath of Jay's Treaty had espoused a pro-French and anticlerical policy. One could have anticipated that a faction or party advocating strict separation at the state level would become a conspicuous feature of Pennsylvania politics.

In actuality, controversies over church and state at either the Federal or state level played little role in Pennsylvania politics after 1800. The leading historians of the periods of Federalist and Jeffersonian ascendency in the Commonwealth do not even mention church-state issues.[47] The Jeffersonians in power made no changes in state laws affecting religion. Thomas McKean, formerly chief justice and governor for three terms beginning in 1799, was a conservative and Scots-Irish Presbyterian.[48] In 1807 James Ross was again a Federalist candidate for governor and he was again pilloried as an enemy to Christianity. After McKean most of the governors of Pennsylvania for the next twenty-five years were Germans. None was antireligious and one, John Andrew Schulze (1823–29) was an ordained Lutheran minister.[49] Prominent Republicans include William Findley, who defended the Presbyterian church, and Dr. Michael Lieb, for a time a friend of William Duane and later a leader of the Quid faction, who was a vestryman at Philadelphia's Reformed church. Peter and Frederick Muhlenberg, sons of Reverend Henry Melchior Muhlenberg, became ministers but left the parish ministry in the Revolution and later became prominent Jeffersonian politicians. Henry Augustus Muhlenberg (1782–1844), another Lutheran minister, became president of the ministerium; but from 1829–38 served as congressman and later candidate for governor.[50] The only Republican forum of mild anticlericalism was William Duane's Philadelphia *Aurora*,[51] but Duane's erratic pursuit of power within the very diverse Republican coalition by and large ignored church-state issues.

There are only scattered indications of dissatisfaction. Pennsylvania's governors, whether Federalist or Republican, issued thanksgiving proclamations recommending voluntary abstention from work and attendance at a worship service. In the *Democratic Press* in November 1818, a correspondent attacked these proclamations as "Political Religion" complaining that the governor was not the "religious head of the community" and that the courts and post office should not have closed.[52] That same month, when Robert Murphy was convicted of blasphemy, the *Franklin Gazette* announced a public meeting to protest the decision. Because the editor's notice was bracketed with that of the annual meeting of the Female Missionary Society, the paper showed his impartiality between evangelicals and freethinkers.[53]

The impression left is that before 1820 virtually everyone was satisfied with the Pennsylvania tradition of separation of church and state combined with laws punishing vice and breaking the Sabbath. The Federal and state government passed no laws evangelicals saw as hostile to religion. Quakers issued mild protests against militia training laws, but neither they nor others expected to change the state's policies.

In the 1820s the Working Men's party, emerging as a faction in the Democratic-Republican coalition, identified its advocacy of a total separation of church and state with Jefferson. These absolutists were also anticlerical and opponents of the evangelical network of voluntary associations and the Presbyterian church, which they saw as creating an intolerant so-called Christian political party. In Pennsylvania their most prominent spokesman was Thomas Earle (1796–1849), owner and editor of the *Mechanics Free Press and Reform Advocate*.[54] Earle, a birthright Quaker, defended Fanny Wright, Robert Owen, and free thought. He opposed restrictive Sabbath laws (but not having a day of rest), religious tests for office, the antiblasphemy act, and prayer at public functions. He criticized the infant school movement and the Sunday School Union because both provided sectarian education and he advocated, as an alternative, government supported nonreligious common schools.[55] Earle's newspaper proved one could be moralistic without being evangelical, because he condemned lotteries, drunkenness, prostitution, and the unequal burden that Sabbath laws placed on the poor.[56]

The clergy along with bankers and lawyers belonged to the parasitic classes feeding off of productive farmers, mechanics, and workingmen. Earle's paper consistently supported the Working Men's party, one of whose planks was "No Legislation on Religion."[57] The Working Men's party and Earle advocated radical changes in banking laws, reform of courts, and better treatment of the poor.

The Working Men's party, centered in Philadelphia, had little support elsewhere. Earle seemed to have a promising political career until he became a strong supporter of the right of Negroes to vote. His newspaper failed in 1835 and his membership in the 1837 convention to revise the Pennsylvania constitution was his last political office. After 1840 Earle edited *The Pennsylvanian,* an abolitionist newspaper, and accepted an invitation to run for vice-president on the Liberty party. Earle's career shows that he could not maintain a constituency based upon radical religious, social, economic, and racial beliefs.

Russel Canfield published a radical newspaper, *The Temple of Reason,* in Philadelphia in 1836 and 1837. The prospectus promised opposition to the Christian party in politics, but the primary focus was theological with attacks on the Bible and revealed religion. Still, there was no moral relativism. "Seneca" claimed that although the Bible was mostly non-sense, nine of the Ten Commandments were "self-evident, and hence divine commands." Canfield attacked the Universalists for orthodoxy and proclaimed his faith in "Nature," not God, providence, or chance.[58] The paper attacked the American Sunday School Union as being guilty of "Clerical Intolerance" and termed Christianity "dangerous to Civil Liberty." Canfield scorned Bible societies, Sabbath laws, judicial oaths, and the "Test Act" in the new Pennsylvania constitution.[59]

Benjamin Webb began publishing a radical newspaper, the *Delaware Free Press* in 1830. Webb was a Wilmington Hicksite Quaker, whose espousal of complete subjectivity in religion and opposition to having authoritative beliefs and a disciplinary procedure in the meeting led to his disownment.[60] The *Delaware Free Press* was similar in tone to the *Mechanics Free Press,* though less oriented to workingmen's causes and even stronger in its anticlericalism. The *Delaware Free Press* celebrated Thomas Jefferson, Tom Paine, Fanny Wright, and Robert Owen. It opposed Sabbath legislation, paid chaplains, and laws against blasphemy.[61] Because all religion was a product of the conscience and conscience could not be coerced, a law against blasphemy was an attempt to coerce conscience. The *Delaware Free Press* took up the cause of William Michener in a court case in Chester County in 1831. Michener was called as a witness in a case of trespass. He was asked whether he believed in God prior to taking an oath. Because Michener did not, he was not tendered the oath.[62] This was a religious "inquisition" in court. The *Delaware Free*

Press insisted that "the salvation of our country depends upon the exclusion of all theological controversies from our political councils."[63] The newspaper was both antislavery and anti-Catholic.

The radical-workingmen-liberal religious perspective on church and state never died out.[64] Universalists, Unitarians, some Hicksite Quakers, and freethinkers continued to oppose what they defined as the evangelical attempt to erode the distinction between church and state and the political hegemony of the Presbyterian and evangelical associations.

In 1827 and 1828 the Pennsylvania legislature debated incorporating the American Sunday School Union, a lay-controlled nationwide organization with headquarters in Philadelphia, that sponsored charity schools on Sunday to teach basic reading, writing, morality, and Christianity to children who were poor, idle, or who worked six days a week.[65] Normally, charitable, educational, and religious institutions whose charters preserved the usual forms and limited the amount of income from property received incorporation on a pro-forma basis. The opposition to incorporating the Sunday School Union came from those who feared that the separation of church and state would be jeopardized by the power of the Presbyterian church and the growth of Protestant voluntary organizations working for the reform of American society. They feared a Presbyterian conspiracy aimed at destroying or changing basic values. The themes and rhetoric first used to accuse the Presbyterians would later be employed against Mormons, Masons, and Roman Catholics.[66] Ironically, both those who sponsored the schools and others who feared them worried about the strength of American institutions and sought to impose correct values.

The Sunday School Union's petition for incorporation occurred during a period of intense political strife among factions seeking to control the Democratic-Republican party, an organization that had controlled the legislature and the governorship for thirty years. Now those who were already divided over issues of internal improvement, tariffs, and banks superimposed support for President John Quincy Adams or challenger Andrew Jackson.[67] Politicians maneuvering for power and creating what would become the Democratic and Whig parties did not relish the idea of a religious-political organization as a rival.

The leadership for such a party would come from Pennsylvania's Presbyterians.[68] The Presbyterian Church, U.S.A., whose periodicals, headquarters, and General Assembly were in Philadelphia and whose primary college was at Princeton was a very visible institution. Delegates from all over the country attended the General Assembly. Unlike most newspapers, the Presbyterian magazines had a nationwide circulation. Presbyterians were so closely allied with New England Congregationalists that outsiders could detect no differences. Delegates from Congregationalist consociations and from the Presbyterian General Assembly visited each others' annual and statewide gatherings. Since 1801 the two churches had worked together in a Plan of Union that allowed a mixed church polity in the attempt to proselytize frontier settlements. Methodists, Baptists, Lutherans, Reformed, and Episcopalians joined with Presbyterians and Congregationalists in Bible, tract, home- and foreign-missionary societies, and the Sunday School Union, but the officers and paid employees of the voluntary organizations tended to come from the latter two denominations. The two denominations had just demonstrated their political clout by organizing a massive petition campaign to Congress against transporting mails on Sunday. In Philadelphia the Presbyterians were the dominant church and they also were strong in those areas of Pennsylvania settled by Scots-Irish. Most members of the legislature and governors in early nineteenth-century Pennsylvania were either Scots-Irish or Germans. A party of the members of the major evangelical denominations joined by like-minded individuals from the Lutheran, Episcopal, and Reformed churches would constitute a formidable force, and it would be a force controlled by clergy and devout laymen, not party manipulators.

Today much of the supposed power of the Presbyterian church in 1829 appears a product of the imagination of fearful politicians. They did not foresee that controversies over new methods in revivals, the definition of Calvinist orthodoxy, cooperation with the Congregationalists, participation in interdenominational voluntary societies, and slavery – to a minor extent in 1837 but not in the 1850s – would split the Presbyterian church into Old School and New School and then into northern and southern branches. The result would be years of bitter feuding, additional schisms, and dissipation of influence.

In New England the Unitarian controversy and the disestablishment of the Congregational church in Massachusetts weakened that denomination. The network of interdenominational societies also showed strains. Episcopal, Methodist, and Baptist churches created their own Bible, tract, and Sunday School associations to advance denominational goals.[69] Baptists and Methodists already were growing more rapidly than Presbyterians and their move to create or control colleges like Bucknell and Dickinson and establish well-edited magazines showed the growing maturity of these churches. As the Baptists and Methodists gained stability and respectability, their ministers more directly addressed moral issues that had political implications. The most important and explosive of these issues was slavery. The slavery controversy would eventually split the Presbyterian, Methodist, and Baptist organizations. Yet although the evangelicals' institutional churches lost power at the national level, by mid-century

Pennsylvania politics and law appeared more uniformly sympathetic to Christianity than in 1800 or 1830.

The American Sunday School Union first came to the attention of the Pennsylvania legislature in 1824, when it petitioned for state aid to purchase books and stationery for poor children. A Senate committee turned down the request, arguing that a small appropriation would only discourage private charity. The Sunday Schools already furnished supplies for all children and to introduce a distinction between regular and poor scholars would disrupt the good feeling and equality now existing in the schools.[70]

In 1827 the House in a committee of the whole procedure voted against incorporation of the American Sunday School Union. No debate and no vote tallies appeared in the records because of the parliamentary procedure. The next year the bill was reintroduced, sent to committee, amended, and voted on. The legislature received at least forty-one memorials, twenty-six against, before it began to debate. The most important item in the Senate debate was the content of a speech of the Presbyterian minister Ezra Stiles Ely entitled *The Duty of a Christian Freeman,* delivered on July 4, 1827.

Even the occasion showed the evangelicals' concern for moral order. Earlier patriots celebrated July 4th by parades and feasting during which the participants imbibed alcohol freely, a practice that resulted in brawls and riots. In an effort to treat the nation's birthday with appropriate solemnity, Philadelphia's pious laity and clergy began the custom of having a prominent clergyman give an address. Ely, a Presbyterian evangelical who was a friend of Andrew Jackson, echoed in his oration the beliefs of most evangelical Protestants. He praised American democracy, endorsed the separation of church and state, discussed no specific political issue, even suggested that the clergy should not discuss politics or vote if such practices disturbed their congregations, and defended the constitution's prohibition of a religious test for public office.[71]

Following the traditional Presbyterian position, Ely asserted that ultimately all political power came from God and was based on the moral law. Because God judged a nation and its rulers, a people who had the right to vote should select magistrates likely to seek and follow God's will. Politicians, like other citizens, should have their moral qualities scrutinized by the people, though Ely warned that past transgressions, if later atoned for, were not a disqualification.[72] Thus far, Ely's sermon said little that was not a cliché, but now he frightened Pennsylvania's politicians.

Ely called for the creation of a new "Christian party" based not on platforms or constitutions but Christian commitment.[73] Its followers asked candidates whether they were baptized, read the Bible, prayed, took the sacrament, and observed the moral law. Christians dwelling in a country founded for Christian principles and with a majority of Christians had a right to seek Christian candidates. Ely argued that non-Christian communities in America and elsewhere would have the same right to apply their religious principles. Such screening violated no constitutional principle because it would be done by voters to determine suitability for office and was not a legal disqualification. The Presbyterians alone, Ely promised, if united could deliver one half million votes. When their votes were combined with those of Methodists, Baptists, Episcopalians, Congregationalists, and Reformed (no mention was made of Quakers, Roman Catholics, Unitarians, and Universalists), Ely boasted that the combination would be irresistible.[74] Ely advocated a generous injection of evangelical morality into politics.

The sermon became a cause célèbre and was used for years to show the political aims of the clergy, who intended to destroy religious liberty. Ely was a strong supporter of the American Sunday School Union, had participated in its annual meeting, and written its annual report at least once. He was not an officer of the organization, because all the trustees and other officers were laymen. But opponents read the Sunday School Union's annual reports and claimed to discover the same design of creating a Presbyterian political party whose existence and aims would destroy the separation of church and state.

On Feb. 7, 1828, just before the scheduled vote in the Pennsylvania Senate, all members received a printed flier containing carefully chosen excerpts from Ely's sermon and the annual reports. The flyer's quotations revealed the youth educated in Sunday Schools would in twenty years have the "POLITICAL POWER OF OUR COUNTRY" and could implement reforms. The organizers of the schools wanted to become "DICTATORS TO THE CONSCIENCES" of the children.[75] So the Union carefully selected and edited materials, screening out passages unsuitable for children. The Union had between 1824 and 1827 issued a total of 3,741,849 publications. In Pennsylvania alone the Sunday School Union had 480 schools, 4,459 teachers, and 34,261 scholars.[76] In New York the teachers had their pupils sign petitions against Sunday mails. Ely, the Presbyterian church, and the Sunday School Union had engaged in a massive conspiracy to blot out freedom of thought, destroy the separation of church and state, and create a new political party.

Even the proponents of the Sunday School Union in the senate disassociated their views from Ely and claimed that his overzealousness for Jackson had led him to excess. They insisted that support for education was to improve democracy, because tyrants were always against schools. Sunday Schools had existed for years with no threat to America.[77] The debate in the senate focused on the political aims of the evangelicals. The result was a crushing defeat as the senate voted twenty-one to nine against incorporation.[78] The house, therefore, did not vote on the measure at all. Because all members of the Pennsylvania senate claimed to be members of the same party, a political analysis of the voting pattern would prove little. No consistent geographical alignment emerged either. This was neither a city versus country nor an East versus West issue. Most petitions against the incorporations came from the Philadelphia City representative, Josiah Martin, although they need not have originated there.[79] Martin was absent from the final vote, but the other Philadelphia City member voted against the Sunday School Union. Both Chester and Delaware senators voted against it, but the Philadelphia County, Bucks, and Allegheny delegations split.

The vote was against clerical meddling in politics and in defense of the status quo in church and state. But it was not against religion and education. In January 1828, less than a month before the Sunday School Union vote, the senate committee on education reported that education "is conceded to be the most powerful means of furthering the cause of morality and religion; and its importance to a country possessing a republican form of government is universally admitted."[80]

In 1837 the citizens of Pennsylvania voted by a very narrow margin to call a convention to amend the 1790 constitution. When the convention met it was almost evenly divided between Democrats and a Whig-Anti-Masonic party alliance. Ultimately, the convention made no changes in the religious clauses in the 1790 constitution, but on two occasions the delegates, after debating religion, proceeded to a roll-call vote. An analysis of these discussions and the votes provides an indication of the feelings of the delegates, who were well aware of the constitutional issues of separation of church and state and liberty of conscience.

The convention opened and held the first half of its sessions in Harrisburg, then moved to Philadelphia for the remainder. At the beginning a motion passed without a division asking the clergy of Harrisburg to open each day's proceedings with prayer. Shortly before the convention was to move to Philadelphia, Thaddeus Stevens moved that the clergy of Harrisburg who had prayed be paid $350. This motion, which Stevens assumed would be noncontroversial, occasioned a debate and amendments that were summarized in thirteen pages of the *Proceedings and Debates*. The debate, Stevens wryly observed, cost more than the clergy.[81]

Those favoring the motion thought it only just to pay the clergy for professional services rendered at the request of the convention. It would be dishonorable to take the clergy's time without compensation and to discuss the matter was insulting to them. These politicians did not see the matter as a church-state issue or as establishing any kind of precedent.[82]

Opponents presented a diversity of perspectives. Some thought the

$350 was too much money, because it granted to each clergyman three dollars per attendance and the prayers took only a few minutes to deliver. The delegates were receiving only three dollars per day. When one delegate suggested that the money be taken from the per diem allowance for each delegate, that amendment was quickly rejected. Another suggestion was to rely on voluntary contributions from delegates. One man saw the paying of the clergy as a divisive measure. Religion had caused wars since antiquity but separation of church and state precluded such catastrophes in America.[83] The most able opposition speech came from Thomas Earle, editor of the radical *Mechanics Free Press*. No taxation for the payment of clergy had been allowed in Pennsylvania since the time of William Penn. Any use of tax funds to pay the clergy violated liberty of conscience and established a dangerous precedent. Earle opposed not only the payment of the clergy, but even the opening of the sessions with prayer. Prayer was a private act, which could be used in church, but should never occur in a governmental function.[84]

The variety of perspectives expressed in debate make difficult an interpretation of the vote on the resolution to pay the clergy. A vote against could have been all or one of the following: anticlerical, antireligion, absolutist position on the separation of church and state, or concern for precedent. A vote in favor could signify accommodationist position of church and state, courtesy to the clergy, no precedent, or no principle involved. The final vote was close, 60 to 58 in favor of paying the clergy. When the convention was first organized, the Whig-Anti-Masonic candidate, John Sergeant, was elected president over the Democrat James Porter, 66 to 63.[85] A comparison of those voting for Sergeant and against Porter disclosed that the Whig-Anti-Masons voted two to one (36 to 17) in favor of payment and the Democrats three to one (39 to 12) against payment. That voting pattern supports historians who argue that the Whigs had support from the evangelical Protestants and favored accommodation of church and state.

A second roll call came on a motion to appoint a special committee to consider several petitions requesting that the "civil rights, privileges or capacities of any citizen, shall in no way be affected, diminished, or enlarged, merely on account of his religious opinions."[86] The issue here was the 1790 clause requiring of officeholders belief in the "being" of God and of a future state of punishment or reward for one's deeds. A related issue was whether people who did not believe in hell could be tendered an oath because their testimony in court might not be accepted.[87] Those advocating a change desired an absolute separation between church and state, and disliked what they saw as a religious test that discriminated against freethinkers, Universalists, and some Unitarians.

A committee of the convention, chaired by Democrat James Porter, had already recommended against any changes in the religious clauses. Porter argued that his committee had rejected proposed amendments against enforcing the Sabbath, outlawing duels, and forbidding lotteries because they were already subjects of legislation and needed no constitutional sanction. His committee had already considered provisions on religious tests similar to that in the memorials and had rejected them.[88]

The vote was not a straightforward referendum on changing the constitution. Some delegates opposed any additional committees as a needless expense and a dangerous precedent for the convention to adopt. Others did not want any change in the religious clause of the constitution, but believed that in a democracy so many petitioners should have their wants carefully considered by a special committee. A delegate could have voted for amendment because he wanted stricter legislation that could be used against Mormons, Masons, and those who fought duels and gambled in lotteries. Or he could have supported the opposite and wanted no religious tests.

The convention rejected the special committee by a vote of 65 to 44. The Whig-Anti-Masons split evenly (27 to 24), the Democrats voted against the resolution (16 to 34) or by a two-to-one margin, preferring to keep the test. Of the 16 Democrats who voted for a special committee, only 14 had opposed paying the praying clergy. Of the 27 Whig-Anti-Masons who supported the special committee, only three had opposed paying the clergy. It seems reasonably certain that the Whig-Anti-Masons who approved paying the clergy and wanted a special committee wanted to strengthen the moral and religious articles in the constitution. There was also a hard core of support for complete separation of church and state whose advocates wanted no payment of clergy for prayers and no religious tests, but they numbered no more than seventeen delegates out of 130 and had a minority role even in the Pennsylvania Democratic party.

Normally, the power of the churches was expressed through the dominant political parties rather than in a separate Christian organization. The House of Representatives in 1841 graphically demonstrated the Christian ascendancy. The House received a resolution, similar to that rejected by the constitutional convention, signed by 119 men asking repeal of all laws "against blasphemy and the violation of the Sabbath Day." The House was outraged, labeling the petition "disreputable to the Legislature of Pennsylvania" and refusing to entertain it. A resolution to this effect passed 81 to 1. The preamble, which passed 85 to 0 was vitriolic:

the members of this body are deeply impressed with the belief that the doctrines contained in the said petition are destructive, not only of all the ties which bind men together as civilized beings, but of all the obligations which unite man, to

GOD the Creator and Governor of the Universe: *And Whereas,* we are unwilling that any inference should be drawn, from the fact of such petition having been received without any motion having been made for a disposition of it, that the members of this House, can in the remotest degree, give countenance and currency to infidel opinions and principles, which strike at the foundation of all civil government.[89]

The member who voted against the resolution, but not the preamble, made clear that he opposed the substance of the petition. His vote expressed his belief that a member's duty was to present all memorials to the House "no matter to what subject they relate." The constitutional issue was whether any petition in correct form should be labeled "disrespectable." He would have preferred the resolution to state that the memorial met the "decided disapprobation" of the House.[90]

In 1800 Pennsylvania's Republicans countered Federalist charges that Jefferson was a dangerous atheist or deist by linking their candidate to William Penn's heritage of religious liberty and attacking the New England linkage of church and state. In elections after 1800 Jefferson, Madison, and Monroe carried the state and the Jeffersonian party controlled the governorship, the legislature, and, eventually, the courts. In power, the Pennsylvania Republican-Democrats made no attempt at the state level to implement the absolutist views of Jefferson and Madison. The state's religious policies remained uncontroversial because virtually everyone approved of the religious clauses of the 1790 constitution and the antivice laws. In the 1820s the Working Men's party and a few freethinkers challenged these policies that they saw as mingling church and state. Evangelical clergymen who appeared to advocate a religiously based political party and wanted to use Sunday Schools to indoctrinate pupils also seemed to demand change. The politicians in major parties ignored workingmen and rebuked the evangelicals. Similarly, the motion to pay clergy at the 1837 constitutional convention and the petition for the legislature to repeal Sabbath legislation threatened the status quo. Pennsylvania's politicians thought they had already reached the best possible policy on religious liberty. They would keep a distance but not erect a wall between church and state. The state needed the moral foundation provided by organized religion, but it did not need politician ministers. In the 1840s even advocacy of the Jeffersonian absolutist position in the state legislature brought condemnation. Freedom of religion no longer gave the liberty to criticize the religious foundation of the Commonwealth.

CHAPTER VII

The Churches and Religious Liberty

After the Revolution Pennsylvanians celebrated their religious liberties with eloquent slogans that passed over difficult issues. They approved of churches free from governmental control, a state separate from church and clerical politics, and the positive interaction of republican and Christian virtues in undergirding the society. The government sought and received the churches' support, and the churches needed and gained a fostering role by the state. Obviously, in such an ambiguous situation the clergy needed to define carefully their responsibilities on political-moral issues. This chapter examines church responses to the new constitutions, the one serious debate on the advisability of new constitutions' provisions on religion, and the ministers' actions on political-moral controversies, concentrating upon the regulation of alcoholic beverages.

The churches did not comment on changes in the religious clauses in the 1790 Pennsylvania constitution. All denominations saw the government as ratifying the status quo in which the state remained separate from the institutional church, and made laws to encourage moral living. Quakers complained that the new constitution did not treat conscientious objection to serving in the military as an absolute right. But they and the Mennonites and German Baptists made their peace with the state and Federal governments, accepted the new constitutions, and had their voting rights and ability to hold office restored.[1] From then on, however, the sectarian churches withdrew from direct political activity, some of their members refused to vote or hold office, and the remainder played a negligible role in the political life of the Commonwealth.

During and after the Revolution, Baptists John Leland in Virginia and New York and Isaac Backus in New England joined in advocating disestablishment, but Pennsylvania's Baptists stayed apart from these crusaders who attempted to gain elsewhere the liberties that had been customary in Pennsylvania for one hundred years.[2] The burgeoning Methodist move-

105

ment issued no declaration on church and state. Like the Pennsylvania Baptists, their ministers preached the necessity of new birth, remained preoccupied with revivals, and found no reason to publish political manifestos or books of political theory.[3]

The Methodist Discipline of 1798 advocated no bribery in elections and observance of the Sabbath. Although not wishing "to intrude upon the proper religious or civil liberties of any of our people" the Methodists announced their intention to treat any individual's sale or gift of "spirituous liquors" as immoral conduct to be "cleared, censured, suspended, or excluded."[4] The Baptist Confession of Faith, reprinted in 1798, identified the moral law as equalling both the natural law imposed on Adam and "delivered by God upon Mount Sinai." Christ in no way dissolved, but only strengthened its imperatives. Obedience to this law should be universal, or, in other words, there was no right to unbelief. To espouse anything contrary to the Word of God and the moral law was to "betray true liberty of conscience." Sinning was destructive of Christian liberty, because true liberty came from Christ's deliverance from sin.[5] In 1788 the Philadelphia and New York Synod of the Presbyterian church offered a similar understanding of liberty of conscience.[6] For both churches, God was ruler of conscience; the state, by allowing the churches their rights of autonomy, would gain a population endowed with Christian obedience.

Clerics in all churches agreed with the Republican position in 1800 that organized religion and politics should be separate. The clergy should not allow their message of God's redemption to be submerged in the muck of partisan politics. The minutes of the conventions, associations, general assemblies, and synods of the Pennsylvania churches before and after 1800 show that they did not endorse political parties or candidates. After the inauguration of George Washington in 1789, most denominations issued declarations in support of the new government and saw its establishment as providential. Washington responded by thanking them for "uniting reverence" to the government and "obedience to its laws with the duties and exercise of religion." On occasion churches in colonial Pennsylvania had presented formal welcoming addresses to new governors. This custom originated in the address to the throne by the dissenting churches of Great Britain upon the ascension of a new king. John Adams and later presidents received no such formal addresses.[7]

The 1789 declarations of the General Assembly of the Presbyterian church, the Reformed Coetus, and Philadelphia Yearly Meeting of the Society of Friends indicate the sentiments of three Pennsylvania denominations. The addresses of the Presbyterian and Reformed conformed to the contours of republican religious liberty. "Public virtue is the most certain means of public felicity; and religion is the surest base of virtue." "Reverence" to a just and lawful government was a part of the "exercises of religion" and strengthening good citizenship was "an acceptable service to God."[8] The Quakers sent two letters, one to George Washington and another to the President, the House, and the Senate. Friends told Congress that a government based upon "Oppression and Violence" risked God's judgment and called for an end to the slave trade. The address to Washington professed loyalty to and prayed for God's blessing on the new government, but made clear that Friends would not participate in any war. Friends desired to be in harmony with all other religious denominations and called on the President to preserve toleration and freedom of worship while suppressing "Vice, Infidelity, and Irreligion."[9] Friends did not specify how the new government would accomplish such contradictory goals. The declarations of the two churches proclaimed that the new government already exemplified justice and law; the sect instructed the magistrate on how to attain a just society.

In the early years of the new Republic there were few occasions of direct involvement of the churches with government. In the first printed rules or Discipline of Philadelphia Yearly Meeting, Friends argued that refusal to accept any political office or to engage in any act against their religious testimonies would preserve "inviolate that liberty of conscience which is essential to our union and well being as a religious society." In addition, the Society of Friends petitioned Congress repeatedly over militia service, slavery, and the slave trade, and also over Indian policy.[10] Friends obtained an endorsement from the Federal government of a plan to settle a few Quaker families among the Seneca Indians in order to teach farm methods and provide schools. Under the Articles of Confederation, Congress had authorized importation of Bibles and in 1782 appointed a committee of three who, with the assistance of the chaplains of Congress, examined the accuracy of a new translation of the Bible. The Pennsylvania Assembly advanced Robert Aitkin seven hundred dollars to complete his Bible, the first edition of an English Bible produced in the United States. In 1792 the Lutheran Ministerium and the Coetus of the German Reformed Church joined in a petition to Congress initiated by Boston ministers asking that "no edition" of the Bible be published without a "close examination as to its correctness."[11] Congress had just passed a copyright law and American printers were now issuing editions of the Bible, including Matthew Carey's edition of the Roman Catholic Douai Bible. Before the Revolution American printers could not produce Bibles in English, because a British firm had an official monopoly. The American ministers' desire was ostensibly for quality control, not censorship, because of the importance of accuracy in the Bible. The petition, if it was ever presented to Congress, had no results.

The churches in Pennsylvania observed fast days and thanksgiving days, whether initiated by the President, the governor, or by churches themselves. In 1813, in the midst of war, the German Reformed Church decided to petition the governor to have a fast day and invited the Lutherans to join with them. The Lutherans responded favorably, but with the proviso that a presidential proclamation would take precedence. The German Lutheran and Reformed churches' most direct action involving politics came in 1796.[12] When the assembly seemed intent on creating a system of free schools, both denominations opposed this as injurious to the German schools, "especially in regard to the religion taught in them." The Reformed saw the measure as "threatening the overthrow of the instruction of the youth in the true Christian religion."[13] The Coetus' statement is very revealing. The churches in Pennsylvania saw religious liberty as operating in a Christian context that could not be preserved in government schools. There was no relativity of truth on fundamentals. Left unanswered in the 1790s but a central issue in the 1840s was whether the Roman Catholic Church accepted "true" Christianity.

After 1789 the only debate as to the advisability of religious liberty in Pennsylvania occurred among branches of the Presbyterians. Ministers of the Reformed and Associate Presbyterian churches continued to worry about whether the absence of references to God in the United States Constitution proved that America was not in a religious covenant. Politicians and ministers from the Presbyterian Church, U.S.A. used the Pennsylvania constitution of 1790 and laws to show the state's religious dimensions. A careful examination of this controversy between Presbyterian churches will show different interpretations of what separation of church and state and religious liberty meant in early nineteenth-century Pennsylvania.

A continuing prerevolutionary era debate over church and state in Pennsylvania occurred in the small Reformed and Associate Presbyterian churches. These "Seceder" churches had split away from the established Church of Scotland in the late seventeenth century in order to maintain the validity of the Solemn League and Covenant taken at the beginning of the English civil war. Because that oath remained binding on following generations, the Seceder ministers refused to take an oath to the king or even an oath of abjuration.[14] Insisting on the continued efficacy of all sections of the Westminster Confession, the Seceder or Covenanter churches became intensely anti-Roman Catholic and antirevival, opposing George Whitefield's platform of unified Christianity as latitudinarian.

The first known Seceder minister in colonial Pennsylvania was Alexander Gellatly (ca.1720–61), who arrived in 1753 and shortly thereafter helped organize two congregations and three ministers into the Associate Presbyterian Synod of Pennsylvania. Gellatly reacted against the religious freedom practiced in Pennsylvania and criticized other Presbyterians for selling out the faith. The predictable result was a pamphlet war between Gellatly and several spokespeople for Old Light and New Light Presbyterians.[15] Gellatly's original tract does not survive, but according to his critics it asserted that the magistrate had an obligation not to tolerate error. In the highly charged religious animosities of the mid-1750s, the Seceder's vision of church and state confirmed the worst fears of Quakers of what the growing power of the Presbyterians might mean. In this context, Gilbert Tennent's sermon of 1759 on Christian liberty attempted to distance the main body of Presbyterians from the Seceders as well as to reassure other religious communities.[16] Francis Alison also attacked the Covenanters.

In 1782 two American branches of the Seceding church attempted to unite in the Reformed Presbyterian presbytery. They could agree on everything except Articles XX, XXIII, and XXXI of the Westminster Confession, which defined the magistrates' role; eventually disagreement here led to a division between the Reformed Presbyterians and others who became the Associate Reformed Church. Robert Annan, the Reformed minister in Philadelphia, sought to unify the two churches in 1783 by composing a commentary on the Westminster Confession and a summary of beliefs.[17] His synthesis, which remained the position of the Reformed church until the Civil War, showed the impact of American beliefs about liberty of conscience and denominationalism upon traditional Calvinistic interpretations of church and state.

Civil government, Annan argued, originated in God's moral and natural law. These laws of reason (the existence of God, the punishment of evil, the reward of the good, eternal life) were summarized in the Ten Commandments and contained within the Christian religion, but they could be discovered apart from revealed religion.[18] Thomas Hobbes wrongly saw the origins of government in fear and force; such an interpretation ignored the essential nature of humans as made in the image of God. John Locke and those who saw the social compact as a purely man-made device were also wrong. God was present in the original covenant for government among men who took an oath to obey. The "sense of obligation" in the oath to abide by the covenant derived from man's rational and moral agency; that is, his God-given nature.[19] All government existed to keep God's moral order, but a government among a Christian people had additional obligations because they knew the true religion.

The purpose of government was to preserve order by punishing vice and preventing crime. The magistrate was a minister of God, but not a lawgiver, because God is the sole lawgiver; the magistrate merely implemented the law of God in civil society. Law penalized criminals, but the prevention of crime through the promotion of virtue was of more importance to the survival of the state.[20] The Christian religion fostered virtue and the government for its own well-being should protect it without playing any role in the church. The church's foundation was the law of God as revealed through Christ, and the minister's role as a magistrate within the church was analogous to that of the magistrate in the state. The separation of church from the state protected the church from the state, but both agencies worked together under the providence of God to foster mankind's moral well-being.

Annan approved of liberty of conscience rightly understood, but he complained that Americans mistook liberty for anarchy. Liberty of conscience required that conscience exist as more than subjectivity. Conscience or "the voice of God in the soul" had an objective content derived from "religion and moral excellence." Full freedom of conscience allowed liberty for all "speculative opinions," and "modes of worship," but did not allow for relativism in matters of the moral law.[21] The universal law contained in nature, the moral law, the Ten Commandments, and Christianity required that the government foster true religion. Annan wanted support for no distinctive tenets of any particular church but for the essentials of Christianity upon which all could agree. The state helped Christianity through laws against vice, the promotion of education, and by the magistrates' example of godly living.[22] A secular state was an impossibility; all states supported some religion. The basic religion of Americans was Christianity and all magistrates should be Christians. Non-Christians who obeyed the moral law should receive their full civil rights, but these did not include the right to serve as an officeholder.

Samuel Brown Wylie (1773–1852), born in Ireland and educated in Scotland, migrated to America in 1797 and beginning in 1803 served as pastor of the Philadelphia Reformed Presbyterian Church for nearly fifty years. Wylie became professor of Greek and Latin at the University of Pennsylvania and professor of theology and Hebrew in the Theological Seminary of the Reformed Presbyterian Church.[23] In an 1803 tract Wylie, starting from the same premises as Annan, spelled out the implications of living under state and Federal constitutions that supposedly did not recognize civil authority as deriving from God, did not view magistrates as ministers enforcing the moral law, and guaranteed full religious liberty to heretics.

For Wylie, the Federal Constitution would have been bad in a heathen land; in a country inhabited by Christians it was idolatrous and all authority coming from it illegitimate. The Constitution did not mention God, established no religious test for officeholding, and ignored the magistrates' responsibility to enforce the moral law. The Pennsylvania constitution had similar flaws in addition to recognizing the authority of the Federal government.[24] Like Annan, Wylie denounced the false conception of conscience imbedded in the Pennsylvania constitution. Full liberty of conscience made conscience a law-giving power superior to God. True conscience reinforced God's moral law and supported those churches that followed the revealed commands of God.[25]

What was the responsibility of Christians living in an American state in open rebellion against God's law? For Wylie, their first obligation was to mourn before God the "prevailing abominations" and to pray for reformation. Next, they should do no act that would honor or reinforce the legitimacy of authority lest believers become participants in its criminality. This meant taking no oath of allegiance, not voting, not serving in any public office where an oath was required, and not being on any juries. Wylie supported most of Pennsylvania's law code with three exceptions. He disapproved of the Pennsylvania statute incorporating St. Mary's Roman Catholic Church, he disliked the provisions allowing a person guilty of second degree murder to be sent to prison rather than being put to death as Deuteronomy stipulated, and he denounced all laws supporting slavery as against God's law.[26]

Even with all its faults, Wylie viewed the United States government "as the best now existing in the Christian world." Reformed Presbyterians desired "nothing more than its reformation, happiness, and prosperity."[27] When challenged that his principles would lead to religious persecution, Wylie replied that a state that followed the precepts of God could not persecute. The magistrates' destruction of idolatry was not persecution; persecution was what happend to God's faithful. The main virtue of the American system was that the church was perfectly free from state interference.

Wylie's treatise was reprinted in 1806, 1832, and 1850 – the last long after its author had repudiated his negative view of the United States government. Within the Reformed and Associate Reformed churches, the views of Annan and Wylie continued to be debated. James Wilson, the Cameronian minister of Albany, New York, agreed with Wylie and pronounced George Washington "an infidel."[28] Joseph Cooper, a pastor of the Second Associate Presbyterian Reformed Church in Philadelphia, in 1845 declared that a Christian magistrate is bound to enforce "an external conformity [to those] principles that are founded upon the moral natural law, and the recognition of which is essential to the happiness of civil society. The Christian religion is a *natural* religion in so far as it enforces the precepts of the moral natural law or the decalogue."[29]

Gilbert McMaster, minister of the Reformed Presbyterian Church in Duanesburgh, New York, in an 1832 tract shows how over time the Reformed Presbyterian position approximated that of the Old School and New School Presbyterians. McMaster began with the premises of Annan and Wylie and ended by arguing for the legitimacy of the American government. McMaster argued that any government that kept and preserved order was legitimate according to the moral law. A state's obligations remained the same whether or not it was inhabited by Christians, so Wylie was wrong in seeing the state and Federal governments as illegitimate.[30] He was also incorrect in misunderstanding their relationships to Christianity.

At the Federal level the oath of office, chaplains for Congress and the armed services, adjournment of Congress on the Sabbath, proclamation by the executive of fasting, prayer, and thanksgiving days all constituted official recognition of Christianity. Though the Constitution did not name God, it provided for oaths that did, and the Declaration of Independence recognized the providence of God. Most important, McMaster insisted, the defects in the Federal government were supplied by state governments.[31]

A citizen had most contact with the state government, and New York State's constitution, laws, and court decisions confessed God and His providence, secured liberty of worship while opposing licentiousness, allowed no lotteries, outlawed slavery, supported public education, acknowledged the Christian Sabbath and preserved its sanctity, exempted ministers from various civil obligations, and secured church property. The state courts prosecuted for blasphemy and declared that Christianity was the religion of the state.[32] By adding the state and Federal governments together, McMaster announced, New York and America were "not only a moral system, but also a Christian government, in actual and voluntary subjection to [the] Messiah."[33] The Reformed Presbyterians in Pennsylvania could have used virtually the same arguments. By 1830 to the Reformed Presbyterians like McMaster, the American government, because it ruled according to the natural and revealed word of God, was not idolatrous and illegitimate, though Sunday mails showed a need for further actions. Reformed Presbyterians could vote and enter into civil life with a clear conscience.

J. H. McIlvaine, an Old School Presbyterian who became a professor at Princeton in 1860, agreed with those absolutists who saw chaplains and religion in public schools as contradicting the essence of the Constitution. The Federal Constitution exalted the "idea of religious liberty" over the need for "national unity, liberty, and responsibility." The small minority who disbelieved, said McIlvaine, overrode the wishes of the majority who practiced Christianity, because there was no constitutional safeguard against infidels and Mormons. In order to give Protestants the legal right to the religious liberty they now enjoyed, the Constitution should be amended to read "We, avowing ourselves to be a Christian and Protestant nation, do ordain and establish the Constitution. . . ."[34]

William Findley, a Republican member of Congress and a Presbyterian, wrote in 1813 a five-hundred-page answer to Wylie. Findley's treatise gains importance because as an influential member of the Pennsylvania constitutional convention in 1789 he had offered an amendment and engaged in debate over the meaning of the religion clause. Unlike Mc-Master, Findley repudiated Wylie's presupposition, denied that America was a Christian state, and insisted its authority was legitimate.

According to Findley, the American government, like that of all other nations, was founded upon the moral law of God as revealed in nature and repeated in the fifth commandment ("Honor thy father").[35] The United States was not founded upon Christianity, which was a revealed religion. Jesus created a spiritual kingdom and offered salvation, not statute law. The Old Testament precedents on crime and idolatry cited by Wylie were irrelevant to America because God ruled Israel directly in a fashion applicable to no other nation. Under the Christian dispensation, a person sinned against God's law and God did the punishing. The state recognized no crime against divine law and no sin. Instead, it made civil laws derived from natural law and enforced them by coercive physical power. Violators were criminals against the public peace and not viewed as sinners.[36]

Wylie and the Associate and Reformed Presbyterians misunderstood the American system of government. Because the originator of all government was God, America recognized the deity, and statutes on marriage and the Sabbath attempted to embody the unchanging natural law. The Pennsylvania constitution did not legislate toleration, for in America no government granted toleration. Rather, the people withheld from both state and national government any jurisdiction over religion. The right of conscience was anterior to the formation of government.[37]

Conscience was not a law-giving power at all. At the Pennsylvania constitutional convention Findley, because of ambiguity in the meaning of conscience, proposed substituting the phrase "contrary to his own knowledge and judgment of his will." The convention voted down this amendment because they knew what conscience was. Americans defined conscience as "an exercise of mind of every man possessed of reason. It is not even a faculty of mind. It is the exercise of memory, recollecting what the person has done; and of reason, comparing our conduct with the law; and of judgment, drawing a conclusion."[38]

The Pennsylvania constitution did not exalt conscience above God or make conscience a law-giver. Rather the convention's declaration meant that *"no man should be compelled to worship God agreeably to the dictates of the consciences of any other man or body of men."*[39] To do otherwise would bind conscience to the will of the state. Such restraint happened under the Roman emperors or the Pope, and the practice of all established churches proved that coercing conscience led to false worship and persecution.

America's separation of the institutional church from the state guaranteed, according to Findley, what all wanted: the freedom of the church.

The church went beyond the state in bringing salvation. The only authority in the church was from Christ, and from His precept and example the
minister had to learn to be a servant, not a lawgiver.[40] On occasion,
church and state cooperated, because God was the source of both, but
they operated from different premises. The United States Congress had
no authority over any state's "religious affairs," and neither the Federal
government nor Pennsylvania could be a Christian state; there was no
such phenomenon. But Pennsylvania did follow the moral precepts of
God in laws punishing blasphemy, protecting marriage, preserving the
Sabbath, forbidding murder and theft, and protecting only the worship of
almighty God, not that of Baal and Moloch.

Annan, Wylie, McMaster, and Findley agreed on one belief: Government
rested upon the civil, natural, or moral law and had an obligation to obey
it. No Pennsylvania clergyman asserted otherwise in the pre-Civil War
period, though there were disagreements as to the content of that moral
law. Virtually all the Pennsylvanians who wrote on church and state
before 1830 were Presbyterians, but the views of other denominations
expressed in their periodicals before 1860 showed no significant difference in emphases.[41]

Government could not be neutral toward religion. The moral law and
the Ten Commandments called on all to "have no other gods before me."
The Federal and state governments enforced the moral law, though most
responsibility rested upon the states, and their motivation was civil order,
not religious commitment. Domestic peace and republican government
required a virtuous citizenry capable of electing good officials and willing
to obey the law. Organized religion buttressed the society by preventing
murder, theft, adultery, and supporting obedience to rightful authority –
parents, teachers, and magistrates.

The Protestant clergy saw God judging nations according to their enforcement of the moral law. God's requirements for America were the
same as for other nations. In discussions of church and state, Pennsylvania
ministers did not invoke millenialism or suggest that America had a special destiny or favored relationship, or equalled a new Israel.[42] Instead,
the prevalence of Christianity meant that the natural law was reinforced
and clearly known by Americans, not that it was in any way changed.
Christianity also meant that there was an ample supply of good men to be
elected to office. The clergy told their parishioners to select Christians,
because such moral men could more safely be entrusted with power and
should rule for the benefit of all.

All denominations agreed that the church must be kept free from the
state.

The sentiment of entire freedom in religion; of perfect liberty to worship God according to our own views of right; of universal toleration, or rather of entire *equality* in this respect – for the word *tolerate* does not meet the idea; the belief that religion is to be kept separate from the state, and is safe when the state shall in no way attempt to regulate its movements – is the *last point* which society is to reach in this direction.... It is impossible to conceive that there is to be anything *beyond* this which mankind are to desire in their progress toward perfectness.[43]

Jesus Christ founded the church and the power of his realm was purely spiritual. God operated directly upon each person through his or her conscience, and the believer had to be free to follow God's directions. The church could structure this process by guiding and counseling the person, because God through Jesus had entrusted the keys to His kingdom to the church. But the state had no role. State involvement in the internal affairs of the church led to idolatry, persecution, and hypocrisy. The government should neither endorse nor condemn the distinctive tenets of any Christian church; it was "neutral" and favored no denomination. The state's only role in the institutional church came if there were a serious problem the organization could not solve on its own or without endangering the peace. In such cases, when requested by members of the church, the courts might determine the previous policies and practices and restore order. The courts or the legislature were to make no policies for the church.

Neutrality toward denominational peculiarities did not entail neutrality toward religious worship or Christianity. Christianity was the religion of the people, and the government for civil purposes should encourage the people to worship. Such encouragement showed through tax exemptions, the special status of the clergy in being free from military service or jury duties, and in public ceremonies at which the clergy prayed or participated. The clergy's obligation on such days was to provide a generalized Christian belief, not to proselytize for the distinctive beliefs of their denomination.

The primary function of the clergy was to save souls, and they should allow nothing to deter them from proclaiming the promise of salvation. Preaching was on spiritual subjects, not politics. Ministers were never to discuss matters of partisan politics in church nor to endorse candidates from the pulpit. Samuel Fisher, the Presbyterian minister of Moorestown, New Jersey, crossed the permissible line in his fast-day sermon of 1812. He published the sermons to show he had preached morality, not politics.[44] His congregation thought otherwise and Fisher lost his pulpit. His successor, Albert Barnes, who became the most prominent Presbyterian

New School leader in Philadelphia and an important antislavery advocate, first endorsed a political candidate in 1861.[45]

James Abercrombie, one of the ministers at Christ Church and St. Peter's in Philadelphia, breached the invisible barrier on several occasions. In 1798 during the quasi-war with France and upon the President's proclamation of a fast day, Abercrombie complained about infidelity in high places in America, denounced the atheists of France for making war on Christianity, and called for support for the President. Even so, Abercrombie's preface apologized that a minister's introduction of politics in sermons is "in the highest degree improper. But, uncommon exigencies require unusual exertions" and the oration was "to show the necessity of religion to the support of good government."[46] The *United States Gazette* denounced the sermon as a partisan utterance unbefitting a pastor. Abercrombie's sermon in 1800 denouncing Thomas Jefferson has already been mentioned; his fast-day sermons during the War of 1812 also brought controversy. The *Democratic Press* called one "seditious" and wondered if the sermon were "intended as a signal, a tocsin for *another St. Bartholomew's.*"[47] Abercrombie denied any "seditious intention" and proclaimed the right of a clergyman to express sentiments upon political subjects, even though the pulpit was a "most improper place." Evidently, Abercrombie thought the preface to the published text of the sermons was a proper place, for it was openly political, denouncing France and Napoleon and deploring a "destructive and unnecessary" war caused by a "blundering and feeble administration."[48] After the preface, the two sermons seem very tame and not very political. Still, after a declaration of war, a sermon showing considerable sympathy to Great Britain, opposition to France, and praying to avert the evil of war could appear incendiary. Abercrombie did not lose his pulpit, perhaps because the Philadelphia Episcopalians thought him right but indiscreet. Still, he never became rector of Christ Church nor held a parish on his own. Fisher's and Abercrombie's difficulties came from fast-day sermons during wartime. Such occasions could cause difficulties because they were proclaimed by Presidents for bewailing sins and beseeching God's particular providence. The Administration wanted the clergy to be court preachers rather than prophets.

All churches felt compelled to take a stand on moral issues. Neither congregations nor politicians objected to ministers preaching about daily life. But even here there were proper forms to be followed. A sermon against covetousness or dishonesty in business was legitimate, but not one on paper money, tariffs, or banking reform. These were not moral issues, except when banking failure due to speculation and greed brought distress to the general community. And the preaching on moral issues must be done in such a manner as not to identify individuals and to persuade the congregation to change, not drive them away from the church.

Obviously a minister needed to pick his moral targets carefully, particularly in an election year or if there were political ramifications, because zeal without discretion would accomplish little. Like politicians, the clergy had to lead as well as listen to the public. Still, there would be little difficulty if the preacher selected as topics those areas that the public expected the church to be interested in. Traditionally, the church served as moral arbitrators on the family, giving advice on rearing children, the sanctity of marriage, divorce, and education. The clergy applied biblical precepts to masters and servants and honesty and justice to the market economy. Ministers advised the rich to give to charity and to treat workers fairly, and advised laborers to live soberly and to work hard.[49] Churches developed positions against duels, Indian removals, lotteries, and drunkenness, the latter testimony becoming more stringent after 1830.[50] In the early nineteenth century religious periodicals praised and reported the activities of the American Colonization Society.[51] The fear of disrupting denominational unity and opposition within the congregation meant that most preachers ignored abolitionism until mainline Protestant churches divided into northern and southern branches.

Theoretically, outside the pulpit a minister could discuss moral issues relying upon only the natural law. But within the church the minister could freely mix revealed and moral truths, because both originated from God. The complications arose when the moral topics involved legislation.[52] The pulpit and even the religious press were no place to discuss laws or the power of the state.

The election of 1824 ushered in a long period of political maneuvering between the supporters of John Quincy Adams and those of Andrew Jackson. Historians generally describe the Presbyterian church as the denomination in Pennsylvania that due to its traditions and involvement in bringing the Revolution was most likely to be involved in partisan politics. The *Christian Advocate,* the major Presbyterian religious periodical, was edited by Ashbel Green, a minister in Philadelphia, and published in the city. A careful study of the *Advocate* in the period before the Presbyterians became involved in controversies leading to schism provides a test case for showing how the institutional church dealt with politics.

The *Advocate* in the election of 1824 took no position beyond decrying partisanship and animosity. One correspondent thought it ironical that Presbyterians would seek to pray for the President, but not pray for wisdom in electing a President. After all, God heard prayer and had the wisdom to bring to the United States a man of "pure morals and sound principles."[53] Green praised John Quincy Adams's inaugural address because his references to God did not seem just tacked on, but condemned Henry Clay's participation in a duel while he had been Speaker of the House of Representatives.[54] The *Advocate* showed displeasure over the wrangling and the irreligious comments of the opponents of sending delegates to the Panama Congress.[55] Georgia's claims to Indian lands and Sabbath mail brought strong editorials. The election of Andrew Jackson brought no comment beyond favorable notice of his recently proclaimed opposition to dueling.[56]

In 1829 the nation according to the *Advocate* faced four moral evils: slavery, intemperance, Sabbath profanation, and Indian oppression.[57] The *Advocate* showed its tepid antislavery sentiments by occasional comments and regularly printing the proceedings of the American Colonization Society.[58] Temperance was a state problem. The Sabbath issue should be addressed by "appeal" to the "conscience, or moral sense of the people" rather than Federal legislation. The government's sponsoring Sunday mail meant that it was legislating on the subject and such laws could be opposed.[59] Eleven Presbyterian missionaries who had supported the claims of the Cherokees were imprisoned by Georgia. Indian rights, as the *Advocate* defined it, was not a partisan issue:

Into mere party politicks we have never dipped our editorial pen, and we never will. But no fear of being charged with meddling with party politicks, should make us forget or forego our duty and character as a *Christian Advocate*... And in that character we say most deliberately, and after close and careful investigation, that we think the contemplated removal of the Indians, is a measure at war with every principle of Christianity, with every dictate of humanity, and with all regard to national character – a measure for which we shall, if it take place, suffer the reproach of all civilized nations, and the frowns and chastisements of the God of the whole earth. . . .[60]

The *Advocate* took no position on the reelection of Jackson, declined to discuss the tariff, would not comment on the changes in Jackson's cabinet because these were political matters. Editorials did support Jackson on nullification.[61] The *Advocate* asserted that Presbyterians were as strong opponents as any "Owenite, or other infidel" of a "union of church and state." Yet the United States of America claimed to be a Christian country and it was incumbent upon the community to elect representatives who would not "outrage every Christian feeling, and expose their country to the judgments of Almighty God."[62]

The Presbyterian periodical devoted more attention to politics than other religious journals. Pennsylvanians believed that the pulpit was purely for salvation and not discussing policies of the nation. In church ministers discussed subjects in religious language and sought to influence their congregations to voluntary compliance. The only exceptions to this generalization came in the few printed sermons by black ministers on slavery and by Quaker women ministers on slavery and women's rights.

The black clergy addressed the issues of slavery as well as of religious liberty in addresses given every January 1 in commemoration of the ending of the foreign slave trade in 1808. The clergy normally coupled a strong call for abolition, a vivid description of the evils of slavery with a plea to members to live responsibly in order to show that free blacks made good citizens. Occasionally religious liberty was mentioned, and always in a manner that showed Pennsylvania blacks receiving its benefits. The black Episcopalian, Absalom Jones, in 1808 praised God for "the privileges we enjoy, of worshipping God, agreeably to our consciences, in churches of our own."[63] Russell Parrott, a second black Episcopal minister, in 1812 praised "the mild influence of the laws of Pennsylvania" and in 1816 saw America as a "land of liberty and equality" in which those whom "religious intolerance" had forced into exile could be "free in the profession of religious tenets." Parrott blamed the slaveholders for withholding from blacks the right to read Scripture and to receive the "consolations of religion."[64] The few published orations of black ministers need to be interpreted cautiously. Although printed at the request of the black congregations, the sermons addressed an audience of white patrons, who needed to be persuaded of the necessity of abolishing slavery in the South. Still, black clergy seem to have served as their congregations' spokesmen with a freedom not available to white ministers.

Women occupied a special position, numerically not a minority but legally not enjoying full equality. The law did not allow them to hold office or vote in political elections, and married women could not hold property in their own name. Within the church they did not serve in the vestry or as trustees, and most had no vote in parish elections. The Quakers always and the Methodists and the Disciples of Christ (Christians) occasionally allowed women to preach. The main role of women within and outside of the church was in the benevolent societies through which they helped orphans and the poor by providing charity, education, and moral examples. Even here there were liabilities. One unincorporated Philadelphia female benevolent society required its treasurer to be a single woman, thereby finessing the legal strictures on the property rights of married women. The state issued no charters to separate women's churches, but it did incorporate women's benevolent societies.[65] Pennsylvania neither officially recognized nor forbade women from exercising power in churches, with Friends coming closest to giving women equal rights in church government. Women recognized their importance in religious organizations. Mary Still, a black member of the African Methodist Episcopal Church, proclaimed in 1857 "when female labor is withdrawn the church must cease to exist."[66]

Pennsylvania women played a major role in feminist agitation before the Civil War. When women reformers protested their subordinate role in the church, they attacked the male-centered exegesis of the story of Eve or St. Paul's admonitions. Sarah Grimké, during the time she was a Quaker, argued that the Scriptures portrayed women as morally equal to men and entitled to preach.[67] Grimké and Lucretia Mott satirized the hierarchical pretensions of the clergy. Mott accused the ministers of a false idolatry of the Bible, superstitious reverence for Sunday, neglect of temperance, support of war, discrimination against women's education, and opposition to women's equality.[68] She did not divorce politics from religion, and explicitly linked her faith to support for temperance, abolition, and women's rights. Because Quakers had no "hireling" preachers, Mott saw her duty as a Quaker minister to preach divine truth rather than to hold a congregation together and irritate no one; so she addressed openly in meeting for worship highly controversial moral-political-religious subjects. Although she often spoke for changing laws to give women equality, Mott never discussed church-state issues as a constitutional or legal subject. Rather, she contrasted liberty of conscience with idolatry, superstition, and priestcraft, all of which she identified with evangelical Protestantism.[69] She claimed for blacks and women the freedom to participate equally – if they so desired – in politics, education, and religion.

When the Christian clergy and laity wanted to influence the legislation or the general community, they joined voluntary associations. These organizations, relying upon moral suasion at first, in time began lobbying in Harrisburg for specific legislation. The strengths and limitations of the clergy's role are illustrated in their efforts to obtain a moral law on alcohol.

Pennsylvania has always had difficulty in dealing legally with the sale and consumption of alcohol. It has not found an easy way to limit the sale of alcohol in order to curtail the abuses coming from overindulgence, or to persuade the citizens that the social pathology stemming from social drinking is serious enough to merit prohibition. Since the colony began, alcohol has been a source of political patronage, tax revenue, corruption, crime, poverty, as well as good times and merriment. The alcoholic has been a comic as well as a tragic figure, a product of a disease and his moral failings.

In the late colonial and early national period the emphasis in the churches' teachings and in the statutes was on control, not abolition of drinking. The Quakers had moved from temperance to total abstinence of hard liquor, but they were no longer a political force. The Methodists who originally had strong antislavery and antialcohol testimonies gradually became accommodating on both issues. The cheapness of distilled spirits, the myriad business and social occasions on which they were consumed, and the prodigious amounts consumed in the period after the Revolution prompted one scholar to describe the new nation as "The Alcoholic Republic."[70]

Pennsylvania's antivice code contained fines for drunkenness, and also a demand for stringent licensing of taverns. Even so, in 1808 the legislature repealed the 1721 law's provisions on licensing taverns, but not the sections limiting the amount of credit an innkeeper could extend for drinks.[71] The lawmakers seemed more concerned with appointing inspectors to grade the size of barrels of whiskey than to curtail consumption.[72]

At first, reformers focused on the devastating effects of alcoholism on a respectable person's family. In 1819 and 1822 laws allowed the courts to determine if a man were an habitual drunkard and, if so, to permit trustees to control his property for the benefit of his wife and children. Any tavernkeeper who sold alcohol to a known drunkard was subject to a heavy fine.[73] Humanitarian reformers debated whether the state should create an institution in which the courts could confine habitual drunkards for periods of a year or two so that they could exist in a good environment while developing the stamina to resist alcohol.[74]

Under the impact of the Second Great Awakening, Presbyterians, Baptists, Methodists, and Low Church Episcopalians discovered that drinking was an evil. They first advocated only abstinence from hard or spirituous liquors but, being charged with outlawing the beverages of the poor but not those of the wealthy, moved to proscribe wine and brandy. In the 1830s churches staged successful campaigns to persuade members against making, buying, selling, and drinking alcoholic beverages, even beer and cider.[75] Their initial tactics relied almost exclusively upon individual commitment, and temperance advocates disdained the use of law. Still, the churches' growing opposition to drinking of alcoholic beverages appeared almost immediately in new laws.

In 1830 all applicants for tavern licenses had to obtain recommendations of their good character from twelve citizens; courts became obligated to limit the number of taverns and inns to a "sufficient" number and to ensure that all such establishments provided suitable accommodations for eating and putting up travelers. The fee for tavern licenses was set at a minimum of $10 per year plus a 4 percent tax on sales over one hundred dollars.[76] In 1832 previously unregulated oyster cellars could sell quantities of alcohol smaller than a quart (that is, a drink) only if they also sold raw and cooked oysters too.[77] The 1834 law forbade innkeepers from accepting credit for sales of alcoholic beverages, harboring servants or apprentices, or allowing any devices for gaming on the premises. The regulations showed a hostility toward tavern culture, and assumed that control of saloons would end intemperance.[78]

When the existing laws failed to stop drunkenness, reformers turned to local option. In 1846 the legislature allowed eighteen counties the right of local option. Before the Civil War thirteen states passed so-called Maine laws outlawing the sale of alcoholic beverages.[79] Temperance advocates in Pennsylvania brought pressure upon their lawmakers for a similar law. In order to duck taking a stand on such a controversial issue and/or to follow the precedent of county local option vote, the state in 1854 scheduled a referendum. After a bitter campaign and an extremely heavy voter turnout for an off-year election, the results showed the state split about equally: 49 percent in favor of going dry; 50 percent opposed; one percent so unconcerned that they did not mark their ballots.[80] After this result, which some temperance advocates claimed was really a victory because some drys voted "no" on constitutional grounds, the legislature passed a fainthearted measure restricting the sale of liquor in small quantities, – the quart "jug" law. The law was unpopular, hard to enforce, and was soon repealed.

The evangelical churches created and sustained the prohibition movement in Pennsylvania, but their campaign was not seen as an infringement upon separation of church and state. Hicksite Quakers, Unitarians, and Universalists who denounced Sabbath legislation as destructive of liberty of conscience and who feared the evangelical clergy supported prohibition. Those who opposed the referendum cited personal freedom, not church and state.[81] Why? The answer seems to be that clergy changed their style of address depending upon the audience. Sermons and tracts addressed to church members pictured drinking as a sin and trumpeted conversion as a cure. But the language the clergy employed in temperance conventions and addresses to the legislature downplayed religion and portrayed the drinking of alcohol as a social and moral problem, not a sin. Drinking led to social pathology, which cost the Commonwealth money. Revenues gained from tavern licenses fell far short of what the state had to spend on prisons, asylums, and poor relief. The protemperance clergy, physicians, and lawyers, by relying upon medical studies, statistical evidence on the number of persons inhabiting Pennsylvania's prisons and asylums who had drunk excessively, and calculations of revenue and cost, managed to convert religious and moral outrage into a moral and political reform. The state's responsibility to curtail sales rested upon its police power to protect citizens. Church and state were not at issue.[82]

The clergy's defeat over prohibition was an exception. In the pre-Civil War period on other moral issues in which the clergy united – against duels, opposing lotteries, approving of a strict Sabbath – legislation supported their position. The clergy understood the separation of church and state as restricting them from speaking out on what they and their parishioners defined as purely political or economic issues. They did not discuss tariffs, internal improvements, banking, political parties, and individual candidates. Churches still remained the arbiters of morality and defenders of the family. Ministers proclaimed their responsibility to use religious or moral language in the pulpits and moral or social rhetoric in advocating laws. The churches and ministers had reason to look upon the Revolution as providential. Under the state they had more influence than previously under the Quaker-dominated colonial government. The churches flourished because they were self-supporting and self-governing, and government exercised a benevolent neutrality toward all religious institutions in order to foster the commonweal.

In the early nineteenth century, the clergy and the politicians agreed that God's moral law undergirded society, and the politicians agreed that statutes should embody the moral law. No one – radical worker, black clergyman, conservative Presbyterian, abolitionist, feminist, industrialist, Whig, or Democrat – disagreed on these fundamentals. God's moral law was Pennsylvania's civic religion. The controversy came on the relationship of Christianity, the church, and the state to the moral law. Paine, Jefferson, Findley, and Earle thought freedom of religion required an official ignorance, or separation from both the insitutional church and Christianity. The state dealt only with the moral law. A few Reformed Presbyterians and Old School Presbyterians agreed that this strict separation was the legal status quo and they worked to change the constitutions so that Christianity was given official recognition. More commonly, politicians and ministers claimed that Christianity as a system of beliefs already enjoyed official recognition, and the separation was only between the institutional church and the agencies of government. The clergy proclaimed their understanding of church and state in sermons or tracts on which no one voted; the politician in and out of government spent little time discussing religious liberty, concentrating instead on social, economic, and, occasionally, moral issues. The ultimate arbitrators of actual practices in the state were the courts.

CHAPTER VIII

The Legal Implications of Religious Liberty

The rhetoric of religious liberty had to be translated into law and jurisprudence to be meaningful in practice. The state and the courts sought for a definition that would show a fostering benevolent neutrality, treat all religious institutions equally, preserve the religious fabric of the Commonwealth, and protect individual and group freedom of conscience. Court cases illustrate very clearly the dilemmas Pennsylvanians encountered with their contrary, if not contradictory, attitudes toward religious freedom and separation of church and state. An analysis of cases of property rights, blasphemy, and the Sabbath will show how the courts protected and fostered religion by defining the churches as corporations advocating morality. This legal fiction enabled the Commonwealth to have no religion and to be religious at the same time.

In 1731 the Pennsylvania Assembly passed an act enabling "Religious Societies of Protestants Within This Province" to purchase land and hold property.[1] A later act allowed the religious societies to specify an association or creed whose adherents would retain control of the property. Some colonial Pennsylvania churches sought charters of incorporation from the proprietors, but many more had trustees who controlled the property. The sectarian groups (Quakers, Mennonites) in colonial Pennsylvania did not seek charters and never used lotteries to finance the erection of structures. Before 1776 Reformed, Lutheran, Presbyterian, and Anglican churches had received charters along with the college, a hospital, learned societies, and a religiously based insurance company.

A policy of free incorporation by legislative act began with independence, but few churches sought charters during the war years. In 1791 the legislature sought relief from too frequent petitions of incorporation of churches, and allowed the attorney general to receive applications.[2] If he determined that the stipulations were legal, he forwarded the documents to the Pennsylvania supreme court, which granted the incorporation. The attempt to ease the burdens of the assemblymen was only partially successful. Churches, seminaries, and academies continued to receive charters from the state legislature. In general, the state followed a policy of allowing the applicants to put in their charter as much or as little as they wanted, with only a few regulations.

The courts held that according to the 1731 act "religious societies" were distinct congregations or communities that belonged to larger organizations. The Presbyterians or Methodists could not obtain a charter for the denomination; a local habitation was required. A trust created for the members of the Methodist Episcopal Church in the United States of America was not valid, because its members were not resident in Pennsylvania.[3] The legislature also restricted the amount of money from rent or other properties that could be earned by the church or charity.[4] When the legislature passed special acts of tax exemption the properties tax exempt were always limited, normally to the church buildings and five acres of land (such as a graveyard).[5] The charters also often stipulated that moneys earned by the church or charity be for the exclusive use of the purposes specified in the charter. In 1831 the legislature decreed that property of charitable and religious organizations was tax exempt. The church building and up to five acres were tax free. All land beyond this and income from stocks and bonds were rateable.[6] The court later argued that the Pennsylvania equivalent of the English common-law statute of mortmain was the limitation in each charter on the amount of tax-free income a church could receive.[7] In 1841 the legislature passed a law taxing the salaries of officers of corporations. An officer of a bank received a taxable salary because his compensation was related directly to his position in the chartered corporation, but a minister's salary was tax exempt because he was a corporate officer only in his temporal capacity, and received his compensation for spiritual ministrations. A tax upon a minister's salary was really upon the contribution of parishioners and would hinder the practice of religion.[8]

Church charters specified who controlled the property, the times of election for trustees, and regulated the collection of pew rents. After the Methodist Annual Conference of Pennsylvania was incorporated, the Methodists drew up a form to be used by their churches. The Episcopalians did the same, and once rejected a church's application to join convention because the necessary stipulations on clerical power had not been included.[9] The court determined that the charter of a Baptist congregation took precedence over the general polity of Baptist churches, because each Baptist church was independent.[10] In 1813, four years after being chartered in Philadelphia as an independent German Reformed Church, the congregation joined the Dutch Reformed Church in order to have English-language sermons. When in 1860 the congregation, named the First Dutch Reformed Church, wished to leave that denomination in order to call a former Methodist minister, the court held that the 1813 decision was binding even though now a majority of the congregation wished to terminate the relationship with the Dutch Reformed. The polity of the denomination bound an individual church.[11]

A dissenting opinion held that the church had originally formed in 1809 to practice faith according to the Heidelberg Confession. That purpose took priority over the decision to join the Dutch Reformed Church in 1813. The original charter allowed a majority to vote to determine to end a denominational relationship. The Synod of the Dutch Reformed had rejected the ex-Methodist minister because he was an Arminian. The Dutch Reformed Synod might insist upon a belief in predestination, but the Heidelberg Confession did not. The judge insisted that the court in this case must take cognizance of theology because it determined the property rights. The original purposes of the church could be best served by allowing the Methodist minister.[12] In all such cases, the intentions of the charter applicants must be decisive.

The courts tried never to rule on theology or spiritual matters, and in general they were successful. Instead, they relied upon enforcing the letter of the charter. If there were two ministers who claimed to be the elected or chosen pastor of a church, according to the court the majority of the congregation would not prevail if the charter entrusted that responsibility to the vestry or trustees. If a minister were to be dismissed and another called, only the duly constituted authority could do so.[13] When a church member brought a suit against another for disturbing the worship service by his manner of singing, the court dismissed the suit saying that only the duly constituted authority could bring such an action.[14] When an old man who had been a member of the Reverend George Rapp's communitarian group left all his money to Rapp, the sons brought suit. The court held against the sons, in spite of the fact that the man was old and feeble and Rapp had brought pressure. The court said that although the father had accepted Rapp's claims it was not evidence of an unsound mind. Because there was no religious belief or dogma established by law in Pennsylvania, English precedents did not hold, and consequently there could be no such legal phenomenon as superstitious usage.[15]

The state courts had to settle some disputes over church property and procedures when there was no incorporation. Two of the most important such cases involved schisms: the Society of Friends into Orthodox and Hicksites, and the General Assembly of the Presbyterian Church into Old School and New School. The Friends divided in 1827 and because local meetings had deeded their property to trustees, in general the majority of the people in a meeting determined who kept the land and structures. Controversy concerned Westtown School, trusts, and other property owned by the Yearly Meeting. The crucial case was tried in New Jersey and involved a trust claimed by both Orthodox and Hicksite members. The court based its decision on narrow, technical grounds. The cause of the separation was the decision by the clerk of Philadelphia Yearly Meeting in 1827 to accept the appointment of visiting committees, a device aimed at purging the Hicksites. Although the Yearly Meeting had been in an uproar and the Hicksites denied the legality of the decision because there had been no sense of the meeting, the Hicksites, rather than withdrawing immediately, had stayed in the session until another action was taken and the Yearly Meeting ended. The court held that by not walking out at the time of the committee's appointment, the Hicksites had accepted the legitimacy of that Yearly Meeting session, and so all actions of the Yearly Meeting were valid and the Orthodox had title to the property.[16] The fact that the Hicksites had numerical domination did not stop them from being schismatic.

The breakup of the Presbyterian General Assembly in 1837 came after several years of bitter struggle between Old School and New School delegates in which the New School had held a majority. But in 1837 the Old School had a majority because the moderator refused to recognize the credentials of synods formed under the Plan of Union with the Congregationalists. The Old School majority remaining upheld the moderator, thereby depriving some 60,000 Presbyterians of representation and membership in the General Assembly. The lower court sustained the New School, rebuking the moderator for carrying out an unjust judicial action. The state supreme court reversed on the grounds that the moderator's decision was legislative and legal according to Presbyterian canons. The previous year's moderator remained legally the moderator until a new one was chosen, and he was not obliged to grant an appeal of his decision to exclude the Union congregations. Repealing the 1801 Plan of Union between Congregationalists and Presbyterians was constitutional because the merger had been an interim measure for the frontier and did not change the definition of what it meant to be a Presbyterian. So the Old School majority had the legal right to purge the mixed Congregationalist-Presbyterian synods formed in New York and the West under the Plan of Union. The court insisted that it could deal only with the legality, not the wisdom, of the excision.[17]

Each side claimed vindication from the courts. The New School claimed the lower court vindicated the injustice of the Old School's proceedings and that the supreme court reversed on a technicality. The Old School used the supreme court to show the un-Presbyterian nature of the Plan of Union, the illegality of the steps the New School had used to create a new General Assembly, and that they were the only real Presbyterians. Both the Old School and New School organized rival general assemblies, each claiming to be the Presbyterian Church in the United States of America. Little property was involved because the General Assembly was unincorporated. The courts normally did not worry about duplication of names. In a 1829 case in which two parties claimed the right to style themselves the First Baptist Church of Philadelphia, the court declined jurisdiction because no property right was involved.[18] In 1858 in a case involving property rights the court said there should not be two First Presbyterian Churches of Harrisburg, because of confusion, and that the new church should select a different name.[19]

A second Old School/New School case involved a local church in which the Old School minority claimed the right to the property on the basis of being the only true Presbyterians. The court sustained the New School, and refused to define whether either party was legitimately Presbyterian.[20]

As early as 1798 the Pennsylvania courts guaranteed the right of a Roman Catholic bishop to control individual congregations. The case involved the income from an endowment to support a priest who served a parish and said masses for a deceased member. An ordained German priest claimed he did not need the permission of the bishop to say the masses and collect the stipend. The court disagreed, holding that church officials – Episcopal bishops, Presbyterian elders, Catholic bishops – had equal right to exercise the power bestowed on them by their denomination. The Roman Catholic Church was defined by hierarchical control: "Every Catholic congregation within the United States is subject to his [the Bishop's] inspection, and without authority from him, no Catholic priest can exercise any pastoral authority."[21]

A technicality determined the court's decision in the St. Mary's Roman Catholic Church case. Here property was owned by a priest, although neither side made reference to this fact. The dispute concerned the right to choose priests. The original charter joined eight elected lay trustees plus three clerical members, one of whom was the bishop, in the corporation. The causes of the dispute, involving ethnic tensions, the desire of Roman Catholic laymen to emulate the forms of church organization practiced by their Protestant neighbors, and the attempts of bishops to follow European practices, did not concern the court. When the bishop and the laity could not agree on who was to be the priest at St. Mary's, the laity hired William Hogan.[22] When Father Hogan did not leave voluntarily, the bishop excommunicated him. In response, the laity amended the charter to abolish the bishop's power over the selection and dismissal of the church's priests and to remove all priests from the board of trustees. The trustees demonstrated the popularity of their position by winning congregational elections over the bishop's supporters, and obtained confirmatory legislation from the state government with the proviso that the courts had to approve the changes in the charter. At first the court sent the trustees' revisions of the charter back to the church to make sure the provisions represented majority opinion. Eventually the case came to the state supreme court. The legal question was whether Father Hogan's assent to the charter's revision satisfied the original incorporator's desires.

James Commiskey, a regularly ordained and appointed priest at St. Mary's, presided over trustees' meetings, even after the withdrawal of the bishop. (The court did not agree upon or rule whether the bishop's absence from the trustees' meetings was voluntary.) When William Hogan attended meetings, the lay trustees recognized him as senior pastor and made him chairman over Commiskey. Commiskey protested this action and did not attend the next three meetings. So the trustees decided and notified Commiskey that he was no longer a trustee. The court unanimously agreed that this proceeding was illegal. All amendments passed after the exclusion were invalid. The original charter created two classes of trustees, laity and clergy, and both must be present and agree before a charter could be amended.

Over virtually every other issue, the justices differed. In three signed opinions the state court debated the nature of the Roman Catholic Church in America, the rights of bishop and laity, the intent of the original charter and of the legislature's act of incorporation. How much power could a foreign temporality (the Pope) have in the United States? Could control of temporals be divided from that of spirituals? The decision, while favoring the hierarchy, came with an admonition to both sides to settle their differences out of court. Chief Justice William Tilghman concluded the majority opinion:

It is scarcely possible that the *Roman Catholics* of the *United States of America*, should not imbibe some of that spirit of religious freedom which is diffused throughout the country. If those who govern that church, exercise their power with moderation; if they are not too forward in assuming the direction of temporal affairs; if they consult the reasonable desires of the laity both in the *appointment*, and the *removal* of pastors, in all human probability they may long retain their dominion. But if things are carried with a high hand – if, trusting to the authority of the church, they disregard the wishes of their congregations, it is easy to foresee how the matter will end. That church possesses neither property nor temporal power in this country. The laity have both. In a struggle, therefore, between two orders, the issue cannot be doubtful.[23]

The response of the trustees was again to use the legislative process. After an involved debate, the legislature passed a revised charter, but the governor's veto foreclosed that option. The St. Mary's case showed that a charter recognizing the power of a Roman Catholic priest or a bishop over a congregation was legal. Even if the charter gave the bishop authority over the appointment of ministers and vestries and made the laity subordinate in all matters, the courts enforced it. If the trustees had sole power, the court enforced their rights. In all property cases the courts attempted to ignore the religious implications of their decisions. Legally, the church was merely a special kind of incorporated property.

In colonial Pennsylvania there was no religious liberty for blacks to form institutions to practice their beliefs brought from Africa. Slaves might have practiced African religious rituals in private or in cemeteries, but no one recognized any of their rites as religious. The Quakers periodically held special meetings for blacks, but did not allow them to become members until 1796.[24] After 1741 the Anglican clergy of Philadelphia sought out, catechized, baptized, educated, and married free blacks and slaves. In response virtually all the blacks who joined a church became Anglican.[25] The church's sanction of a marriage did not stop the relationship from being severed if the master sold either the husband or wife to an out-of-state owner. When in 1780 Pennsylvania passed a gradual emancipation law, with the preamble invoking reason, freedom, and God's providential deliverance during the Revolution, those advocating abolition had not addressed the issue whether religious freedom allowed separate black churches.[26] When black Episcopalians and then Methodists sought to form separate congregations, their white patrons, after some reluctance, granted their request. The legislature faced a request from black church members and the parent denomination for incorporation.

In 1787 St. Thomas's African Episcopal Church received a charter. In the inaugural discourse for the new church, the white Episcopal minister, Samuel Magaw, boasted that the members had the right to "fix upon, or adopt such system, order, and mode of worship as may be most agreeable to you."[27] The charter granted the vestry, wardens, and minister full legal powers. It did not mention race, but the constitution of St. Thomas restricted membership to blacks and required the submission of ecclesiastical affairs to the Protestant Episcopal Church.[28] This clause meant that the worship had to be according to Episcopal methods and the minister an ordained priest, but the members retained the power of choosing the minister. The vestry had full control over all financial affairs of the church. When Bishop William White ordained Absalom Jones in 1794, the convention waived requirements for a knowledge of Greek and Latin for Jones but did not permit him to have a voice in its deliberations. (In 1849 after a bitter debate, the convention reiterated this policy of exclusion of black priests.)[29] After Jones's death in 1824, St. Thomas had difficulty in obtaining an ordained black Episcopal priest. In theory at least, the vestry and congregation had the same powers as other Episcopal churches.

Bethel Church's quest for equality within the Methodist Episcopal Church took much longer and, after court involvement, ended with the creation of a separate denomination.[30] Bethel's charter of 1799 granted control of revenue and property to trustees elected by members, all of whom were black, but gave the white elder of St. George's the right to preach once on Sunday and once during the week, to nominate the minister of Bethel, and to license other black ministers to preach. If two thirds of the black trustees were unable to agree, the elder of St. George's had a vote and his decision – whether favoring the majority or minority – became final, except on an issue involving money.[31] Richard Allen, the black minister who was ordained deacon by Bishop Asbury in 1799, and the members later claimed that the charter did not reflect their wishes. So, in 1807 they drew up a supplement to the charter that Bishop Asbury accepted and the legislature granted, but which neither St. George's nor the conference endorsed. The supplement restricted the power of the elder of St. George to interfere with either church property or internal church discipline, and allowed the black trustees to license preachers in the quarterly conference.[32] Bethel became more self-governing than any other Methodist church.

Distressed at the amount of black control over Bethel, a new white elder of St. George's, with the support of dissident Bethel trustee Robert Green, attempted to assert his authority over the church. Allen and the members resisted. The results of the dispute are clear – by 1816 Bethel was an independent church – but whether the Pennsylvania courts gave justice to its members is uncertain. In the first case, decided in January 1815, the Pennsylvania supreme court decreed that Bethel's manner of dismissing trustee Robert Green was illegal, because only an indeterminate number and not the full membership had made the decision.[33] The court here ruled against the church on a matter in keeping with its other decisions enforcing charters.

No other verdicts have been found, but there appears to have been at least one more case. Papers of lawyers Joseph Hopkinson and Samuel Shoemaker dated April 6 and April 24 concern the mandamus and the validity of the supplement.[34] Either a second court ruling was against Bethel and in favor of the white elder, or the mortgage was foreclosed, or there was an out-of-court settlement. On June 12, 1815 the property of Bethel, including both land and building, was sold at sheriff's auction. Richard Allen offered $10,125 in the winning bid for the building and lot. Tradition has it that Allen frustrated the white Methodists by outbidding them. Exactly where he obtained the substantial sum is not known. The defendant, perhaps the Methodist church, received $4,925; $2,186 went to satisfy the principle and interest of the mortgage (held by Allen) and $3,012 came from sales in "satisfaction of his Execution."[35]

A lawyer's opinion dated Dec. 16, 1815 indicates that there may have been more litigation. The black preacher, Daniel Coker of Baltimore, in a sermon preached in 1816, gave thanks for a favorable court decision allowing Bethel to become independent.[36] After 1816 there was no question but that a black church with a charter had the same rights and immunities as a white church. The survival of Bethel, which became the mother church of the African Methodist Episcopal denomination, paved the way for black churches to function within white denominations or to become independent. By the Civil War there were eighteen black churches in Philadelphia alone, with seating capacity of 11,000, and 4,254 communicants.[37] Blacks also created their own network of charitable organizations. Pennsylvania's blacks lost their right to vote in the 1837 constitutional convention. There was no abridgement of their right to religious liberty. The racism black Christians encountered in the white ministers and parishioners prompted black withdrawal and white acceptance of separate but equal institutions. Independent black churches came to symbolize for both races the desire of Pennsylvania blacks for justice. Perhaps that is why on two occasions before the Civil War mobs burnt a black church.

The closest the state came to an outright endorsement of Christianity was in blasphemy and Sabbath law cases. In 1822 Abner Updegraph was tried, convicted, and fined for violating an act of the Pennsylvania Assembly, passed in 1700, which stipulated that "whosoever shall wilfully, premeditatedly and despitefully blaspheme, and speak loosely and profane of Almighty God, Christ Jesus, the Holy Spirit, or the Scripture of Truth, and is legally convicted therefore, shall . . . pay . . . ten pounds." Updegraph appealed to the Pennsylvania supreme court for a ruling on the law's constitutionality. The court could have dismissed the case on a technicality. It found the indictment defective because there was only a summary, not a quotation, of Updegraph's words and because the charge of blasphemy was a crime in England but not a part of Pennsylvania law.[38] The attorney-general did not defend the lower court's action, either because it was unnecessary or because he would have had difficulty proving that Updegraph's actions were caused by his "being moved and seduced by the instigation of the devil."[39] The court implied that the case was a set-up to obtain a constitutional ruling, and, recognizing that the case raised important questions, in 1824 defined the legal meaning of Pennsylvania's heritage of religious liberty.

Updegraph's lawyer argued that the 1700 statute on profanity was now unconstitutional. The Pennsylvania constitutions of 1776 and 1790 guaranteed freedom of opinion and outlawed religious tests. Christianity was not in the parts of the English common law exported to the colony and had not become part of the common law of the United States, because America had outlawed religious persecution. Finally, counsel insisted that even if the 1700 law were in force, it was not applicable in this case because Updegraph spoke neither loosely nor profanely but in a discussion society.[40]

The court began by refusing to reconsider the jury's finding that Updegraph's words were loosely and profanely spoken and fell within the scope of the 1700 act. Even the existence of his debating club was deplorable, perhaps even actionable, as a threat to the public peace. A group which treated Christianity "with so much levity, indecency, and scurrility" would prove to be "a nursery of vice, a school of preparation to qualify young men for the gallows, and young women for the brothel."[41] The court's lurid point of reference was the social effect of allowing loose and profane talk about religion.

Chief Justice Duncan now addressed the main issue: the "constitutionality of Christianity." He quoted Penn's preamble to the laws passed at the first meeting of the Pennsylvania Assembly in Chester in 1683, which linked Christianity and civil liberties. English common law merged Christianity with the state and led to persecution; Pennsylvania's common law, begun by Penn, incorporated liberty of conscience with Christianity. The foundation of Pennsylvania's law was revealed and natural law. In 1700 infidels were not the issue, because there were few in the colony. The law of 1700 on profane speaking had never been repealed. Neither the Revolution, the Pennsylvania constitutions of 1776 and 1790, nor the United States Constitution had changed Pennsylvania's common law on religion and freedom of conscience. Duncan cited English precedents and Justice James Wilson's lectures on law to prove that God was the basis of all law and that the common law contained the "essential principles" of revealed and natural law. To attack Christianity, therefore, was to attack the law and endanger the foundation of society.[42]

Pennsylvania's constitutions guaranteed freedom of opinion, and the courts did not recognize heresy. The law protected serious discussion of religion, and also preserved public peace. Pennsylvania's statutes on marriage, family, divorce, oaths, the Sabbath, and morality rested upon religion. Therefore, the state must oppose any opinion with "dangerous temporal consequences likely to proceed from the removal of religion and moral restraints." One test of criminality was the speaker's intention. If Updegraph had been engaged in a serious theological discussion for the "benefit" of others, his speech was protected. But if he had maliciously sought to undermine the peace by destroying the "outward respect" due Christianity, he was guilty. The second test was whether the issues Updegraph discussed were against fundamentals: (1) "Denying the being and providence of God," (2) "Contumelious" reproach of Jesus Christ and profane scoffing at scripture, (3) "Certain immoralities tending to subvert all religion and morality, which is the foundation of all government."[43] Profane speech had to meet the same tests as immorality. Not all immorality was a crime, but when immorality weakened the bonds of society it became illegal. The law on profaneness, like that on the Sabbath, was not punishing "sins or offenses against God, but crimes injurious to and having a malignant influence on society."[44]

Pennsylvania's upholding of a blasphemy law in 1824 was not unusual. Courts in New York and Massachusetts upheld similar laws. What was unique was that the Pennsylvania court rested its decision upon William Penn's declaration, the content of colonial Pennsylvania's common law, and James Wilson's lectures. The court viewed Wilson's role in the Pennsylvania convention as so important that his lectures provided the key to understanding its constitution. Because the lectures had not distinguished between the foundations of the Federal and state constitutions, the court could have cited Wilson's views as illustrative of Pennsylvania's understanding of the Federal Constitution.

The court viewed liberty of conscience as a Christian concept allowing for religious pluralism within a context of fundamental agreement. Liberty of conscience meant that there would be no discrimination because of a person's religion or lack of religious belief. Even infidels benefited from the stability of society, which religion undergirded. The court decisively rejected what has come to be known as the absolutist or the secularist position that religion either in its institutional form or as a system of beliefs has nothing to do with the state and the state is neutral to all religious beliefs. The main importance of the 1824 decision did not involve profane speech for there were no other blasphemy cases that reached the Pennsylvania supreme court. Rather, the court used the reasoning in Updegraph to settle a wide-ranging series of cases on economic activities on the Sabbath.

Virtually no one opposed some kind of Sunday legislation in either the colonial or early national period, and every state had some restrictions.[45] For centuries theologians and political theorists had justified laws to enforce Sabbath rest as required by both revealed law and natural law. The need to keep one day holy was even a part of the creation story. Exodus 20:8 "Remember the sabbath day to keep it holy. Six days you shall labor, and do all your work; but the seventh day is a sabbath to the Lord your God; in it you shall not do any work." All Christendom believed in special legislation for Sunday, and the so-called Continental Sabbath appears relaxed only in comparison with the restrictions of Calvinist Geneva, Scotland, and New England. The Reformed clergy insisted that all the Ten Commandments were part of the eternal moral law, and Sabbath restrictions were as binding as the prohibitions against stealing, murder, adultery, and blasphemy.[46]

The church people who wished that America was a country in which Christianity was officially recognized used the Sabbath as their litmus test.[47] In insisting that Sunday was the day to make normal activities like work taboo, the clergy did not insist that there were intrinsic qualities to the day that made it different from others. After all, the Jews had kept the seventh day as the Sabbath; the early church had initially kept the same day and had only gradually changed the celebration to the first day to commemorate the Resurrection of Jesus. Although the Seventh-Day Baptists disapproved of the substitution of the first day, revolutionary lawmakers gave their protests short shrift. In this they followed colonial precedent, for both Johann Beissel at Ephrata and the Moravians had been criticized by their neighbors for keeping Saturday holy and profaning Sunday, and they had eventually conformed.[48] In 1850, when the Pennsylvania Senate passed a bill granting the Seventh-Day Baptists relief, the House refused to concur, saying in essence that the general perception and customs of the majority took precedence over a minority's dissent in moral questions.[49] The official rationale for Sabbath legislation – when the state finally provided one – had to do with the necessity of a day of rest. That the day of rest coincided with divine commandment made the restrictions even more important.

The main controversy over Sabbath legislation did not occur in Pennsylvania, where legislation was on the books and remained so throughout the nineteenth century; the dismantling of many restrictive Sunday practices has taken place only within our lifetimes. The serious debate over whether Sabbath laws infringed the relations between church and state took place at the Federal level. A general post-office law of 1810 had provided for the transportation of mail on Sunday and also for local post offices to be open. Attempting to ease potential conflicts with religious groups, the postmaster general allowed offices to remain open only one hour on Sunday and that not at a time of church services.[50]

Led by the Presbyterian and Congregational clergy, church people attempted to bring pressure on Congress to repeal the law. The Presbyterian General Assembly suggested that petitions be sent to Congress and insisted that the 1810 law was an attempt to enact irreligious legislation and, thereby, to destroy the separation between church and state.[51] Federal statutes undermined the state laws protecting the Sabbath, and the clergy advocated allowing the states to determine such matters as Sunday mail transportation. The clergy's jeremiads against Sunday mails warned that the Lord should not be mocked. Protestantism created a free and prosperous land, but the official profanation of the Lord's Day would bring his wrath – a judgment the events of the War of 1812 seemed to vindicate. The literature of Sabbath observance furnished graphic illustrations of God's punishment of Sunday violators.

The anti-post-office law crusade flourished and waned over a thirty-year period, with the petition campaign being very strong between 1828 and 1831 and again in the 1840s. The tactics used in the Sabbath campaign, similar to those employed by evangelicals for other moral causes like temperance, included sermons by clergy, small tracts, weighty tomes, national, state, and local voluntary societies, conventions to generate mass support, and petitions from state legislatures to Congress. The evangelical movement experienced total defeat in its campaign to change the post-office law and even generated a backlash from those who feared the powers of the various moral crusades of the 1820s and 1830s. Colonel Richard Johnson, senator from Kentucky and a strong Jacksonian supporter, as a member of the U.S. Senate in 1830 composed a classic defense of the separation of church and state at the Federal level. His strong stance did not hurt him politically, because, at Jackson's behest, he became Van Buren's running mate in 1836.[52] Ironically, the present-day practice by which mail can be picked up and transported but not delivered on Sunday was proposed as a compromise measure by a House committee in 1830. That position is exactly halfway between the two camps. It does not stop some Federal workers from labor on Sunday, but it does protect the general public from the temptation of going to the post office on the Lord's Day.

In Pennsylvania the antivice law of 1794 outlawed all ordinary labor on Sunday except for works of charity and necessity, and the statute specified as works of necessity taverns serving travelers, the delivery of milk before 9:00 a.m. or after 5:00 p.m., etc. The state courts did not question the constitutionality of Sunday laws. They insisted that the law required that no legal business be transacted on Sunday. A wager on the strength of a horse on Sunday was invalid. If a man rented a horse on Sunday and damaged the horse, the man was not responsible because the original transaction was illegal.[53] But if a man rented a horse and went to visit his father on Sunday and damaged the horse, the man was liable because the visiting of a parent was a work of either charity or necessity, but not of business.[54] The courts held that a jury could deliberate on Sunday, but that on the first day a traveler could not be sold a glass of beer. The tavernkeeper could rightly plea that fixing a meal was a necessity, but not selling of alcohol.[55] Labor done within the house escaped the wrath of enforcers. Although justices of the peace had summary jurisdiction and viewing of a forbidden activity was sufficient grounds for judgment, an official could not forcibly enter a home in order to see what was going on.[56]

The increasing complexity of economic activities caused difficulty for the courts as well as those who believed in a strict interpretation of the law. At a Sabbath convention one ironmonger confessed that he had no difficulty in closing his forge but that letting the fires in the furnace go out occasioned great inconvenience.[57] Moralists denounced Sunday newspapers and before the Civil War the few attempts to create one for Philadelphians failed, but the government did not prosecute those who prepared the Monday morning newspaper.

The 1794 statute exempted as works of necessity the operation of ferryboats and the docking of ships. Individual land travel was not outlawed, unless it was done as a normal business activity. After the 1830s the state had to decide whether the men who worked on turnpikes, canals, and railroads should be exempt as performing a necessary service or prosecuted for carrying on their regular labor. The legislature passed in 1845 a law protecting from liability suits those canal workers (and railroads) who chose to close on Sunday, and there was no effort to penalize those who worked the locks.[58] A lockmaster remained exempt because his work was considered necessary. It was not his task but that of the civil authorities to determine whether those traveling on the canal on the Sabbath were guilty of ordinary labor. Canal pilots, however, whose normal occupation was the guiding of boats through locks and dangerous passages had to cease from this labor on Sunday.[59] A significant number of canal locks did close on Sunday, but one report indicated that often the boatsmen operated locks anyway. There were complaints from canal-boat operators that if they halted on the Sabbath, other boats went around them and were first in line on Monday, when the locks reopened.[60]

In 1849 stockholders of the Pennsylvania Railroad voted that there would be no Sunday trains; they reversed that position a year later. By the 1850s railroads scheduled Sunday trains into and from Philadelphia and Pittsburgh and horse-drawn omnibuses appeared in these cities. Some of the vehicles transported people to church; others allowed city dwellers to reach the countryside. Three major cases in 1853, 1859, and 1867 on Sunday travel reached the state supreme court. These cases show the court struggling with and disagreeing over the purpose and extent of Sabbath regulation.

In all these cases the court agreed that Christianity had been part of the common law of England and, thereby, became part of the common law of colonial Pennsylvania.[61] English religious law was altered, however, by Penn's declaration of liberty of conscience, colonial laws, the state's constitutions, and later acts of the legislature. The court cited both the practices and statutes of colonial Pennsylvania in attempting to understand the reasons for the 1794 prohibition. That law had provided no rationale for its provision that no person "shall do or perform any worldly employment or business whatsoever, on the Lord's Day, commonly called

Sunday." That stipulation was more stringent than English tradition and colonial legislation in Pennsylvania. In the nineteenth and early twentieth centuries Pennsylvania gained a reputation for blue laws because the 1794 statute remained on the books and enforced.

By calling Sunday "the Lord's Day" the 1794 law could have been endorsing a view associated with the Presbyterians, who saw the government's role as designed to prevent worldly employment in order to foster religious worship. Alternatively, a rationalist or secularist saw the prohibitions as fostering a day of rest as a necessary element of civilized life. Here the government adopted a policy of strict neutrality toward worship and the religious aspects of the first day. If the court could determine the justifications for the colonial and 1794 Sunday statutes, it would also gain insight into the meaning of William Penn's and the Pennsylvania constitution's declarations on religious freedom.

Until the 1850s the court used language that could be interpreted as religious or secular, sometimes in the same decision. In 1815 Sabbath-breaking was "a violation of a divine as well as a human law."[62] In 1834 actions were referred to as being "sinful" and illegal.[63] Yet, the state extended recognition to no religious dogma and in 1848 declared that the true basis for the Sunday law was "a temporary cessation of labor" without any "religious obligation."[64] In 1853 the court merged secular and religious language: "Rest one day in seven was enjoined by the precept and example of the Author of our existence, and government, founding itself on Divine appointment, has made it a civil institution."[65] Here "rest" as well as worship originates in religion and the government makes the obligation civil.

The implications of the court's decision were spelled out in 1853 in Johnston versus Commonwealth. The court declared that a man who drove an omnibus, that is, a public vehicle, in Pittsburgh on Sunday as part of his normal work committed an illegal act, even though part of the public that rode the omnibus was on the way to church. The driver's employment on Sunday was wrong and he neither did nor could be expected to determine whether the use of his vehicle was for works of charity or necessity.[66] The court did not address other issues of Sunday employment, but did expand the definition of Sabbath laws.

Sunday legislation drew upon "Divine command and Human legislation" in order to "enforce an observance of the Sabbath" as a day of "*rest* and *public worship.*"[67] Such laws did not infringe upon religious liberty; rather, they secured religious freedom by allowing no interference with those who wished to worship. The law was auxiliary to religion, not neutral, not unconcerned. It neither penalized nor compelled irreligious people to agree to the Sabbath's divine origins, but opponents of the law had no right to interfere with the liberty of conscience of Christians, even if they thought the whole Sunday observance was a superstition. The court would not enforce Christian observance of the Sabbath, but it would oppose violations of the peace.[68]

In Nesbit versus Commonwealth (1859) the court allowed a servant who was a coachman to take his master's family (and himself) in a private vehicle to church on Sunday, even though it was his normal employ. Building upon the Johnston case, the court again declared that the purpose of the 1794 law was to foster "rest" and "worship of God" and all means necessary for this were allowable by the civil law.[69] The labor of clergymen and sextons on Sunday had never been penalized; no legal business took place on Sunday but marriages performed that day were valid. Using the coachman for a drive to church might be against divine law, but it was not against Pennsylvania's law, and the court was responsible only for the latter.[70]

Again, the justices expounded a theory for Sunday laws. Neither in the colonial past nor the present did the people distinguish "clearly between religion, morality, and the law." So their rationale for their "moral" wants was also an amalgam with the predictable result that "their political institutions must be more or less theocratical or religious. No amount of rational principles, set in array in bills of rights, can prevent them."[71] Of what significance then were Pennsylvania's declarations of liberty of conscience? They were "a moral ideal to which all government ought to approach as nearly as possible, rather than a positive principle of legislation." The colonists claimed freedom of religion because they assumed the existence of Christian values and they never thought of "tolerating Paganism" with its human sacrifices, infanticide, and orgies. They sought to protect the "pure, moral customs" originating in Christianity and would have been appalled to see liberty of conscience misapplied to permit "concubinage, polygamy, incest, free love, and free divorce." They did not wish "phallic processions . . . obscene songs, and indecent statues, and paintings of ancient or modern paganism" to be introduced under the pretense of religion to offend "moral modesty" and to corrupt youth.[72] Freedom of religion in Pennsylvania was possible because Christianity undergirded the society's norms.

Sunday laws and other laws against vice and immorality were not to enforce religion. They were to protect "our customs," even if such originated from religion, "for they are essential parts of our social life." The courts did not enforce divine law; their province was the civil law, which expressed "the common sense and common morality of the country." Civil and divine law were distinct in origin and enforcement but "it is impossible to make a complete separation." Law "is essentially founded on the moral customs of men, and the very generating principle of these is most frequently religion."[73]

The Johnston and Nesbit cases clearly assumed an accommodationist view of the relation between church and state. Because both cases dealt with specific subjects, the justices had not addressed the issue as to whether operating railroads on Sunday was a work of necessity. Under the 1794 law the penalty for Sabbath violation was $4, an amount trivial to a major corporation. In an effort to stop repeated offenses, residents along the lines sought to obtain injunctions.[74] A court-ordered injunction could presumably restrain a railroad before an illegal act was committed. In 1867 the legality of a court-ordered injunction, obtained without a jury trial, was tested in Sparhawk versus Union Passenger Railway Company.

Church members and residents living along the route of the Union Passenger Railway Company in Philadelphia claimed that the noise from the Union Company's Sunday omnibus trains (horse cars drawn along tracks) jeopardized their property rights as homeowners and pew holders. The bells, shouts, and general commotion supposedly made it difficult to hear a minister or to conduct Sunday devotions in peace. The suit was an equity case and the lower court ruled for the plaintiffs and granted an injunction. In 1867 the Pennsylvania supreme court reversed in a three to two decision. Running passenger cars on Sunday was a clear violation of the 1794 law and should be punished by the state's penal code.[75] But there was no equity case. In order to be sustained the property owners needed to demonstrate that Sunday trains affected their property's "capacity for *ordinary use and enjoyment.*" Courts could not assign a monetary value to a diminished ability to worship because of noise. The court agreed that the purpose of the Sunday law was to allow peace and quiet, but disruption and noise were not crimes. Normal labor constituted the only part of the law enforceable by the courts.[76]

In the concurrent opinion Justice John Meredith Read agreed with Chief Justice Duncan that there was no equity case, but disagreed that running Sunday trains violated the law. Instead, he argued that having trains on Sunday was a work of necessity. He based his conclusion on an alternative view of the purpose of liberty of conscience, colonial laws, and the 1794 statute. Read asserted in an erudite commentary that the Pennsylvania court in the 1850s had erred in accepting a Jewish interpretation of the meaning of the Sabbath. The Christian Sunday marked a decisive break with the Jewish customs. Paul, early Christians, Martin Luther, John Calvin, Robert Barclay, William Penn, and the early law codes of Pennsylvania opposed declaring any day holy or the exclusive time to worship and prescribed rest from ordinary labor on Sunday as a custom or convenience.[77] The law of Pennsylvania had always been designed to provide a break from labor, not to foster worship. Sunday was a civil, not a religious, holiday. The Pennsylvania supreme court was wrong, therefore, in the Johnston and Nesbit cases in treating Sunday as a day "set apart by divine commandment." The courts had no right to enforce any religious obligation; the Commonwealth required only a "temporary weekly cessation from labor."[78]

Running railroads on Sunday was a work of necessity. In England and other states of America trains ran on Sunday, and it had been the practice in Pennsylvania for seventeen years. In carrying people to church an omnibus was no noisier than carriages on cobblestone. The plaintiffs asked to enjoin all trains from running for twenty-four hours so that they could worship for four hours. And even they did not maintain that omnibus noise prevented worship in churches or in their homes on weekdays. The rich had carriages; the poor had omnibuses.[79] Allowing Sunday trains permitted the poor in the cities to go to the country for rest and relaxation and fulfilled the purpose of the law. The Presbyterian version of Sunday was not, declared Read, the law of Pennsylvania.

No other justice agreed with him. Two of the justices favored the injunction; two more declared Sunday trains a violation of the law. Still, in essence the sabbatarians lost the battle and won the war. Trains and omnibuses continued to run on Sunday. Even in the Nesbit case the court had declared parts of the manufacture of iron and glass as works of necessity and declared that there could be no hard and fast line between convenience and necessity, because conditions changed. Still, throughout the rest of the nineteenth century the court would not allow milk, meat, soda water, or newspapers to be sold on Sunday (though they could be delivered before nine or after five) or even permit a professional baseball game.[80]

The sabbatarian cases in Pennsylvania showed the closest relation between the government and religion. Such a relationship was made possible because the law and courts were not dealing with the institutional church. Rather, the court was upholding a law based upon moral judgment. And the courts found two utilitarian reasons for the Sunday laws, custom and the universal need for rest from labor. Even so, particularly in the 1850s, certain language of the supreme court went beyond the relaxation theory and implied that the Commonwealth accepted the Christian affirmation that Sunday was a holy sanctified day. Even when the courts were most Christian, they were never evangelical. That is, they never agreed that the law could require people to spend Sunday in Bible study, prayer and meditation, and going to services. Even the evangelical clergy acknowledged that their vision of a religious Sabbath could be obtained only by voluntary compliance. Every citizen was free to relax on Sunday within the privacy of his own home and outside as well so long as his fun did not involve commercial activity.

Opponents of Sunday legislation began with an obvious liability. They opposed the blue laws for contradictory reasons and did not wish to end a day of rest. (In our day, when Sunday laws are ineffectual, the number of legal holidays is increasing. We are returning to the medieval customs when Sunday was downplayed because of the importance of holy days. And the holidays now occur on Monday so they do not disrupt the workweek.) The pre-Civil War dissenters were not enamored of American commerce. Yet, they had to argue that utility was as strong a sanction against exploitation of labor on a rest day as religion.[81] The antisabbatarians insisted that they were neither antireligion nor antimorality, just anticlerical and opposed to state-enforced religion. They also attacked the theological and natural law arguments for the Sunday Sabbath.

Who in Pennsylvania opposed Sabbath laws? The Democratic party (however factionalized), which dominated Pennsylvania politics from 1800 until the Civil War, had a tradition of anticlericalism and distrust of the institutionalized church inherited from Jefferson and Madison.[82] The vocal opponents of Sabbath laws in Pennsylvania included Unitarians, Universalists, and Hicksite Quakers, groups that opposed the evangelicals for theological reasons.[83] In addition, there were freethinkers and followers of Robert Owen and Fanny Wright, who included some workingmen and radical mechanics.[84] Neither Jews nor Seventh-Day Baptists played a significant role in the 1830s. The role of Roman Catholics in the antisabbatarian movement in Pennsylvania is uncertain, but the bishops clearly supported a restrictive Sunday. The Protestant clergy did not attack the Catholic church on this issue; perhaps its minority status made them a negligible factor. John Bodo is very perceptive in characterizing the primary opponents of Sabbath legislation as extreme religious individualists. Lucretia Mott and the Working Men's party typified the antisabbatarians' commitment to freedom for individuals to develop their fullest potentialities.[85]

The Pennsylvania courts in the pre-Civil War period managed to accommodate religion and to separate absolutely church from state. They could do both because the colonial, revolutionary, and constitutional heritage of freedom of religion allowed for inconsistency in the practices of the Commonwealth. No one could be guilty of the crime of heresy, because the state recognized no orthodoxy. The courts judged cases involving church property, the duties of vestries, elections to church boards, ministering disputes, and the rights of laity on the basis of the intention of the founders of an individual congregation, a charter, prior agreements by the group with a denominational authority, or majority rule. Theology was irrelevant, unless specified in the charter, and the courts' test was not truthfulness but adherence.

All religious bodies had equal standing before the law. The legal rights of a Presbyterian church, a synagogue, and a Roman Catholic cathedral were the same. The courts remained neutral toward any specific church, but favorably disposed toward all religions. This benevolence did not violate the separation of church and state, because the courts extracted from all religions a set of core values undergirding civic religion. This civic religion originated in a nondenominational Christianity reinforced by reason and natural law. This reductionist essence of religion incorporated Protestantism, Catholicism, and Judaism in so far as these faiths supported a common morality and republican institutions, while making no claim that others' differing dogmas reduced their civil rights. All true religions affirmed the existence of God. God as the source of Christianity, reason, and natural law unified the civic religion, unified the various churches, unified the citizenry, and unified the state. The civic religion of the Founding Fathers, drawn from William Penn or James Wilson, underlay all order and law. The court and the legislature utilized the common civic religion to write and enforce laws penalizing vices, proscribe blasphemy, enforce the Sabbath, support the family, and allow tax exemptions for schools, charities, and churches. These three institutions created the moral citizenry necessary to insure the survival of republican government. At first the government's indirect support of these institutions occasioned little controversy, because all were private. The legal equivalence ended when Pennsylvanians decided that the state should create and finance a governmental system of common schools.

CHAPTER IX

Religious Liberty and the Catholic and Jewish Minorities

In one sense all denominations and all ethnic groups in Pennsylvania were minorities. No nationality or church had numerical dominance, and during the history of the colony and the state virtually every group complained at some time that it was mistreated. Still, after 1783 the mainline Protestant churches – Presbyterian, Lutheran, Reformed, Episcopalian, Baptist, and Methodist – established the tone of society, and their members occupied prominent positions in government, commerce, and education. Grumblings from these denominations meant that they perceived some threat to their hegemony. The sectarian churches – Friends, Moravians, Amish, and Mennonites – enjoyed prosperity and the prestige of priority of settlement in Chester and Bucks, Lehigh, and Lancaster counties. Because of their small numbers the sects' distinctive beliefs and practices did not threaten the major evangelical denominations' political or cultural dominance, and they enjoyed a quiet existence among the world's peoples.

Jews, the only organized non-Christian population in the state, wished to be free to practice their distinctive rituals and not feel treated as aliens or second-class citizens. Roman Catholics sought during the Revolution to remove the British imposed barriers to becoming citizens and full political participants. In the early Republic Jews and Catholics enjoyed good relations with their Protestant neighbors, who attended their services on special occasions, donated to building funds, and granted them legal equality. By the 1830s the religious leaders of the Jews and Catholics viewed with alarm the increasing power of evangelical Protestants reflected in demands for Sunday observances and religious exercises in public schools. The salient difference determining the reaction of the Protestant majority to the two groups was that the Jews remained a miniscule portion of the population with less than 5,000 adherents in the state, but the number of Catholics increased rapidly after 1820. Anti-

Catholicism focused on Irish immigrants and the alleged intolerance and temporal power by priests and papacy.

Before the Revolution, the oaths or affirmations required of officeholders meant that Jews could not hold political office. After 1740 the British government allowed Jews to obtain citizenship by taking an oath on the Pentateuch.[1] The test oath in the 1776 constitution, inserted at the request of the Protestant clergy, required belief in the divine origin of the Old and New Testaments. The clergy wanted to eliminate the possibility of free-thinkers, Muslims, heathens, and Jews from becoming officeholders.

In 1782 Rabbi Gervase Seixas and several members of Mikveh Israel, the synagogue in Philadelphia, petitioned the council of censors, the body responsible for recommending amendments to the 1776 constitution, to revise the test. Seixas argued that Jews did not wish to hold political office, but regarded the oath as a "stigma upon them and their nation and their religion" and as inconsistent with the declaration on the right of conscience elsewhere in the constitution. The petition enumerated the contributions that Jews had made during the Revolution, announced that "Jews are as fond of liberty as other religious societies," and insisted upon their "right" to legal equality.[2] In 1782 the council of censors did nothing, probably because allowing Jews full equality would raise the issue of other amendments to the constitution. During the Federal Constitutional Convention in Philadelphia, the delegates received a petition from Jonas Phillips asking that there be no religious tests against Jews. Two weeks earlier in secret session the Convention had agreed to have no religious qualification for officeholding.[3] The Pennsylvania constitution of 1790 revised the religious tests of the 1776 document to allow a deist, Muslim, or Jew to hold office if he believed in divine providence, but still precluded atheists from service.

Jewish religious organizations enjoyed legal equality. The assembly granted charters of incorporation to synagogues and passed a lottery for fund-raising. In 1825, when a synagogue was consecrated in Philadelphia, Bishop William White of the Protestant Episcopal Church and other Philadelphia clergy, as well as the chief justice and the associate justices of the Pennsylvania supreme court attended, "all manifesting by their presence and demeanor, that, however we may differ upon certain points, that great truth is recognized and acted upon, that we are all children of a common and eternal FATHER."[4] The description of the service in Poulson's *American Daily Advertiser* boasted about the full political equality of Jews in Pennsylvania. Six years earlier Poulson had reprinted from the *Baltimore Chronicle* an attack upon Maryland's refusal to allow Jews to hold political office.[5] In their discussion of the involvement of Jews in the social and intellectual life of pre-Civil War Philadelphia, Edwin Wolf 2nd and Maxwell Whiteman label as "atypical" an incident of anti-Semitism.[6]

Philadelphia Jews supported the creation of a public-school system, seeing in it an alternative to the religious instruction offered in private institutions. They opposed requiring the reading of Christian Scriptures in the public schools, but were willing to have written prayers "which might be termed universal and uniformly acceptable, embracing all the necessary ideas of divine moral government."[7] Rebecca Gratz helped create a Jewish Sunday School to offer religious training to Jewish children who either attended public school or worked during the week. In time the Jewish Sunday School proved inadequate to teach Hebrew, and the rabbis and congregations created separate Jewish academies.

When in 1848 the Pennsylvania supreme court upheld the validity of Sunday legislation with the judges claiming that Christianity underlay the laws of the state, Rabbi Isaac Lesser vigorously protested:

If the Constitution of Pennsylvania declares Sunday-keeping, trinitarian Christianity, to be the foundation of the social compact, then for one, we do not profess to know the meaning of words. . . . There are, in the words of the Declaration of Right, no earthly supports for the opinion that Christianity is the law of the land. Is it the only religion which believes in the existence of God and rewards and punishments.[8]

According to Lesser, the Pennsylvania constitution did not exclude Seventh-Day Adventists, Muslims, and Jews from equal rights. It did not bestow upon legislature or judges the ability to decide for a Jew what constituted the Sabbath. The 1790 Pennsylvania constitution and the federal Constitution put all "profession of religion" on a "perfect equal basis" and forbade any kind of favoritism. The 1794 statute was unconstitutional because it established a religion by outlawing profaning of the "Lord's Day." Unlike many other Jews, Lesser opposed allowing Seventh-Day Adventists and Jews to substitute Saturday as a day of rest. Any legislative enactment, he argued, would deny freedom of conscience to the person who desired to labor on all days.[9]

Philadelphia rabbis denounced the effort, led by the Presbyterians during and after the Civil War, to declare in the constitutions that Pennsylvania and the other states and the Federal government were Christian states. They complained when Pennsylvania's governor invoked Christianity in a Thanksgiving proclamation. The protest was not against the proclamation, but the exclusive nature of the language. (The governor apologized for the mistake.)[10] Often the rabbis' position was accommodationist, with equality for Jews in the public sphere. On occasion, however, the Jewish interpretation of church and state approached the Jeffersonian position of a wall between them at all levels of government. "Religion and Government, or to use the current term, Church and State, in order to remain pure and free, each in its own dominion, must be kept separate from one another, and naturally guard themselves against intrusion."[11]

The American traditions of religious liberty drew upon English precedents, and that legacy included anti-Catholicism. The 1689 Act of Toleration bestowed freedom of worship on orthodox Protestants and allowed no such latitude to Roman Catholics. Parliament passed the toleration law in the aftermath of the Glorious Revolution as a means of uniting all Protestants against an alleged Roman Catholic threat led by the deposed Stuart king in alliance with the French. The long series of wars between Great Britain and France reinforced English and colonial negative stereotypes of Rome. Throughout the eighteenth century Americans juxtaposed Protestant against Catholic as exemplifying contrary ways of life. Protestantism supposedly fostered liberty, education, and prosperity while Catholicism led to tyranny, ignorance, and poverty. The Church of Rome supported absolutism and intolerance by opposing freedom of thought, keeping the population poorly schooled, and fostering blind obedience in church and state. Catholic worship with its images of saints, crucifix, candles, stained glass, incense, prayer beads, veneration of the Virgin Mary, and Latin liturgy seemed little better than idol worship. As the American Revolution approached, the Quebec Act revived colonial fear of subordination of liberty to Catholic power. Anti-Catholic stereotypes survived the Revolution, though played down after 1777 in deference to the French alliance.[12]

Pennsylvania's definition of republican religious liberty built upon an intellectual foundation common to Protestants and Catholics. For centuries Christian thinkers had described the Ten Commandments as a summary of the moral law, which could be derived from nature and/or revelation. They also had insisted that the will of God legitimized statute law and government. One role of religious institutions was to inculcate the moral law and thereby undergird the social fabric.

In Pennsylvania Catholics and Protestants differed over the source of authority for discovering truth. Both orthodox Protestant leaders and freethinkers in the state separated the institutional church from religious beliefs. James Wilson, Benjamin Rush, Samuel Stanhope Smith, and William White found the source of truth in the Bible as interpreted by individual conscience. Coercion of that conscience led to hypocrisy in the church and persecution by the state. Whether the person arrived at truth through reason, a moral sense, or the Bible did not matter, for each method ended with a common conclusion composed of republican ideals and a generalized Christianity. Each church was free to hold its peculiar theological tenets and the state (and often the churches as well) could treat these differences as unessential.

The subjectivism and individualism in the republican definition of religious liberty went against the Catholic emphasis upon the Church as the source of revealed truth. The apostolic succession from Peter to Pope guaranteed the preservation of Christianity, and true liberty came in submission or obedience to unbroken tradition. Roman Catholicism could not be defined as one religion among many, all of which had equal claims to legitimacy. Catholic truth and Protestant error did not have the same status.

In America during and after the Revolution, Catholic leaders proclaimed their support for republican liberty, separation of church and state, and freedom of religion. They argued that the Catholic church's position on revealed truth did not lead to unique privileges in the political realm. The Church adapted to diverse societies and in America the best situation was separation of church and state as well as legal equality of all denominations. Free competition would allow the truth to prevail. Pennsylvania Catholics identified their Church's traditions with civil liberties, autonomy for the Church, and support for legitimate authority.[13]

Such assurances carried weight in republican Pennsylvania, where Protestants and Catholics had traditionally enjoyed good relations. Ferdinand Farmer, Jesuit priest at St. Mary's in Philadelphia, was an intellectual who became a member of the American Philosophical Society and a trustee of the College of Philadelphia.[14] Thomas Fitzsimmons became Philadelphia's first Federalist Congressman, and Mathew Carey was a prominent printer and author. Protestants often contributed to building funds for churches they were not members of; they did the same for Roman Catholic churches. George Washington headed a list of subscribers to St. Augustine's church. Protestants and Catholics attended each other's private schools. Catholics mingled with their Protestant neighbors in a wide variety of situations and organizations.[15] A ceremonial procession was likely to include clergymen from Baptist, Lutheran, Roman Catholic, Presbyterian, and Episcopalian churches (all of whom had specially ordained ministers) but not representatives from the Moravians, Quakers, and Mennonites. In republican Pennsylvania nativism remained a muted strain and Protestants accepted Catholics as neighbors because of their minority status and endorsement of American values.

In the early nineteenth century the bishops, priests, and laity of the American Catholic church supported the nation's republican system of government and endorsed the separation of the institutional church from the state.[16] The Vatican, operating within a European context, did not make similar declarations and, on occasion, repudiated both democracy and liberty of conscience. The Vatican was still reliving the French Revolution, during which the republicans used concepts like freedom, equality, rights of man, and separation of state from church in a spirit of anticlericalism and anti-Catholicism. Before and after the Revolutions of 1848, the Catholic church in Austria, France, and Spain supported monarchy.[17] Therefore, American bishops often saw the need to remind the curia that republicanism, democracy, and religious liberty in America had no anti-Christian context.[18] The priests and bishops in Pennsylvania, virtually all of whom were immigrants, had to learn here to forget the European scene.

The American bishops remained committed to political democracy, but they opposed republican ideas in the Catholic church. Because there was no bishop in America until after the Revolution, there had been little episcopal supervision in colonial Pennsylvania. Laymen originated, built, and paid for Philadelphia's Catholic churches, St. Joseph's and St. Mary's, and in most places trustees controlled deeds to the property. Colonial Catholic churches, like Protestant ones, experienced a substantial growth in the power of the laity and a democratic flavor insofar as the pewholders elected trustees to care for church temporalities. Trustees, who often included the priest (ex officio), set salaries and exercised a de facto if not de jure role in the selecting and dismissing of priests.[19] When after 1790 Roman episcopal authority was established in America, the bishops confronted a laity accustomed to exercising power.

The conflict between bishops and laity over control of the temporalities of the church is known as the Trustee Controversy. Disputes occurred in most major centers of Catholicism in the United States: New Orleans, Charlestown, St. Louis, Buffalo, and most especially in Philadelphia.[20] They began in 1787 over the selection of the pastor in the German Catholic parish of Holy Trinity. John Carroll of Baltimore, prefect apostolic at the time but to become bishop in 1790, and the congregation disagreed over who was to be priest. The laity asserted the canonical *jus patronatus*, a right of patronage, in which the person who paid for and supported the church (generally on the basis of a fixed endowment) nominated the priest.[21] In 1787 the matter was compromised, but, after the creation of the diocese of Philadelphia in 1808, disputes between the bishops and the trustees continued sporadically until Holy Trinity received an amended charter in 1859 giving the bishop the right to appoint trustees and priests. A similar dispute occurred in St. Mary's parish between 1820 and 1832.[22] These disputes occurred because the laity could find priests and on one occasion a bishop who sympathized with them.[23] The bishops' disciplining of the congregations and of the priests occurred at the same time.

The acrimony between bishops and trustees occurred in full view of their Protestant neighbors and on several occasions spilled over into the courts. The trustees appealed to Rome citing canon-law precedents, but they were always overruled. They wrote pamphlets and newspaper articles seeking public support and arguing that all they wanted was religious liberty in the church. Giving full power to one man was against America's republican tradition. They cited the Episcopal church as an example of combining the bishops' spiritual prerogatives with lay responsibility.[24] The trustees claimed that they were good Catholics and that their demands in no way diminished the spiritual authority of the bishops.

In Francis Patrick Kenrick, third bishop of Philadelphia 1830–51, the trustees encountered an able opponent who vanquished them. Kenrick, Irish born and educated in Rome after the French Revolution, viewed the trustees and their supporters as not really Catholics. They were instead, he argued, covert Protestants trying to undermine Catholic tradition. Kenrick's style was confrontation. He announced to the people at St. Mary's that he had designated that church as his cathedral church, and told the vestry what support he expected. When the trustees demurred, he placed an interdict that banned all services there.[25] On his visitations throughout the diocese of Pennsylvania, he would refuse to bless the church if the deeds were not to his liking. Kenrick sought to have congregations name him as sole trustee of the property, and gained a law in 1844 allowing the bishop to be a corporation sole. He also attempted to persuade churches to permit him to name trustees.[26] When churches proved recalcitrant, he relied upon court decisions or allowed a religious order, such as the Jesuits, to staff the church or built competing churches. More importantly, the rapidly growing Catholic population due to Irish immigration helped the bishop. Kenrick instituted a vigorous building program that saw the number of Catholic churches in his diocese increase from twenty-two to ninety-two (erecting nineteen buildings in Philadelphia alone) in his thirty-year rule, and in all the new parishes the episcopacy was supreme. The congregations with independent trustees became a much smaller percentage. The bishop would not allow peace to be restored except on his terms, and in time Kenrick and his successors such as Bishop John Neumann gained total control over priest and parish.

Republican ideology originally seeped into the Church, so Kenrick believed, because of the influence of Protestants. So the bishop attempted to reduce the interaction between Catholics and Protestants. The new tone of Catholicism can be shown by an incident that occurred in Holy Trinity Church in 1834. The German priest, Father Lemke, was a former Lutheran minister. On the Sunday following a Lutheran commemoration of the Reformation, Lemke preached an anti-Luther sermon. After mass, Lemke was visited by the trustees: "Your Reverence, that was a very fine sermon you delivered to-day, but as we wish to live in peace with our Protestant neighbors, we have come to tell you that you must not preach any more sermons like that in this church." Lemke, jumping to his feet, grabbed a poker from the coal shuttle and shouted "You tailors, you blacksmiths, you carpenters! How dare you come here to tell me what to preach. Get out of here." Father Lemke asked for a transfer from Holy Trinity because he disliked the trustee system.[27]

In the early nineteenth century Philadelphia Catholics joined other Americans in voluntary organizations, some of which were secret societies. The Masons, the most prominent of such organizations, had long been condemned by the Catholic church. Bishop Kenrick refused to allow a funeral service for Stephen Girard in St. Mary's when the Philadelphia Masons appeared in ceremonial dress to honor their deceased member. He did allow burial in consecrated ground because Girard had been a baptized Catholic.[28] In a letter to the Vatican Kenrick argued that unlike European secret societies such organizations in Pennsylvania were rarely anticlerical or engaged in subversive political activities. Instead, they often did good works and the only secrecy might be a handshake or slogan. Still, Kenrick worried about Catholic participation in such organizations, which often had religious ceremonies. Promiscuous mixing with Protestants in religious exercises would erode the distinction between truth and error and leave the impression that morals based on "natural reason" and virtues obtained outside the true church were efficacious.[29] The Vatican responded to Kenrick's letter by forbidding Catholics to belong to secret societies.

Even when Catholic and Protestant worked for the same ends, Catholics should remain separate. Bishop Kenrick despised drunkenness and was a strong advocate of temperance, even endorsing total abstinence.[30] Yet he had reservations about welcoming the Irish temperance reformer Father Mathew to Philadelphia.[31] In England and Ireland Mathew's crusade had joined Protestants and Catholics and some interpreted the pledge as a work of man unaided by supernatural grace. On his arrival in Philadelphia, Mathew provided the assurances that Kenrick sought about directing his movement to Catholics.

Bishop Kenrick approved of the organization of Catholic voluntary societies to support orphanages, hospitals, and charities. He commended the priests and sisters who administered to Catholics and Protestants during the cholera epidemic.[32] But the interaction had to take place in a context expressive of Catholic hegemony. There was no such phenomenon as a neutral religious setting that was neither Catholic nor Protestant.

Kenrick used theological debates as a means of gaining converts and of solidifying the Catholic community. He had been a vigorous and successful controversialist in Kentucky before becoming bishop of Philadelphia. Because Catholics and Protestants perennially baited each other, there was no shortage of clergy in both camps willing to enter the fray. Each side worried its opponent with boasts about the number of converts. Bishop Kenrick followed the events in the Tractarian, or Oxford, movement in

England and rejoiced in the conversion of John Henry Newman to Catholicism. Seeing a similar debate between evangelicals and High Churchmen in the American Episcopal church, Kenrick and the Episcopal bishop of Vermont, John H. Hopkins, debated in 1837 which tradition exemplified true Christianity.[33] An equally acerbic debate occurred between a young parish priest, John Hughes, later bishop of New York, and the Presbyterian minister, John Breckinridge, in 1833. The debate, printed in religious periodicals of both denominations over many months, soon descended to a level of obscurity over the interpretation of patristic texts that would bore anyone except a connoisseur of nineteenth-century theological polemics. Hughes and Breckinridge agreed in advance that the central focus would be on the source of authority. Hughes claimed that the Catholic church guaranteed truth and order and that Protestantism led to subjectivity in religion and moral chaos. Breckinridge countered that the Bible gave truth and that the Catholic reliance upon the papacy inevitably led to tyranny over conscience and persecution.[34]

Catholic-Protestant debates in early nineteenth-century Pennsylvania, which began on theology, often ended discussing religious liberty. The Catholic image of Protestants took the basic American value system of freedom of religion and separation of church and state and showed how these flourished better under Catholicism. Protestantism inevitably led to Erastianism, which was what the Protestants were trying to create in America. Luther, Calvin, Cromwell, the Puritans – all these Protestant reformers persecuted the true faith. Catholics pointed to Germany and England as proof of the inevitable loss of freedom of the church in Protestant countries. Ireland showed the intolerance of Protestant England.[35]

The Protestant clergy – all the major evangelical denominations printed anti-Catholic material – insisted that freedom of religion and separation of church and state were antithetical to the Roman church. The American Protestant Association declared in 1843, "Popery in its political aspect, is essentially anti-republican, and totally at variance with the genius of our Institutions." The Inquisition, St. Bartholomew's Day massacre, bloody Mary Tudor, and the recent history of Spain, Italy, and Latin America showed the results of giving the papacy power. America was a Christian Protestant country in which Catholics were free to worship. American Protestants had sufficient power to keep the country free, but they should be aware of the machinations of the papacy and the subtle measures Catholics used to gain political power.[36]

Catholics and Protestants had mirror images of each other. Each group claimed to have no political ambitions. Both insisted that the spiritual calling of the clergy precluded comment on purely political issues.[37] Both supported temperance and Sabbath restrictions. The Roman Catholic strength was increasing due to Irish migration; Protestant numbers were increasing due to the attractiveness of evangelical emphases and successful revivals. Both claimed that the basic values of the Republic – religious liberty, civil liberties, morality – were safe only in their hands. The rivalry could have stayed a slightly unfriendly competition; instead, it culminated in a series of riots, caused by differences over religion in the public schools.

Priscilla Ferguson Clement characterizes the treatment of the poor in nineteenth-century Philadelphia as a mixture of humanitarian uplift, social control, and economy.[38] Such motives dominated much social legislation of the early nineteenth century, and religious values helped shape both of the first two categories. The clergy and the legislators frequently praised religion as a guarantor and generator of morality and virtuous character. Those parts of the population the legislature saw as needing reforming or shaping – children, the poor, the insane, the criminal – would be helped by religious instruction. Religion brought honesty, hard work, reverence, self-discipline, and perhaps even salvation, though politicians rarely discussed salvation. The legislature created institutions in which a good environment would seclude problem people from evil influence and allow moral people (that is, religious people) to create good citizens. Most of these institutions still survive as state-funded agencies: special schools for the blind and deaf, asylums for the insane, penitentiaries, "homes" for juvenile delinquents, the common school.[39] The Pennsylvania experiments in criminal reform resulted in penitentiaries in which solitary confinement was combined with frequent visits by good men and women, who would help the prisoner to reflect on his or her errors and learn to be strengthened in virtue.[40] At first the clergy provided their services to the prison on a voluntary basis. The legislature, after a prolonged debate, eventually passed in 1829 and 1838 acts to employ moral teachers in the prisons. These were clergymen but the law termed them "moral instructors," thereby preserving the distinction between church and state.[41]

The survival of democracy in Pennsylvania depended upon the character of voters; all children – but particularly those whose parents were poor and immigrants – needed to be trained for the responsibilities of citizenship. If children grew up without the Christian virtues, if they were illiterate, immoral, and undisciplined, Pennsylvania could neither prosper nor remain free. The legislators wanted schools to teach reading and writing, but also to give good habits. Before the Revolution there had been no state-funded education in Pennsylvania. Even though the 1776 and 1790 constitutions gave the state responsibility for schools, no action was taken until after 1802.[42] Before this time, everyone who received any formal education attended a private school and virtually all of these were church-controlled. In fact, until the French Revolution, everywhere in Western society people assumed a religious content for education. In Pennsylvania the Bible was used as both a devotional tool and as a primer.[43] When the state began supplementing private funds to educate the very poor, it either had to create its own schools, provide subsidies for new Sunday School or Charity School societies, or pay for the education of a few of the poor in already existing religious schools. In terms of religious instruction, it did not make much difference, because the Lancastrian monitorial schools established for the poor in Philadelphia and Lancaster taught basic Christianity as well as steady habits.

The religious and moral emphasis continued after the creation of the common-school system. After a long debate, the legislature created a fund for common schools in 1824 and 1834, and gave localities virtual control of how it was spent.[44] After its first two years of operation, the school law had to be redrafted because less than half of the school districts had created common schools. The law was a success in the western and northern parts of the state, but not in the east, where religious schools predominated.[45] So the legislature stipulated that any religious school that wanted to become part of the common-school system could do so by educating at state expense a few of the poor. The state asked only to have visitors come to the private schools; the trustees of each school would continue to control the education.

Many schools founded by religious groups merged into the public system. Theoretically, Roman Catholic as well as Protestant schools could have been incorporated. In actuality, this did not happen, because the schools of St. Mary's and Holy Trinity catered to an upper-class population that did not patronize public schools.

In debates on the advisability of a common-school system, in the laws, and in the reports provided by the state superintendent to the legislature there is rarely a direct reference to religious instruction. The religious content was assumed but not prescribed by law. Local control protected Germans wanting to maintain the Old World language and Protestants desiring to preserve the existing pattern of education. So, after 1840, when Bishop Kenrick raised a challenge to the Protestant orientation of the schools, those Pennsylvanians who had merged their church schools with the common schools felt betrayed and reacted angrily.[46] For Kenrick challenged a basic assumption of most Pennsylvania Protestants: that there could be a nonsectarian, religious, and moral education that did not violate the separation of church and state.

The Catholic critique of the Philadelphia common schools drew upon the provisions in the Pennsylvania constitution guaranteeing religious liberty. Catholics, like Protestants, paid taxes for schools. But the schools fostered hostility to Catholicism and favored the Protestants. All people agreed that conscience should not be coerced, but the common schools coerced the consciences of Catholic children, a group unable to defend itself. They were forced to read from the King James Bible, not the Catholic Douai version. They participated in religious exercises using Protestant prayers and hymns and their textbooks contained anti-Catholic and pro-Protestant passages.[47]

When Bishop Kenrick raised the issue of the fairness of religion in public schools, he could have envisaged several outcomes. Perhaps the public schools could continue as before, but the state would furnish money for a separate system of Catholic parochial schools. In this way both Catholic and Protestant would achieve religious instruction and freedom of religion. In New York City in an earlier dispute over the Protestant orientation of the schools, Bishop John Hughes, a protégé and friend of Kenrick's, initiated the crisis with the School Aid Society because he wanted public funds for Catholic schools.[48] The American hierarchy, including Bishop Kenrick, had called for the creation of a Catholic school system.[49] And because Pennsylvania's common-school law guaranteed to the Germans, Quakers, and other denominations that local trustee boards could continue if their schools became part of the state system, Kenrick had legal precedents for his position. The main difference was that the private schools became the common schools, and there were not two different school systems envisaged.

A second alternative was that Kenrick would support common schools for all, but work to make them less Protestant. Given the financial difficulties of the diocese, in which most congregations were heavily in debt because of new church buildings, Kenrick could have wished to settle for a half measure.[50] However, his previous actions with regard to secret societies and the trustees show that compromise did not come easily to Kenrick. His proposal asking that Catholic children use the Douai Bible seems to envisage compromise. But his complaints about Protestant hymns and prayers were more far-reaching. There is nothing in Kenrick's writings to suggest that he favored a secular non-Christian education or wanted all Bible reading ended in school. But taken to an ultimate conclusion Kenrick's complaints struck many Protestants as requiring a secular or nonreligious form of education. And if there was no possibility of a common undergirding civic religion stressing Christianity, republicanism, and moral virtue, then a basic premise supporting democracy and freedom of religion was specious.

The Philadelphia common-school board did not give Kenrick the opportunity to compromise. It initially responded positively to the bishop by seeking to make adjustments in textbooks and eradicate any anti-Catholic sentiments.[51] In Baltimore the authorities decided to provide Catholic pupils with a Douai Bible. The Philadelphia board decided that any version of the Bible was satisfactory so long as it did not contain commentary. Whether or not the board understood the issue, their decision excluded the Douai Bible because the Church insisted that it be printed with notes. When Kenrick protested the board's decision, opponents of any compromise insisted that the Catholics aimed at taking the Bible out of the public schools. If they had instead said teacher-led prayers and hymns, their position would have been more accurate but less inflammatory.

The Protestant enemies of Catholicism now had a significant issue on which they could focus public opinion: religion in the public school. Taking the Bible out of public schools is a divisive idea today; in the 1840s it was more politically potent in Pennsylvania than antislavery, women's rights, or workingmen's grievances. In 1844 the mainline Protestant clergy formed the American Protestant Association, with leaders from all major denominations except Moravians, Quakers, and Unitarians. The clergy agreed to preach about the Catholic danger to American liberties and to warn their parishioners against patronizing Catholic schools or attending Catholic churches. The Romans allegedly took advantage of mingling with Protestants to make converts.

The American Protestant Association created a climate that led to the formation of the American Republican party, an organization dedicated to keeping Catholics out of power.[52] Without the school issue neither the religious nor political anti-Catholics would have achieved mass influence. Now the Protestants could wrap themselves in the mantle of religious liberty and defend prayer and Bible reading in public schools. American religious freedom began with the Bible, which fostered the religious morality that guaranteed the survival of the Republic. Bishop Kenrick was a foreign-born agent sent to foster absolutism by a Roman church opposed to democracy. Taking the Bible out of schools would weaken democracy and thereby help European monarchy. The Leopoldline Institute in Austria provided funds for Catholic enterprises in Europe and America.[53] Such money proved that the Austrian crown was engaged in a massive conspiracy, using the church as its agency. The images of the hierarchy used by Protestants for centuries and also employed during the trustee controversy now tarred Bishop Kenrick. America's pattern of separation of church and state did not mean either secularity or neutrality toward religion. The Catholic minority was subverting religious freedom in order to deny the majority's rights.

Eventually the increasing shrillness of the debates over Bible readings, prayers, and religious exercises in schools occasioned a series of riots in Philadelphia, in which St. Augustine's Church was burned, men were killed, houses destroyed, and the militia had twice to be deployed. Even though the Protestants did most of the damage in the 1844 riots, the popular press and a grand jury blamed the Roman Catholics and the general reaction allowed the nativists to gain political clout.[54] Still, the courts provided compensation for the destroyed Catholic schools and churches under the theory that the public authorities had the responsibility to keep the peace or make restitution.[55] This policy had not been followed after mobs burnt Pennsylvania Hall and black churches in earlier anti-abolition and anti-Negro riots.

The debate over the political implications of Protestantism and Catholicism and the Bible in schools served the clerics on both sides. They undermined the tradition of good relations and intermingling because of their fear that the assimilation policy was allowing the other side to make converts. Nativist riots secured the public-school system for Protestants and forced the Catholics to create a parochial school system. The clergy of both groups won.

In 1844 female supporters of the anti-Catholic Native Republican Association created a weekly newspaper called *The American Woman.* Like Lucretia Mott, the nativist women addressed political issues, but their justifying rationale was very different. The lady authors of the newspaper's articles – virtually all were unsigned – endorsed the separate spheres of males and females and argued that mothers' moral responsibilities for their children required them to create a virtuous Republic.[56] *The American Woman* favored temperance, relief for the poor, better wages for women, a twenty-one year waiting period for immigrants to become citizens, and the Bible in schools. The "Bible is the foundation and top stone" of America's "liberties." "For it is so interwoven with every department of our government, that take the Bible away, and the government would crumble to atoms in a day."[57]

The nativist women did not criticize the Protestant clergy or the laws on women's property rights. They discussed religious liberty occasionally, because the Roman Catholics allegedly endangered it. Like their male counterparts, these women opposed the temporal power of the papacy and Catholicism as a political system. They claimed to defend freedom of worship for all religions, including Catholicism.[58]

The 1844 riots mark the emergence of nativism as a political force in Pennsylvania. The American Republican party, charged by Catholics and some Protestants with instigating the riots, dominated the city in the next election, posing a dilemma for both Whigs and Democrats. With the decline of the Whigs in the 1850s, the Know Nothings, or American party, appeared as the alternative to the Democrats until differences over slavery divided the nativists and the Republican party emerged.[59] The Democratic political strategy in the 1850s was to portray the Know Nothings as bigots interested in destroying religious liberty.[60] Tolerance for all was a basic American value. The nativists responded that they were the party interested in preserving religious liberty.[61] The foreign hierarchy in the Roman Catholic Church repudiated separation of church and state, and obedient priests manipulated bosses and ignorant Irish immigrants in an attempt to subvert democratic institutions. The nativist parties show that the traditional anti-Catholic foundation of British toleration could flourish in nineteenth-century Pennsylvania.

Anti-Catholic sentiments translated into one law. The trustees of Holy Trinity Church had been battling the bishops for sixty years. In 1854 the trustees experienced a devastating setback when the court ruled, using precedents formulated in 1798, that obedience to the bishop was a requirement of Roman Catholicism.[62] The legislature responded to a petition from the Holy Trinity trustees and in 1855 repealed the law of 1844, which had allowed the bishop to become the sole trustee of church property.[63] The new statute, termed the Price Bill, passed almost unanimously, and required that the bishop hold the property in trust for the congregation. A bishop was now unable to transmit property to his successor in office and, in case of trustee dissent, could not claim the property for a corporate entity entitled the Roman Catholic Church. The bishop was, therefore, a "dry" and not an active trustee. A similar law passed in New York was repealed in 1863, but the Pennsylvania law survived into the twentieth century. The new law had little effect. The priest or bishop selected trustees and he picked men who would not challenge his authority. When Holy Trinity amended its charter in 1859 vesting property in the bishop, trusteeism was dead.

Epilogue: The Dismantling

The major features of Pennsylvania's pre-Civil War understanding of religious liberty endured until the mid-twentieth century. In 1894 the Pennsylvania supreme court upheld the practice of mandatory reading without additional comment of a passage from the Bible in public schools. There was not even a court case on the recitation of the Lord's Prayer that often followed the Bible reading. In 1882 the court declared that a person's testimony in a trial did not depend upon the orthodoxy of his belief, provided that he thought that God punished falsehoods. In 1910 the court affirmed again that the Commonwealth's common-law tradition included a nondenominational Christianity.[1]

The Sunday laws withstood serious challenge until World War II. In 1893 newspapers could not be sold on Sunday. The sesquicentennial fair could not be open on the Sabbath. In the 1920s Pennsylvania continued to prohibit hunting, fishing, and sports on Sunday. In 1927 the court applied the 1794 no-sports-on-Sunday provisions against professional baseball teams. There were exemptions, some granted by the court under the definitions allowed in the 1794 act as works of necessity and transportation and others by acts of the legislature. After 1926 the sale of gasoline was deemed a necessity; utilities could repair machinery and people could engage in "wholesome recreation." Selling soda water was not legal because it was not a foodstuff, but ice cream was. In time baseball on Sunday was permitted, but not in the morning or after 6 p.m. In certain large cities basketball, ice shows, and ice hockey could take place on Sunday evening.[2] Still, laws passed in 1939 and 1959 outlawed merchandising and factory production on Sunday. The Pennsylvania and Federal courts throughout the 1950s upheld the constitutionality of the Sunday prohibitions not on religious grounds but as a secular day of rest and relaxation.

Pennsylvania's understanding of religious liberty faced serious intellectual challenges in the late nineteenth century. In 1680, 1780, and 1880 revealed religion and the academy most often spoke with the same accent. For William Penn and James Wilson the conclusions of philosophy and science, the Bible and nature, intuition and reason formed a divinely arranged harmony. The Ten Commandments summarized obligations all thinking individuals should espouse. Religious commitment created private virtue and led to civic responsibility. Church and state worked in tandem, preserving their separate spheres, and each received the benefits of the well-being of the other. By 1900 the ideas of Charles Darwin, Auguste Compte, Sigmund Freud, and the increasing autonomy and professionalization of history, sociology, economics, and philosophy made the confident harmony of 1790 seem naïve. Religious groups in America had never spoken with one voice, but the disagreements between liberals and fundamentalists over the historical criticism of the Bible made the certainty of what the Ten Commandments represented and their relation to eternal universal values seem problematic. The churches' active role in the creation and then the seeming failure of prohibition prompted some to conclude that morality could not be legislated.

In modern America the restrictive Sabbath seemed less a product of all Christians than of a result of the dominance of Calvinism. By the 1940s the Christian churches no longer spoke with one voice on Sabbath regulations. Mainline church members wanted to attend baseball games, listen to radio, and go to movies on Sunday. Television, the automobile, the forty-hour week, Sunday newspapers, vacations, and the retail revolution brought about by shopping centers eroded the categories of the 1794 law. Neighboring states eased or repealed their Sunday blue laws.

By the 1970s civil service regulations and civil-rights legislation made even asking the religious preferences of a prospective employee or college student illegal. An employee could not be dismissed for any religion or none. The legislature and the courts did not bother to ask whether a person believed that the quality of life after death was determined according to one's behavior on earth. The individual just swore or affirmed to tell the truth or uphold the Constitution.

Apparently, therefore, the dismantling of the Pennsylvania traditions of benevolent neutrality between church and state should have caused little controversy and have resulted from acts of the legislature. In actuality, the courts took the lead, their actions occasioned immense hostility, and religion became a more divisive political issue in Pennsylvania life in the 1980s than it had been since the early years of the colony. The courts and universities jettisoned Pennsylvania's traditions of religious liberty. The people still liked the old ways.

For Pennsylvanians the dismantling began at the end of World War II. In 1940 the United States Supreme Court dismissed a complaint by the

Jehovah's Witnesses claiming liberty of conscience against a Minersville, Pennsylvania, board-of-education ordinance requiring all students to salute the flag.[3] The Court reasoned that the state's right to use the flag saluting ceremony to engender patriotism should not be overthrown by the Court. The Court was not the "school board for the country." In 1943 the Court reversed, holding that making the Jehovah's Witnesses salute the flag violated their religious freedom.[4] The Court utilized the Fourteenth Amendment in order to apply the guarantee of the First Amendment to a state and to a practice in a school. That same year the Court struck down an ordinance of Jeanette, Pennsylvania, requiring a license for Jehovah's Witnesses to sell their religious literature. It again used the Fourteenth Amendment to apply the First Amendment, and it reversed an earlier decision.[5]

In 1963 in School District of Abington (Pa.) Township versus Schempp, the United States Supreme Court ruled against the compulsory reading of a passage of the Bible followed by the recitation of the Lord's Prayer. The Court held that these actions fostered religion, were not neutral, and not justified as moral training.[6] The Court said that the Fourteenth Amendment passed in 1867 had outlawed a practice of Pennsylvania schools followed since the 1830s. Viewed historically, the new premises in the various courts' interpretations of religious liberty were that there was no difference between constitutional restrictions on the Federal and state governments, and that morality could be divorced from Christianity or any religious commitment. Schools could still teach values, but they could not use a ritual act to support morality that also could be construed as endorsing Christianity or fostering any kind of worship. Bishop Kenrick in the 1840s had denied that there could be a nondenominational Christianity that would preserve a Catholic's religious liberty. His solution was to build parochial schools. In the 1960s those parents who wanted education to embody a self-conscious religiously-based morality had to abandon public education and create church schools. The court ruled that a nondenominational Christianity was a religion. Thomas Paine, not James Wilson, understood correctly the Constitution. In other decisions the U.S. Supreme Court struck down a New York State authorized prayer and demanded that the public schools perform no religious practices.

In 1978 the Pennsylvania supreme court, following the precedents of the U.S. Supreme Court's new interpretation of the First Amendment, decreed that Pennsylvania's Sunday statutes were unconstitutional. Even though the legislature had not passed the repeal, the new Sunday liberalization, which brought to Pennsylvania the same tolerance other states had long enjoyed, occasioned little controversy. Ironically, although the courts have extended to atheists, secularists, and religious minorities expanded rights under the First Amendment, there has been no corresponding relaxation of penalties for pacifists. There was more freedom for a pacifist in Pennsylvania from 1680 until 1775 than there is today.

The final outcome of the court-mandated new pattern of church and state in Pennsylvania is still in doubt. One element seems certain: Pennsylvania will no longer be distinctive and the essential decisions on a wide variety of moral-religious issues will be made in Washington. The fundamental problem foreseen by William Penn in the 1680s is still with us. Penn wanted to create a common morality necessary for the institutional church and the state in a condition of religious pluralism. Both church and state needed to be autonomous, and no one's conscience should be coerced so long as peace and order were maintained. Penn found a resolution to his dilemma in natural law, separation of church and state, and benevolent neutrality.

The history of Pennsylvania's experiment in religious liberty contains lessons for modern Americans. The first is that a concentration upon James Madison or the First Amendment distorts the patterns that shaped the United States. Because virtually all Americans saw the Federal government as having no jurisdiction over the states in any matter of religion, the Founding Fathers left to the states the inevitable compromises in creating workable policies. The states in their first constitutions also ignored major problems, because their citizens most wanted to redress past grievances and limit the scope of the government. The provisions in the 1776 and 1790 Pennsylvania constitutions show how their framers fitted new and inherited principles into a tradition created in the early eighteenth century and adapted to changing conditions in the new nation. Later the courts, legislature, and churches modified or created moral or religious customs to deal with unforeseen circumstances like the creation of public schools or development of railroads.

A second lesson is that church and state relations involved the church, law, and politics. The courts shared responsibility with the Pennsylvania Assembly, and religious and nonreligious people elected the legislators. So as political control shifted from the Quakers to the Revolutionaries and then Federalists, Republicans, and Democrats, Pennsylvania's practices evolved. There were always disagreements. The state accepted some degree of coercion in matters that it defined as political-moral but that dissenters saw as moral-religious. Pennsylvania created many traditions of religious liberty and no one normative polity.

A third lesson is that separation of church and state was both an ideology and a practice. The ideology was at times incoherent and the practice inconsistent. Neat formulas did not work well because Americans' wants were and are contradictory: noncoercion of individual conscience and universal agreement on the conclusions of conscience; pressure to live morally and freedom to sin; trust in God and self-reliance.

Still, there were continuities in Pennsylvania's practice from the 1680s until the twentieth century. The state was neutral toward any sect or denomination but was favorable to all churches, because religious practice contributed to the common good by fostering morality, obedience to the law, hard work, and other civic virtues. The state sought to exploit private belief as well as organized religion for the benefit of the general welfare. The churches acquiesced and supported the state that in turn guaranteed their property rights, left them to function, and approved their moral teaching.

The state passed no laws concerning, and made no official pronouncements about, the validity or foolishness of any revealed doctrine. Revelation was the substance of the churches; natural law served an analogous role for the state. If churchgoers wished to blend the conclusions of revealed and natural religion within their denominations, the state would not stop them, but it officially took no cognizance of it. For purposes of the law, a church or synagogue was a special kind of charity that conducted itself according to principles spelled out in its charter. All religious bodies received tax exemption; all could own property, but the state restricted the amount of tax-free property for the good of the Commonwealth. When religious groups claimed that their conscience required them not to fight, not to take oaths, and to modify majority customs of inheritance or private property, the government, in order to avoid religious persecution, sought for an accommodation that would respect the beliefs of the minority while protecting the needs of the majority. Any policy on church and state had to meet the test of reasonableness.

William Penn, James Wilson, and the Pennsylvania supreme court judges saw natural law as furnishing the framework through which the state could solve the political problems caused by the separation of the institutional church from government. Natural law was a product of reason and experience, not revelation, and constituted the foundation of the state. Such law provided a seemingly nonsectarian language through which the society could talk about and settle political issues about religion in a nondivisive manner. By relying on this natural-law vocabulary the state could withstand the dangers of having various segments of society disagreeing over the meaning of religious liberty.

After 1776 a major task for the state was to create a means of interaction between church and government that would allow the Commonwealth to be at the same time benevolent and neutral. Jew, Muslim, deist, Catholic, and Protestant agreed that God was the creator of nature and definer of the law. All adult citizens who could think or experience nature could see the eternal truths. Those truths could be described as equality and justice for all (or life, liberty, and the pursuit of happiness). Other truths included honesty (no false witness), respect for property (not stealing), life (not killing), and the family (no adultery and honor father and mother) – the Ten Commandments. Virtually all Americans in all periods have subscribed to these precepts.

Natural law was and is useful to church and state because of its ambiguity. An atheist or agnostic, deriving principles from reason, the law of peoples – or even the United Nations 1948 declaration on human rights – can join with traditionally religious people in establishing universal norms of behavior. Applying natural law to political-moral issues is part of the American tradition of moral discourse, legitimated by the Declaration of Independence. Those for and against slavery, for and against women's rights, for and against homosexuality, for and against aid to parochial schools have used natural law. Natural law is not going to solve the divisive issues of the twentieth century any more than it did those of earlier centuries. What it does is to provide a common starting point so that newspaper editors, clergy, courts, and politicians can talk the same language, can hear what each other says, and can find the values in each other's position. For example, a natural-law discussion of abortion would recognize that the fetus, the mother, the father, and the society have inherent rights. The issue then becomes what policies can the state follow which recognizes those rights, balances what is most important, and accommodates many perspectives. Proof of a viable policy on abortion would not be based upon revelation or theological dogma, neither of which the state recognizes. Similarly, a natural-law discussion of aid to parochial schools would focus on the role of schools and education in American society and how religion in education adds or detracts from the goals of the general culture.

Applying natural law to contemporary problems may do nothing more than buy time and civility. Still, many of the divisive religious issues of the eighteenth and nineteenth centuries are no longer controversial. Impassioned debates over the political power of the Pope, an Anglican bishop in America, profanation of the Sabbath, and blasphemy are things of the past. Bible-reading and prayer in the public schools and aid to parochial schools are still divisive issues, but unlikely to cause riots such as happened in Philadelphia in 1844.

After the Civil War, Americans expanded the concept of civic religion to include insights derived from Catholics as well as Protestants and, more recently, to become Judeo-Christian. Now the presence of believers in Hinduism and Buddhism, as well as many new made-in-America sects, complicate the definition of religious liberty. Because natural-law advocates must seek a universal standard, they are well-equipped to deal with the plurality in American life.

In the past Pennsylvanians wanted to keep separate the institutions of church and government. They recognized that though churches dealt with salvation and schools with book learning, both wanted to instill or foster morality or values in children. Because most Americans based their moral judgments upon religious beliefs, teaching morality while ignoring God made little sense. Pennsylvanians also recognized that any policy that favored or disfavored religious observances involved coercion of people. Either strict separation or accommodation meant that some individuals were not allowed their free exercise of religion. The state fudged the issue deliberately by using natural law, finding a secular purpose for customs originating in religion, assuming a consensus on morality, and embracing inconsistency. Pennsylvanians reasoned that because individual conscience was left free and all religious bodies were granted equal rights, some degree of discrimination against minorities was permissible in the interests of the state. The government required pacifists, for example, who did not wish to support militarism to pay war taxes. State policies on compulsory education, health care for children, the ability to proselytize in an airport or mall have involved limiting religious freedom. At issue today is whether because of the general welfare a Quaker, a Jehovah's Witness, an Old Order Amish, or a Jew can be made to observe or participate in action against her or his religious beliefs. Or does the protection of minorities override the majority's need to reaffirm the moral precepts and natural law undergirding America's governmental institutions?

The U.S. Supreme Court after World War II argued that in religious matters some, but not all, minority rights took precedence, because the First Amendment applied to the states. Whether or not the Court's interpretation survives, the manner in which it was justified and promulgated jeopardized the complexity of Pennsylvania's evolving traditions. In the past legislators, clergymen, editors, and judges worked together in the political sphere to define the content and practice of religious liberty. No one interest dominated. The present policy has never been submitted to the Congress and the states for adjustment and/or ratification. The result is a polarized atmosphere, a failure of rational debate, neglect of seeking out compromises, and ignorance of the natural-law standards underlying the Federal Constitution and the First Amendment. If the new pattern is to become the American norm, policy needs to move from the realm of judicial review to receive the endorsement of the politicians, the clergy, minorities, and the majority. Otherwise court judgments rather than reason and experience will guide, and the people will not grapple creatively with the United States' heritage of religious freedom.

Notes

Introduction: The Pennsylvania Traditions of Religious Liberty

1. Thomas Jefferson, *Notes on the State of Virginia* (New York, 1964), 154. Jefferson gave no credit to Rhode Island. This is not surprising because Roger Williams' writings on religious liberty were not generally known until rediscovered by Isaac Backus in the 1770s. William G. McLoughlin, ed., *Isaac Backus: On Church, State, and Calvinism, Pamphlets 1754–1789* (Cambridge, Mass., 1968), 17; Thomas Curry, *The First Freedoms: Church and State in America to the Passage of the First Amendment* (New York, 1986), 124; John Webb Pratt, *Religion, Politics, and Diversity: The Church-State Theme in New York History* (Ithaca, N.Y.: 1967) discusses colonial, national, and modern events.,
2. James Madison to William Bradford, Dec. 1, 1773. *Papers of James Madison,* ed. W. T. Hutchinson and W. Rachel Hutchinson (Chicago, 1962), 101.
3. Dietmar Rothermund, *The Layman's Progress: Religious and Political Experience in Colonial Pennsylvania 1740–1770* (Philadelphia, 1961) devoted considerable attention to church and state issues. Patricia U. Bonomi, *Under the Cope of Heaven: Religion, Society, and Politics in Colonial America* (New York, 1986) addresses for all the colonies many of the themes of religion and society raised in this book. After this manuscript was essentially completed, I read Sally Schwartz, *"A Mixed Multitude": The Struggle for Toleration in Colonial Pennsylvania* (New York, 1987). Schwartz focuses on the creation of a religiously and ethnically tolerant society, a topic that is broader but in a time frame narrower than this book. Schwartz' work has the virtues of a revised dissertation: careful argument, copious quotations, and 85 pages of footnotes. I have indicated in footnotes those subjects for which Schwartz provides significant additional information or about which our interpretations differ.
4. William McLoughlin, *New England Dissent, 1630–1833* (Cambridge, Mass., 1971), 2 vols. and *Isaac Backus and the American Pietistic Tradition* (Boston, 1967); Richard Bushman, *From Puritan to Yankee* (Cambridge, Mass., 1971); Thomas Buckley, *Church and State in Revolutionary Virginia, 1776–1789* (Charlottesville, Va., 1977); Charles Kinney, *Church and State: The Struggle for Separation in New Hampshire, 1630–1900* (New York, 1955); Rhys Isaac, *The Transfor-*

166

mation of Virginia, 1740–1790 (Chapel Hill, N.C., 1982); John F. Wilson, *Church and State in America: A Bibliographic Guide* (Westport, Conn., 1986, 1987), using a broad definition of the subject, provides a comprehensive annotated bibliography covering from the colonial period to the present and should be the starting point for future research.

5.   Curry, *First Freedoms,* 74–7, 160–1; William Lee Miller, *The First Liberty: Religion and the American Republic* (New York, 1987), 37–8, 204–5; Leonard Levy, *The Establishment Clause: Religion and the First Amendment* (New York, 1986), 25, 68–9; Michael J. Malbin, *Religion and Politics: The Intentions of the Authors of the First Amendment* (Washington, D.C., 1978). Levy and Malbin have opposing positions on the meaning of the first amendment. Pennsylvania is also slighted in several standard older histories: Mark De Wolfe Howe, *The Garden and the Wilderness: Religion and Government in American Constitutional History* (Chicago, 1965); Sidney Mead, *The Lively Experiment: Shaping of Christianity in America* (New York, 1963) and *The Nation With the Soul of a Church* (New York, 1975). Anson Phelps Stokes, *Church and State in the United States* 3 vols. (New York, 1950) makes many references to Pennsylvania in his compendium of information. Two examples of recent overemphasis on Jefferson: "The Virginia Statute for Religious Freedom became the cornerstone of the unique American tradition of religious freedom and separation of church and state. It served as a model for other American states, both old and new." Jefferson "defined terms for the American debate on the issues of religion in society and church-state relations then and ever since." *The Virginia Statute for Religious Freedom: Its Evolution and Consequences in American History,* ed. Merrill D. Peterson and Robert Vaughan (New York, 1988), ix, 78, 139. The best collection of documents on the American traditions of church and state is John Wilson and Donald Drakeman, eds., *Church and State in American History* (Boston, 1967).

6.   For citations of Pennsylvania in the debates, see Curry, *First Freedoms,* 144, 147 (Virginia), 156 (Maryland), 182 (New England).

Chapter I. The Creation of Religious Liberty in Pennsylvania

1.   Mary Maples Dunn, *William Penn: Politics and Conscience* (Princeton, N.J., 1967), vii, 133–6; Sally Schwartz, "William Penn and Toleration: Foundations of Colonial Pennsylvania," *Pennsylvania History* (October, 1983): 284–312.

2.   Quaker terminology on "spirit" and "conscience" is difficult to interpret because the terms were used in different contexts. The Quaker discussions of sacraments brought the clearest formulations of the spiritual nature of religion. My interpretation of early Quaker thought is influenced by Pamela Oliver, "Quaker Testimony and the Lamb's War," (Ph.D. dissertation, University of Melbourne, Australia, 1977); *Memorable Works of a Son of Thunder and Consolation... Edward Burroughs* (1672), 245–6, 257–8, 268, 343–7; Samuel Fisher, *The Testimony of Truth Exalted* (1679), 4–5, 13, 14; *The Works of the Long-Mournful and Sorely-Distressed Isaac Penington* (London, 1681), 230–2, 236–41, 306–7; George Fox, *Doctrinal Books,* III, *Works* (Philadelphia, 1831), VI, 273, 338–46.

3. Christopher Hill, *The World Turned Upside Down: Radical Ideas During the English Revolution* (New York, 1972); Arthur Morton, *World of the Ranters: Religious Radicalism in the English Revolution* (London, 1970); and *Radical Religion in the English Revolution*, ed. J. F. McGregor and Barry Reay (New York, 1984) provide good introductions to the extensive literature on radicals in the Puritan revolution.

4. Barry Reay, *The Quakers and the English Revolution* (New York, 1986), 49–78.

5. W. K. Jordan, *Development of Religious Toleration in England: From the Convention of the Long Parliament to the Restoration, 1640–1660* (Cambridge, 1938), III, pts. II–IV.

6. Useful secondary sources dealing with Penn's political theory are Dunn, *William Penn*; Hugh Barbour, "William Penn: Model of Protestant Liberalism," *Church History* 48(1979): 156–73; Edward Beatty, *William Penn as Social Philosopher* (New York, 1939); William I. Hull, *William Penn: A Topical Biography* (New York, 1939).

7. William Penn, "An Address to Protestants," *Select Works of William Penn*, (1679) (London, 1825), III, 126, 148–9; idem, "Great Case of Liberty of Conscience," *Select Works* (1670), II, 135, 142.

8. Anne Whiteman, "The Restoration of the Church of England," in Owen Chadwick and Geoffrey F. Nuttall, eds., *From Uniformity to Unity: 1662–1962* (London, 1962), 47–79.

9. Penn's assertion of identity of belief was coupled with a strong attack upon the inconsistencies between other groups' ideas and practices. "This was the purport of their doctrine and ministry; which, for the most part, is what other professors of Christianity pretend to hold, in words and forms, but not in the power of Godliness; which generally speaking has long been lost . . ." quoted in Robert Proud, *History of Pennsylvania* (Philadelphia, 1797), I, 46; Penn, "England's Present Interest," *Select Works* (1675), II, 314–19; idem, "Persuasive to Moderation," *Select Works* (1686), II, 539; "Two Speeches to a Committee of Parliament," in *Papers of William Penn*, ed. Richard Dunn and Mary Dunn (Philadelphia, 1981), I, 535.

10. Penn quoted in Proud, *History* I, 95–6.

11. Penn argued that the disagreements between Anglicans and dissenters were religious, but the differences between Protestants and Catholics were primarily civil. Tests for loyalty should be taken annually by both Catholics and Protestants. Such tests did not infringe upon liberty of conscience because they were about political or worldly matters and the security of the state, and not spiritual affairs. Penn, "One Project for the Good of England," *Select Works*, III (1679), 192–3, 202–4; idem, "England's Present Interest," *Select Works*, II, 271–3, 284–6; idem, "The Great Case of Liberty of Conscience," *Select Works*, II, 133.

12. Penn, "An Address to Protestants," *Select Works*, III, 132; idem, "England's Present Interest," *Select Works* II, 284, 291, 295.

13. Penn, "England's Present Interest," *Select Works*, II, 303–7.

14. Gail McKnight Beckman, comp., *Statutes at Large of Pennsylvania, 1682–1801* (New York, 1976), I, 113. Stephen Webb argued that the clause allowing an Anglican Church was designed to pave the way ultimately for an Anglican estab-

lishment in the colony, " 'The Peaceable Kingdom,' Quaker Pennsylvania in the Stuart Empire," in *The World of William Penn,* ed. Richard Dunn and Mary Dunn (Philadelphia: University of Pennsylvania, 1986), 182–4.

15.   William Penn to Jasper Batt, Feb. 5, 1683, *Papers of William Penn,* II, 348. For a complete discussion of the drafts of the Frames, see II, 135–238.

16.   Beckman, *Statutes at Large,* I, 124, 128.

17.   Beatty, *William Penn,* 126, 157; Penn's attempt to end religious controversy might have derived from Maryland's 1649 Toleration Act, in which anyone "willfully to wronge disturbe trouble or molest" any person "professing to believe in Christ Jesus for or in respect of his or her religion" should pay triple damages plus 20s. Henry S. Commager, ed., *Documents of American History* (Englewood Cliffs, N.J., 1973), 31–2.

18.   Beckman, *Statutes at Large,* I, 117, 128.

19.   Benjamin Furley feared that those who believed that Sunday observances were a human invention would feel obliged in conscience to work on the first day. Furly also wanted servants to have liberty not to be forced to work on the Sabbath. *Pennsylvania Magazine of History and Biography* 19 (1895): 302.

20.   The English Quaker effort was aimed at freeing Friends from prosecution in ecclesiastical and chancery courts, but not at ending the tithe. Norman Hunt, *Two Early Political Associations: The Quakers and the Dissenting Deputies in the Age of Sir Robert Walpole* (Oxford, 1961), 62–72. In the aftermath of the law on toleration, the English government gradually worked out what privileges Friends and other dissenters were allowed. The London Meeting for Sufferings was involved in litigation on the validity of Quaker marriages, imprisonment of schoolmasters, tithes, and affirmations. Penn wanted to avoid such problems in Pennsylvania. London Meeting for Sufferings, Book of Cases, II (1698–1738), 37–9, 60–1, 74–6, 105–7, 112–19. Ms. at Friends House Library, London.

21.   William Penn answers to Board of Trade, Jan. 11, 1704/5, Dunn and Dunn, *Papers of William Penn,* IV, 321.

22.   Ibid. William Penn Requests to Queen Anne, Sept. 1, 1705, IV, 392–3; Draft of a New Patent for Pennsylvania, May 23, 1705, IV, 353–5; To the Board of Trade, June 6, 1705, IV, 359.

23.   Robert Barclay, *Apology for the True Christian Divinity,* 13th ed., (Manchester, 1869), Prop. XIV, paragraph 1, p. 307.

24.   Penn, "England's Present Interest," *Select Works,* II, 314, 317.

25.   Penn, "Address to Protestants," *Select Works,* III, 27.

26.   Ibid., 28.

27.   Beckman, *Statutes at Large,* I, 18.

28.   James T. Mitchell and Henry Flanders, eds., *Statutes at Large of Pennsylvania from 1682 to 1801* (Harrisburg, Pa., 1896–1909), II, 360–3; J. Thomas Jable, "The Pennsylvania Sunday Blue Laws of 1779," *Pennsylvania History* 40(1975): 414–5.

29.   Mitchell and Flanders, *Statutes at Large,* II, 128–9, 133.

30.   Ibid., 130, 132.

31.   Francis N. Thorpe, *The Federal and State Constitutions Colonial Charters and Other Organic Laws* (Washington, 1909), V, 2576–8.

32.   Dunn and Dunn, *Papers of William Penn,* I, 420–1. For London Friends'

reaction, see London Morning Meeting, Minutes, transcripts, 1673–90, 9 mo/11/
1684; 10/15/1684, Friends House Library, London.

33.   There was a Lutheran minister in the colony who, a little later, was said to be
destitute, blind, a drunk, and in need of relief. Israel Acrelius, *A History of New
Sweden* (Philadelphia, 1874), 177, 180, 188. Morgan Edwards found two Baptist
ministers in the colony by 1690, but is vague on whether they held services.
Materials Towards a History of the Baptists (Philadelphia, 1770), I, 9, 11.

34.   "Minutes of the Provincial Council," *PMHB* 11(1887): 156–9.

35.   "The Tryals of Peter Boss, George Keith, Thomas Budd and William Bradford," reprinted in *The Keithian Controversy in Early Pennsylvania,* ed. J. William Frost (Norwood, Pa., 1980), 172–3.

36.   Ibid., 170, 180–1.

37.   Samuel Jennings, "State of the case Briefly, but Impartially given," reprinted
in Frost, *Keithian Controversy,* 268–81.

38.   "Tryals of Peter Boss," Frost, *Keithian Controversy,* 175. The law was useful
for it provided for seizing the press. English Quakers protested against a licensing
law proposed in Parliament in 1702 or 1703. *Some Considerations Humbly
Offered by the People Called Quakers Relating to the Bill for the Restraining the
Licentiousness of the Press* (n.p.n.d.)

39.   "Tryals of Peter Boss," Frost, *Keithian Controversy,* 177–9; William Penn,
The Peoples Ancient and Just Liberties Asserted (1670).

40.   Beckman, *Statutes at Large,* I, 128.

41.   *Minutes of the Provincial Council of Pennsylvania, Colonial Records of
Pennsylvania* (Harrisburg, Pa., 1838) (hereinafter *Colonial Records*), I, 318, 324,
359–60.

42.   Beckman, *Statutes at Large,* I, 212.

43.   Beckman, *Statutes at Large,* I, 39–42; *Colonial Records,* II, 30. It is question-
able that any Catholic would have taken in 1701 "the Declaration appointed by
the Parliament of England, of their abhorrence of that Damnable Doctrine and
Position that Princes excommunicated by the Pope may be deposed or murther'd
by their subjects &c."

44.   Charles J. Stillé, "Religious Tests in Provincial Pennsylvania," *PMHB* 9
(1885):365–406; *Votes and Proceedings of the House of Representatives of the
Province of Pennsylvania, Pennsylvania Archives* Eighth Series (Harrisburg, Pa.,
1931–5) (hereinafter *Votes of Assembly*), I, 402. Robert Quary mentioned that
the oaths given to the Pennsylvania council were not full oaths as were administered in New Jersey. Robert Quary to the Board of Trade, Jan. 1704/5, Board of
Trade Papers, vol. 8, no. 5.

45.   *Correspondence between William Penn and James Logan,* ed. Deborah
Logan and Edward Armstrong, *Memoirs of the Historical Society of Pennsylvania,* IX (Philadelphia, 1870), I, 248, 259, 38, 190–4, 224; *Votes of Assembly,* I,
402–3.

46.   Mitchell and Flanders, *Statutes at Large,* IV, 428–9.

47.   Ibid. II, 490.

48.   Ibid., 465, 489–90; idem, III, 529. The council in 1724 asserted that the
original statute of toleration was in force in Pennsylvania.

49.   Ibid.

50. Ibid. When the bill was first drawn up, the provision of worship did not specify for only Christians. The council insisted upon adding that stipulation. Whether the assembly was careless or motivated by liberal principles cannot be determined. *Colonial Records,* II, 229.

51. See George Whitehead et al., *The Christian Faith and Profession of the People commonly called Quakers, concerning the Divinity or Deity of the Son of God Asserted* (ca. 1693).

52. For a discussion of the basis and evolution of the Quaker testimony on oaths, see J. William Frost, "The Affirmation Controversy and Religious Liberty," in *The World of William Penn,* ed. Richard S. Dunn and Mary Maples Dunn (Philadelphia, 1986), 303–22.

53. Beckman, *Statutes at Large,* I, 152, 188. Fletcher required the council and assembly members to affirm "in the presence of God." *Colonial Records,* I, 324.

54. "The Tryals of Peter Boss," Frost, *Keithian Controversy,* 178; *A Letter From a Satisfied to a Dissatisfied Friend, Concerning the Solemn Affirmation* (London, 1713), 4–5.

55. *A Collection of Acts of Parliament... Relative to Those Protestant Dissenters... called... Quakers* (London, 1777), 57–9.

56. The best narrative of the dispute remains Winfred Root, *Relations of Pennsylvania with the British Government 1696–1767* (1912, reprinted New York, 1970), 222–55. The debate can be traced also in the primary sources. Mitchell and Flanders, *Statutes at Large* II, 39–42, 133, 219–20, 266–72, 355–6, 425–6, 536–40; III, 39–40, 59–60, 199–210, 427–31, 448–9, 457–8, 465, 507–17; *Votes of Assembly,* I, 413–14, 584–5, 769; II, 1177–8, 1190–1206, 1123, 1466–7, 1547, 1584; *Colonial Records* II, 60, 67, 92, 104, 107, 109, 116, 174, 185, 215, 226, 233–7, 474, 476, 537, 564, 607, 634, 644–60; Logan and Armstrong, *Penn-Logan Correspondence* I, 205, 229, 236–7, 242–3, 315, 317–18, 327; James Logan to William Penn 5/4/1712, #1560, Penn Papers Mss. Historical Society of Pennsylvania. See also Schwartz, *"Mixed Multitude,"* 42–6.

57. The best secondary source on Anglicans in Pennsylvania is Deborah Mathias Gough, "Pluralism, Politics, and Power Struggles: The Church of England in Colonial Philadelphia 1695–1789," (Ph.D. diss., University of Pennsylvania, 1978); the most convenient collection of primary materials is William Stevens Perry, ed., *Papers Relating to the History of the Church in Pennsylvania, a.d. 1680–1778* (1871).

58. *Colonial Records,* III, 143; *Votes of Assembly,* II, 1261.

59. The assembly, led by David Lloyd, fought a bitter battle with the governors and council over the tenure of judges and the responsibility for creating courts. When no agreement could be reached, the governors established courts under the provisions of the charter. The leaders of the assembly, without much success, attempted to undermine the legitimacy of these courts. Anglicans also were against the quality of justice given out by Pennsylvania courts, because witnesses who only used the affirmation supposedly lied. In a famous passage in *The Americans: The Colonial Experience* (New York, 1948), I, 47–8, Daniel Boorstin accused Friends of caring more about the affirmation than human life. In 1718 the assembly passed a draconian law code, bringing Pennsylvania statutes into line with English laws. An attempt by two criminals, condemned to death, to gain freedom because of the affirmations used in their trials did not succeed. Boorstin would have been on sounder footing if he had seen the new codes as growing out of a fear of lawlessness and pressures by the British government to make Pennsylvania's laws closer to English practice. *Colonial Records*, III, 41–2; *Votes of Assembly*, III, 1257–8; Roy Lokken, *David Lloyd: Colonial Lawmaker* (Seattle, Washington, 1959), 166–87, 198–9; Gary Nash, *Quakers and Politics* (Princeton, N.J., 1968), 264–5.

60.   The amendment had been defeated in 1701/1702. *Journals of the House of Lords*, XVIII, I Geo. I (June 14, 1715): 168; *Journals of the House of Commons*, XVII, I Geo. I(May 26, June 2, 1715): 139, 161, 168.

61.   When the members of the Meeting for Sufferings went to the king for his support and assent to the law, George stated that the new law came because Quakers had not abused the privileges previously granted.

62.   Mitchell and Flanders, *Statutes at Large* III, 41. The assembly wished to ignore Parliament's declaration and rely upon an as yet unvetoed Pennsylvania statute. Governor Gookin feared that any trials in Pennsylvania using affirmations would be illegal. *Colonial Records*, II, 649.

63.   Beckman, *Statutes at Large*, I, 175; II, 91.

64.   Ibid. I, 195.

65.   Ibid. II, 161. Schwartz, *"Mixed Multitude,"* 53–4.

66.   Pennsylvania Anglicans said the law departed from English practice because the colonial churches could sell lands, but the Church of England could not. David Lloyd in 1709 insisted that dissenters in Pennsylvania could have no protection against the English statute of mortmain, a medieval statute forbidding the gift of property to the church. The Quakers in the assembly may have been trying to establish protection for property of dissenters in case Penn sold the right of government. No Pennsylvania statute mentioned mortmain. *Votes of Assembly*, I, 558, 566, 579, 653–4, 665; II, 797, 890, 901, 910, 918, 974, 1010, 1012, 1017, 1034, 1091, 1119, 1129, 1137–8; III, 2052, 2068–9, 2082–6; *Papers of Governors, Pennsylvania Archives*, Series 4, I, 317; Mitchell and Flanders, *Statutes at Large*, II, 424–5.

67.   Morgan Edwards, *Materials Towards a History of the Baptists in Pennsylvania* (Philadelphia, 1770, reprint 1978), I, 45–6; William Keen, *First Baptist Church of Philadelphia* (Philadelphia, 1899), 29–30.

68.   *Votes of Assembly*, III, 2068, 2081–4; Mitchell and Flanders, *Statutes at Large*, III, 37–8, 448, 462, IV, 208–10. The law was a major departure from English practices. In England an Anglican clergyman owned his living as a freeholder, although there were many restrictions on his disposing of the property without consent of the bishop or ordinary. He even owned the church, though the parish had the right of use and the duty of repair. Property could be given to a church only with the permission of the Crown; otherwise, the statute of mortmain applied. Dissenting meeting houses were owned by trustees whose relationship to congregations, higher ecclesiastical authorities, or creedal standards was ill defined. Friends gained exemption from paying taxes on structures built for worship and used for no other purpose, but not on buildings rented and used for worship. Richard Grey, *A System of English Ecclesiastical Law*, 4th ed.

(London, 1743), 72, 183–4; Meeting for Sufferings, Book of Cases, II, 1700, 60–1, 99–101. For counsel's opinions on the problems of incorporation, 75; on the legal status of an English vestry, 43–4.

69. Ecclesiastical courts would have had jurisdiction if the offense had been perpetrated in England, because the case involved adultery and solicitation of chastity. In addition, while clergymen could be tried under common law for some kinds of felonies, this kind of matter had to be first disposed of in church courts. Benefit of clergy meant that there could be no force on the person. Grey, *System,* 14–18, 429–32.

70. Gough, "Pluralism," 78–92; Perry, *Papers,* 81, 83–98.

71. *Colonial Records,* II, 626.

Chapter II. Pacifism and Religious Liberty

1. Alan Cole, "Quakers and the English Revolution," *Past and Present* 10 (1956), 41; James Maclear, "Quakers and the End of the Interregnum," *Church History* 19(Dec., 1950): 240–70; William Wade Spurrier, "Persecution of the Quakers in England 1650–1714," (Ph.D. diss., University of North Carolina, 1976), 44–51; Reay, *Quakers and the English Revolution,* 88–90.

2. Accounts of the peace testimony are in Peter Brock, *Pioneers of the Peaceable Kingdom* (New Jersey, 1968), and Herman Wellenreuther, "Political Dilemma of the Quakers in Pennsylvania, 1681–1748," *PMHB* (1970): 135–72. See also Robert L. P. Davidson, *War Comes to Quaker Pennsylvania, 1682–1756* (New York, 1957) and Isaac Sharpless, *A Quaker Experiment in Government* (Philadelphia, 1898).

3. Beckman, *Statutes at Large,* I, 115.

4. *Papers of Governors,* Series 4, I, 157, 171; Wellenreuther, "Political Dilemma," 147–55; *Colonial Records,* I, 361.

5. *Colonial Records,* II, 68, 154–5, 198, 211; *Papers of Governors,* I, 288, 302; Logan and Armstrong, *Penn-Logan Correspondence,* I, 88, 124, 152, 299–300, 317–18.

6. *Colonial Records,* II, 251–2, 372–3, 395; *Votes of Assembly,* I, 743–6, 748–50.

7. Pennsylvania's skepticism about the utility of a militia was echoed in England. The leading historian of the English militia labels the period from 1670–1757 as eighty years of decay. The militia was not an effective fighting force and few expected it to defeat a force of regulars. Its main use was to provide internal security when the regular army was engaged in fighting external enemies. For members of Parliament, the militia provided a cheap means of demonstrating concern for the security of the realm. By 1745 the militia could not be used to enforce the law or to suppress smugglers. After the seventeenth century, the English did not introduce a militia bill before 1746, and until convinced of the danger of a French invasion, Parliament did not pass a law until 1757. The 1757 act excused Quakers, hired substitutes for them, and recovered the costs of distraint. J. R. Western, *The English Militia in the Eighteenth Century* (London, 1965), 30, 53–4, 72–3, 115, 251.

8. *Colonial Records* I, 265–9, 361–2; II, 431–9, 441–2, 470–1, 481–2.

9. Ibid. II, 78, 496.

10. Logan and Armstrong, *Penn-Logan Correspondence,* I, 147.

11. *Colonial Records,* I, 264–5, 267–8; II, 252, 432–3, 438–40, 478–9; *Votes of Assembly,* I, 280, 573–6.

12. In the dispute over affirmation, the assembly often invoked the distinctive principles of Friends. The difference with the peace testimony is striking.

13. Penn quoted in Brock, *Pioneers,* 85.

14. *Colonial Records,* I, 264–5, II, 252.

15. Ibid., 258. Penn also used this rationale.

16. Ibid. I, 264–5.

17. Jack Marietta, "Growth of Quaker Self-Consciousness in Pennsylvania," in *Seeking the Light: Essays in Quaker History,* ed. J. William Frost and John M. Moore (Wallingford, Pa., 1986), 79–104.

18. Alan Tully, "Ethnicity, Religion and Politics in Early America," *PMHB* 107(Oct. 1983), 491–536.

19. There are several good general histories of Pennsylvania politics. The different perspectives are set forth in Alan Tully, *William Penn's Legacy: Politics and Social Structure in Provincial Pennsylvania 1726–1755* (Baltimore, 1977); Hermann Wellenreuther, *Glaube und Politick in Pennsylvania, 1681–1776. Die Wandlungen der Obrig Keitsdokrin und des Peace Testimony der Quaker* (Koln, 1972) and Jack Marietta, *The Reformation of American Quakerism, 1748–1783* (Philadelphia, 1984), 131–49.

20. Robert S. Hohwald, *The Structure of Pennsylvania Politics, 1739–1766,* (Ph.D. diss., Princeton, N.J., University of Princeton, 1978) argues that the Quaker party was very fluid and that the Proprietary party did not have a continuous existence.

21. Benjamin Franklin, *Plain Truth: Or Serious Consideration on the Present State of the City of Philadelphia and Province of Pennsylvania* (Philadelphia, 1747); Gilbert Tennent, *Late Association for Defense Encouraged, Or the Lawfulness of Defensive War* (Philadelphia, 1748); idem, *Late Association for Defense Further Encouraged* (Philadelphia, 1748); William Currie, *A Treatise on the Consistency of Defensive War with True Christianity* (Philadelphia, 1748).

22. Samuel Smith, *Necessary Truth, Or Seasonable Considerations for the Inhabitants of the City of Philadelphia and the Province of Pennsylvania* (Philadelphia, 1748); John Smith, *Doctrine of Christianity As Held By the People Called Quakers Vindicated* (Philadelphia, 1748); Benjamin Gilbert, *Truth Vindicated and the Doctrine of Darkness Manifested: Occasioned by the Reading of Gilbert Tennent's late Composure...* (Philadelphia, 1748). After 1748 Quakers defended their pacifism in memorials to the assembly or in defenses by assembly members. John Woolman and Anthony Benezet wrote some of the Epistles of Philadelphia Yearly Meeting and Benezet those of the Meeting for Sufferings. There was no systematic defense of the peace testimony published by a Quaker from 1748 until Anthony Benezet wrote *Thoughts on War* during the Revolution. The tracts issued in 1748 appear an anomaly, for Quakers published few pamphlets defending their political role throughout the colonial period.

23. *Votes of Assembly* III, 2542, 2555; J. W. Frost, "William Penn's Experiment in the Wilderness: Promise and Legend," *PMHB* (Oct., 1983): 577–602.

24.   Frost, "Experiment in the Wilderness," 599–602; W. H. Barber, "Voltaire and Quakerism: Enlightenment and Inner Light," *Studies on Voltaire* 24(1963): 81–109.

25.   *Votes of Assembly,* III, 2544.

26.   Ibid. III, 2555–6.

27.   Ibid. Governor Evans issued in 1704 a proclamation requiring all settlers to enlist in the militia and to have a firelock and ammunition. The settlers ignored his proclamation. Franklin's Association was more successful. Volunteers composed the force and they elected officers who then received commissions from the governor. *Papers of Governors,* I, 195–6.

28.   Gilbert, *Truth Vindicated,* shows the emphasis upon natural rights more than other Quaker pamphlets.

29.   *Votes of Assembly* III, 2555.

30.   *A Testimony and Caution to such as do make a profession of truth, who are in scorn called Quakers, and more especially such who profess to be ministers of Gospel of peace, That they should not be concerned in worldly government* (Philadelphia, 1693), reprinted in Frost, *Keithian Controversy,* 201–12.

31.   *Votes of Assembly* III, 2551.

32.   Barclay wrote a strong defense of pacifism, but granted that for a magistrate "That war, undertaken upon a just occasion, is not altogether unlawful for them." Barclay's caveat meant that the magistrates, who would not be Quakers, remained under an older and inferior understanding of the gospel. *Apology,* Prop. XV, xv.

33.   *Votes of Assembly* III, 2536–7, 2550. The assembly, in a clear infringement of the governor's powers, created a committee to supervise the spending of the money. At the end of the war the money still had not been spent. Anglicans tried to gain the money to support the Church of England in Pennsylvania. One Quaker is alleged to have said in 1709 that he preferred the money donated for the queen's use be spent on war rather than on the Episcopalians. Governor Keith later misappropriated the £2000, or so the assembly later charged. Perry, *Papers,* 52; *Votes of Assembly,* III, 2556.

34.   *Votes of Assembly* III, 2552, 2562.

35.   William Smith, *A Brief View of the Conduct of Pennsylvania* (London, 1756), 76–7.

36.   *Votes of Assembly* III, 2636–7; IV, 4392.

37.   *James Logan to Robert Jordan, and others the Friends of the Yearly Meeting for Business, now conven'd in Philadelphia* (Philadelphia, 1741).

38.   William Smith, "Sermon IV, Preached on the Public Fast, Appointed by the Government of Pennsylvania, May 21, 1756," *Works of William Smith, D.D., Late Provost of the College and Academy of Philadelphia* (Philadelphia, 1803), II, 91, 99–101. Smith's wartime sermons were published in *Discourses on Public Occasions in America* (London, 1762).

39.   *Votes of Assembly,* III, 2537.

40.   Tully, *William Penn's Legacy,* 32–4.

41.   William Read Steckel, "Pietism in Colonial Pennsylvania: Christopher Saur, Printer 1738–1758," (Ph.D. diss., Stanford, Calif., 1951), 142–8, 200–1; A. K. Oller, "Christopher Saur, Colonial Printer: A Study of the Publication of the Press," (Ph.D. diss., University of Michigan, 1963), 157, 274–5; Clair Gordon Frantz,

"Religious Teachings of the German Almanacs Published by the Sauers in Colonial Pennsylvania," (Ed.D. diss., Temple University, 1955), 101–2.

42. Henry Harbaugh, *Life of Rev. Michael Schlatter: With a Full Account of his Travels and Labors Among the Germans in Pennsylvania, New Jersey, Maryland, and Virginia: Including His Services as Chaplain in the French and Indian War, and in the War of the Revolution, 1716–1790.* (Philadelphia, 1857), 270–304.

43. Saur distrusted the rationalism or deism of several of the promoters of charity schools. He was a strong opponent of clerical pretensions and a pacifist. After reading William Smith's pejorative comments about Germans in *A Brief State of the Province of Pennsylvania* (London, 1754), he published them in his newspaper. Steckel, *Pietism,* 47–50, 67, 200.

44. Jack Marietta, *The Reformation of American Quakerism, 1748–1783* (Philadelphia, 1984), 131–86 is the best and most detailed account of the impact of the war on Friends.

45. Beckman, *Statutes at Large* V, 201–12.

46. The law was titled "An Act for the Better Ordering and Regulating Such as are Willing and Desirous to be United for Military Purposes Within This Province," Beckman, *Statutes at Large* V, 197–201.

47. Marietta, *The Reformation,* Chapter 7.

48. William Smith, *Brief State;* idem, *A Brief View of the Conduct of Pennsylvania for the Year 1755* (London, 1756); The Quaker party's military role was defended by Henry Cross, *An Answer to an Invidious Pamphlet, intitled a Brief State of the Province of Pennsylvania* (London, 1755); Francis Jenning, *Empire of Fortune: Crowns, Colonies and Tribes in the Seven Years War in America* (New York, 1988), 226–40.

49. William Smith, *Brief State* (3d ed., London, 1756), 17.

50. William Smith, *Brief View,* 58, 60.

51. William Smith, *Brief State,* 38, 42.

52. Ibid., 42, 44.

53. William Smith, *Brief View,* 72–3.

54. Thomas Penn to Richard Peters, ca. March, 1755. Penn Correspondence IV, 75; Thomas Penn to Gov. Morris, 1/27/1756, IV, 218, 221; 13/13/1756, IV, 245.

55. Mitchell and Flanders, *Statutes at Large* V, 540–3.

56. The governor's objections to the assembly's next militia law are in Mitchell and Flanders, *Statutes at Large* V, 622–33.

57. Thomas Penn to Mr. Hamilton, Feb. 13, 1756, IV, 250; Thomas Penn to Richard Peters, 3/22/1756, IV, 254, 260; *Votes of Assembly* V, 4220; Theodore Thayer, *Israel Pemberton: King of the Quakers* (Philadelphia, 1943), 123–31.

58. Francis Jennings, *The Ambiguous Iroquois Empire* (New York, 1984) 325–46.

59. The report appeared in William Smith's pamphlet and was repeated several times. Nathan Grubb, the Quaker assemblyman from Chester County allegedly quoted, denied ever making the statement. Jennings believes William Smith created the story. William Smith, *Brief State,* 60; Jennings, *Empire of Fortune,* 233.

60. George Franz, "Paxton: A Study of Community, Structure and Mobility," (Ph.D. diss., Rutgers University, 1974) is the best recent study.

61. Brooke Hindle, "The March of the Paxton Boys," *William and Mary Quarterly,* 3d Series, III (1946), 461–86.

62.   David Sloan, "'A Time of Sifting and Winnowing,' The Paxton Riots and Quaker Non-Violence in Pennsylvania," *Quaker History* 66(Spring, 1977): 3–22.

63.   Franz, "Paxton," 85, 116; Schwartz, *"Mixed Multitude,"* 225–9 for a contrary view. John R. Dunbar, ed., *The Paxton Papers*, (The Hague, 1957) contains a good sample of the pamphlet literature.

64.   David James Dove, *The Quaker Unmask'd; Or Plain Truth* (Philadelphia, 1764), 8–9, 11, 13; *The Quakers Grace Prayer, and Thanksgiving* (Philadelphia, 1765).

65.   Thomas Barton, *Conduct of Paxton-Men, Impartially Represented* (Philadelphia, 1764), 9, 12.

66.   Isaac Hunt, *A Looking Glass for Presbyterians* (Philadelphia, 1764), 17; *The Author of the Quaker Unmask'd, Strip'd Start (sic) Naked or the Delineated Presbyterians Play'd Nob With* (Philadelphia, 1764), 4, 6, 9; *Observations on a Late Epitaph, In a Letter from a Gentleman in the Country, To his Friend in Philadelphia* (Philadelphia, 1764), 3–4.

67.   Philadelphia Monthly Meeting disowned the Quaker printer of one of the anonymous tracts who refused to name the author. In both official communications and private letters Friends blamed the Presbyterians for the disturbances. "Fragments of a Journal Kept by Samuel Foulk," *PMHB* 5 (1881): 70. Melvin Buxbaum, *Benjamin Franklin and the Zealous Presbyterians* (University Park, PA, 1975), 195–205, shows how Franklin ignored the Lutherans, blamed the Presbyterians, and sought to gain political advantage from the Paxton affair.

68.   Barton, *Conduct*, 32.

Chapter III.   The Clergy and Religious Liberty

1.   Perry, *Papers*, 559; Patricia Bonomi, *Under the Cope of Heaven*, 168–81.

2.   Ibid., 217.

3.   Henry M. Muhlenberg, *Journals of Henry Melchoir Muhlenberg* 3 vols, ed. Theodore G. Tappert and John W. Doberstein (Philadelphia, 1942, 1945, 1948), II, 295.

4.   Perry, *Papers*, 458–9.

5.   Muhlenberg, *Journals*, I, 67, 99–100, 105–8; II, 476–7.

6.   Perry, *Papers*, 458–9; Muhlenberg, *Journals*, I, 90.

7.   Israel Acrelius, *History of New Sweden: Or the Settlements on the River Delaware*, trans. William M. Reynolds (Philadelphia, 1874), 238; Perry, *Papers*, 196.

8.   Muhlenberg, *Journals* I, 100, 354–5.

9.   *Records of the Presbyterian Church in the United States of America* (Philadelphia, 1904, reprinted 1969), 96.

10.   Ibid. I, 502.

11.   William J. Hinke, ed., *Life and Letters of the Rev. John Philip Boehm, Founder of the Reformed Church in Pennsylvania, 1683–1749* (Philadelphia, 1916), 324, 335. The state did not ask for proof of ordination even from clergymen who administered communion to Protestants seeking to qualify for naturalization.

12.   Muhlenberg, *Journals*, II, 235.

13.   Ibid. I, 198, 690–2.

14.   Ibid. II, 241.

15. *Records of Presbyterian Church,* 347.

16. Muhlenberg, *Journals* I, 544–52, 618–19; II, 512.

17. *Minutes of the Provincial Council, Colonial Records,* V, 378 for a rebuke to Presbyterian justices for allowing religious differences to influence actions.

18. Ibid. II, 101, 252; I, 90.

19. Harbaugh, *Life of Schlatter,* 63.

20. Muhlenberg, *Journals* II, 402–3, 412; James I. Good, "Early Attempted Union of Presbyterian and German Reformed," *Journal of Presbyterian Historical Society,* III (1905–6), 121–37; Perry, *Papers,* 268–9, 287, 367; *Minutes and Letters of the Coetus of the German Reformed Congregations in Pennsylvania* (Philadelphia, 1903), 185–6.

21. Harbaugh, *Life of Schlatter,* 102.

22. Muhlenberg, *Journals,* I, 90, 109, 111–14.

23. Schwartz, "*A Mixed Multitude,*" 77; Joseph Levering, *A History of Bethlehem, Pennsylvania, 1741–1892.* (Bethlehem, Pa., 1903), 147, 210–13, 268–9, 416–19; Brother Lamech, *Chronicon Ephratense,* trans. J. Mack Hark (Lancaster, Pa., 1889), 45, 58–65, 83, 86–7, 139–40, 215–16, 239.

24. *Records of Presbyterian Church,* 398; Guy S. Klett, *Presbyterians in Colonial Pennsylvania* (Philadelphia, 1937), 160–1, 175–6; *Documentary History of the Evangelical Lutheran Ministerium of Pennsylvania and Adjacent States* (Philadelphia, 1898), 31; Charles H. Glatfelter, *Pastors and People: German Lutheran and Reformed Churches in the Pennsylvania Field, 1717–1793, Publications of The Pennsylvania German Society* XIII (Breinigsville, Pa., 1981), I, 222, 255.

25. Perry, *Papers,* 167; *Records of the Presbyterian Church,* 111, 115–16; *Votes of Assembly* III, 2482. Presbyterian ministers discussed throughout the eighteenth century whether the English and biblical rules on consanguinity and marriage should be observed.

26. Muhlenberg, *Journals,* I, 251; Perry, *Papers,* 245; Gottlieb Mittelberger, *Journey to Pennsylvania,* ed. Oscar Handlin and John Clive (Cambridge, Mass., 1960), 47–8.

27. Perry, *Papers,* 243, 245.

28. Glatfelter, *Pastors and People,* II, 321.

29. Muhlenberg, *Journals,* II, 678; Perry, *Papers,* 184, 273, 374.

30. Muhlenberg, *Journals,* II, 18–23.

31. Ibid. II, 273–4.

32. Ibid. II, 54–5, 102–3, 107, 123, 140.

33. Leonard R. Riforgiota, *Missionary of Moderation: Henry Melchoir Muhlenberg and the Lutheran Church in English America* (Lewisburg, 1980), 198.

34. Muhlenberg, *Journals,* II, 190–2.

35. Mitchell and Flanders, *Statutes at Large,* V, 640–2.

36. Muhlenberg, *Journals,* II, 257; Deborah Mathias Gough, "Pluralism, Politics, and Power Struggles: The Church of England in Colonial Philadelphia, 1695–1789," (Ph.D. diss., University of Pennsylvania, 1978), 424–5.

37. Hubertis Cummings, *Richard Peters: Provincial Secretary and Cleric* (Philadelphia, 1944); Joseph Fairbanks, Jr., "Richard Peters, Provincial Secretary of Pennsylvania," (Ph.D. diss., University of Pennsylvania, 1972).

38. Albert Frank Gegenheimer, *William Smith: Educator and Churchman* (Philadelphia, 1943); Horace W. Smith, *Life and Correspondence of Rev. William Smith, D.D.* (Philadelphia, 1879, reprinted 1972) is valuable chiefly for including many letters and documents.

39. Thomas Penn stressed that his policy was to treat all churches equally and that the college must be nondenominational. At times in England and when he appealed to the Presbyterian Synod for funds, William Smith agreed. Thomas Penn to Philadelphia Monthly Meeting, May 10, 1756, 295, and Thomas Penn to William Smith, Feb. 28, 1755, 61, Penn Papers, IV, Mss Historical Society of Pennsylvania; Perry, *Papers,* 574, 578.

40. Gough, "Pluralism," 399–416.

41. Perry, *Papers,* 389–91, 563, 570–1.

42. Ibid., 367, 411, 433.

43. Smith's Preface is reprinted in Horace Smith, *Life and Correspondence,* 110–18; Thomas Barton, *Unanimity and Public Spirit: a Sermon Preached at Carlisle* (Philadelphia, 1755), 2, 9, 10, 12.

44. Horace Smith, *Life and Correspondence,* 115, 117.

45. David Humphrey, *From King's College to Columbia, 1746–1800* (New York, 1976), 23–66; Donald F.M. Gerardi, "The King's College Controversy, 1753–1756 and the Ideological Roots of Toryism in New York," *Perspectives in American History* 11 (1977–8), 145–96; Perry, *Papers,* 570.

46. Guy Klett, *Presbyterians,* 35; Perry, *Papers,* 367–8.

47. Muhlenberg, *Journals,* II, 181, 295. The First Philadelphia Presbytery in April 1775 reported no positions available and suggested that candidates go elsewhere. There were vacancies elsewhere. First Philadelphia Presbytery, Minutes, 189, Presbyterian Historical Society. The Lutheran and Reformed remained dependent on immigrant clergy and continued to have shortages. Glatfelter, *Pastors and People* 148.

48. *Records of the Presbyterian Church,* 229.

49. See notes 21 and 22 in Chapter II for citations of the Tennent and John Smith tracts. Gilbert Tennent, *Sermons on Important Subjects: Adapted to the Perilous State of the British Nation* (Philadelphia, 1758), xxiv–xxv.

50. "Love of Country," Sermons, VI, #1, Alison Mss. Presbyterian Historical Society; Elizabeth Francis Ingersoll, "Francis Alison: American 'Philosophe,' 1705–1799," (Ph.D. diss., University of Delaware, 1974), 106–10.

51. Perry, *Papers,* 564; Franz, *Paxton,* 46.

52. Ingersoll, "Francis Alison," 122.

53. *An address to the Rev. Dr. Alison, the Rev. Mr. Ewing &c Being a Vindication of the Quakers* (Philadelphia, 1765),3, 5, 9, 17; James H. Hutson, *Pennsylvania Politics 1764–1770: The Movement for Royal Government and Its Consequences* (Princeton, N.J., 1972), 153–9, 162–8.

54. Ibid., 170–7; *Votes of Assembly,* VII, 5604–7.

55. Gilbert Tennent, *The Blessedness of Peace-Makers represented; and The Dangers of Persecution considered; In Two Sermons, on Mat. V.9 (Preach'd at Philadelphia ... in May, 1759, before the Reverend the Synod ...* (Philadelphia, 1765), 45. See also Chapter 7, 108–9.

56. Ibid., 20, 32.

57. Ibid., 32–3.
58. Ibid., 20, 32.
59. Ibid., 21–2.
60. Ibid., 23–5.
61. Ibid., 25, 27, 42.
62. Ibid., 35.
63. Ibid., 38.
64. Thomas B. Chandler, *An Appeal to the Public, in Behalf of the Church of England in America* (New York, 1767). Deborah M. Gough provided a detailed analysis of the bishop controversy in Pennsylvania. "Pluralism," 432–507. See also Frederick V. Mills, Sr., *Bishops by Ballot: An Eighteenth Century Ecclesiastical Revolution* (New York, 1978), 62–76.
65. Chandler, *Appeal to the Public* 4–8.
66. Ibid., 34–5.
67. Ibid., 31, 79.
68. Ibid., 76, 79, 108.
69. Ibid., 45, 115.
70. Ibid., 87–8, 104–5, 107.
71. Elizabeth I. Nybakken, ed., *The Centinel: Warning of a Revolution* (Newark, Del., 1980) reprints the Centinel, the Anti-Centinel, and the Remonstrance articles.
72. Nybakken, *Centinel,* 118–21.
73. Ibid., 124.
74. Ibid., 128.
75. Ibid., 112–13, 133–4, 161.
76. Ibid., 107, 149, 219.
77. Ibid., 85, 98–9.
78. Ibid., 92–5.
79. Ibid., 98–100.
80. Ibid., 95, 98, 134, 173.
81. The Anatomist articles were reprinted in *A Collection of Tracts from the late News Papers* (New York, 1768, 1769), II, Anatomist I, 12; X, 82. Smith tepidly endorsed the Pennsylvania pattern of church and state in a 1767 commencement address.
82. Anatomist IX, 78; XI, 87–93; XII, 94; XIV, 104; XV, 121.
83. Ibid., I, 12–13; V, 46; VIII, 74.
84. Joseph Priestley, *Remarks on Some Paragraphs in the Fourth Volume of Dr. Blackstone's Commentaries on the Laws of England Relating to the Dissenters* (Philadelphia, Robert Bell, 1772). Printed together were *Blackstone's Reply to Priestley's Remarks* and *Priestley's Answer to Blackstone's Reply* along with Furneaux's *Letter to the Honorable Mr. Justice Blackstone.* . . .
85. Curry, *First Freedoms,* 125–33, contains a perceptive account of the misleading rhetoric on "establishment" used by Anglicans and New Englanders during and after the bishop's controversy.
86. The 1757 militia act, which did not allow Catholics to serve, was an exception. *Minutes of the Provincial Council of Pennsylvania,* VI, 502, 534 for the assembly's relaxed response to the Catholic danger.
87. In a commencement address at the College of Philadelphia in 1767, William Smith defended the religious establishments in England and Scotland in which

those excluded from political office by religion suffered "no injustice" because all offices came by "Grace and Favor, not Right." A state founded and settled by members of one religion had the legal right to monopolize office. Pennsylvania was a successful experiment showing that persons of different denominations could share political power. William Smith, *Sermons,* IV, 141–3, Smith Mss., Microfilm Historical Society of Pennsylvania.

88. *Minutes of the Provincial Council of Pennsylvania, Colonial Records,* (Philadelphia, 1852), III, 546–7, 564; Schwartz, *"Mixed Multitude,"* 104, 152, 263.

89. Joseph L. Kirlin, *Catholicity in Philadelphia* (Philadelphia, 1909), 77; Mrs. C. R. Howard, "Extracts from the Diary of Daniel Fisher," *PMHB* 27(Oct. 1893): 274.

90. *Minutes of the Provincial Council, Colonial Records,* IX, 596; IV, 502, 534; "Governor Pownall's Reasons for Declining the Government of Pennsylvania, 1758," *PMHB* 13(1889): 444. *Votes of Assembly,* VII, 6295–6. Schwartz, *"Mixed Multitudes,"* 27–8, 97–8, 160–3, 249–50, discusses the colony's policy of naturalization.

91. Some historians argue that Franklin played a major role in creating an American pattern of church and state. This assertion rests on Franklin's persona in the *Autobiography* and in the letter to Ezra Stiles, composed while on his death bed, proclaiming a desire to support all denominations. Melvin Buxbaum demonstrated that early in his life Franklin developed an intense dislike for Calvinist churches and clergy, whom he associated with bigotry and theological abstruseness. On several occasions Franklin portrayed the Presbyterian clergy in a venomous manner. In 1747 Franklin asserted that Quaker pacifism endangered the state, but in 1755 he wrote the militia law guaranteeing the rights of conscientious objectors. In the "Parable against Persecution," written before 1755, Franklin advocated tolerance even for atheists. But in 1776, though personally opposed to religious tests for officeholding, he acquiesced to the clergy's demand for subscription to an oath declaring the divine origin of Old and New Testaments. He also identified Quaker pacifist opposition to the American Revolution with Toryism. The constant in Franklin's positions was a desire to promote a morality that would strengthen the society. Anson Stokes, *Church and State in the United States* (New York, 1950), 293–6; Melvin Buxbaum, *Benjamin Franklin and the Zealous Presbyterians,* 92–111, 200; *The Papers of Benjamin Franklin,* ed. Leonard Labaree (New Haven, 1963), VI, 126–8; Carl Van Doren, *Benjamin Franklin* (New York, 1938), 777.

Chapter IV. Religious Liberty in the Revolution

1. Richard Ryerson, "Portrait of a Colonial Oligarchy: The Quaker Elite in the Pennsylvania Assembly, 1729–1776," in *Power and Status: Essays on Officeholding in the American Colonies,* ed. Bruce Daniels (Middletown, Conn., 1986), 106–14; Schwartz, *"Mixed Multitude,"* 222, cites contemporary opinion on the dominance of Friends in the assembly.

2. Roland Bauman, *For the Reputation of Truth* (Baltimore, Md., 1974) devotes much space to the different styles of Quaker leadership.

3. Benjamin Newcomb, *Franklin and Galloway, A Political Partnership* (New

Haven, Conn., 1972); John Ferling, *The Loyalist Mind: Joseph Galloway and the American Revolution* (University Park, Pa., 1977). Jack Marietta found Galloway's name in the 1760 census of Philadelphia Friends, and there is no record of his disownment.

4.   David L. Jacobsen, *John Dickinson and the Revolution in Pennsylvania, 1764–1776* (Berkeley, Calif., 1964).

5.   In 1730 the Presbyterian Synod had 15 or 16 congregations in Pennsylvania, and in 1776 about 112. Glatfelter, *Pastors and People,* II, 148.

6.   Martha Lou Lemmon Stohlman, *John Witherspoon* (Philadelphia, 1976), Chps. 4–6.

7.   In Chester County, of the 14 delegates to the 1776 convention, 6 were disowned Quakers, 2 were Anglicans, 2 Presbyterians, and 2 Baptists. Rosemary Warden, "The Revolution in Political Leadership in Chester County, Pennsylvania, 1765–1785," (Ph.D. diss., Syracuse, N.Y., 1979), 97; Burton Konkle, *George Bryan and the Constitution of Pennsylvania* (Philadelphia, 1922).

8.   Richard Ryerson, *The Revolution Is Now Begun: The Radical Committee of Philadelphia 1765–1776* (Philadelphia, 1978) is the standard account of the politics of Philadelphia and shows the influence of, as well as the difficulties of explaining, politics on religious grounds. David Hawke, *In the Midst of the Revolution* (Philadelphia, 1958) provides a more general account of events.

9.   In 1748 there were 110 Reformed and Lutheran congregations in Pennsylvania, and in 1776, 249. Glatfelter, *Pastors and People,* II, 145–6, 201–2, 249.

10.   *Minutes of the Coetus of Reformed German Congregations in America* (Philadelphia, 1903); *Reports of the United German Evangelical Lutheran Congregations in North America, Especially in Pennsylvania,* trans. C. W. Schaeffer (Reading, Pa., 1882), I.

11.   Julian Boyd, *Anglo-American Union, Joseph Galloway's Plans to Preserve the British Empire, 1774–1788* (Philadelphia, 1941); Arthur Mekeel, *The Relation of the Quakers to the American Revolution* (Washington, D.C., 1979),84–96.

12.   *Votes of Assembly,* VIII, 7327–30, 7334–7.

13.   Ibid., 7348–50; C. Henry Smith, *Mennonite Immigration to Pennsylvania in the Eighteenth Century, Pennsylvania German Society Proceedings,* (Norristown, Pa., 1929), XXV, 285–7.

14.   *Votes of Assembly,* VIII, 7337–43.

15.   Mitchell and Flanders, *Statutes at Large,* VIII, 511–15, 539, 541, 544, IX, 77, 168. In 1776 the clergy were exempted from provisions of the militia acts. I am indebted to Billy Smith for the information on wages.

16.   In July 1775 the Lutheran and Reformed ministers refused to publish an exhortation to the Germans "to warn them to be watchful because their privileges and liberties are in danger," though a letter was published by the German Society and church council of the two denominations. Glatfelter, *Pastors and People,* II, 363. That same summer Witherspoon wrote a letter to the Presbyterian clergy of New Jersey advocating resistance.

17.   *Records of the Presbyterian Church,* 467–9.

18.   Meeting for Sufferings, Minutes, II, 53–9; Mekeel, *Relation,* 137–40; Jack Marietta, *The Reformation of American Quakerism 1748–1783* (Philadelphia, 1984), 222–5.

19.   Smith served as a member of the Committee of Correspondence in 1774. William Smith, *Works,* Sermon V (1775), 123; Gegenheimer, *William Smith,* 160–81; Perry, *Papers,* 474, 477–80, 483–7.

20.   Henry M. Muhlenberg, *Journals of Henry Melchior Muhlenberg,* 3 vols., ed. Theodore G. Tappert and John W. Doberstein (Philadelphia 1942, 1945, 1948), III, 160–1. Barton had also served as a member of a Committee of Correspondence.

21.   Ibid. II, 700–1.

22.   Ibid. II, 700, III, 99.

23.   Ibid. III, 125.

24.   Ibid., 75–6.

25.   Ibid., 103.

26.   Ibid., 125–6.

27.   Ibid., 55, 125, 158–9; Glatfelter, *Pastors and People,* II, 406–44.

28.   Muhlenberg, *Journals,* III, 56, 102–04, 587.

29.   *Constitutions of Pennsylvania, Constitution of the United States,* ed. Robert A. Weinert (Harrisburg, Pa., 1964), 239–40.

30.   Ibid., 246. Muhlenberg, *Journals,* II, 740–2.

31.   Kenneth G. Hamilton, *John Ettwein and the Moravian Church During the Revolution Period* (Bethlehem, Pa., 1940), 161–2, 345.

32.   Weinert, *Constitutions,* 241, 243.

33.   *The Proceedings Relative to Calling the Conventions of 1776 and 1790. The Minutes of the Convention that Formed the Present Constitution of Pennsylvania,* (Harrisburg, 1825), 53, 117–23; William Smith, *An Address to the General Assembly of Pennsylvania, in the Case of the Violated Charter* (Philadelphia, 1788). Franklin College was established with 40 trustees: 14 Lutheran, 14 Calvinists, and 12 from other denominations including the Roman Catholic priest of Lancaster. Muhlenberg, *Journals,* III, 247, 725; Mitchell and Flanders, *Statutes at Large,* IX, 175–6; William Smith, *An Address to the General Assembly of Pennsylvania, in the case of the violated Charter* (Philadelphia, 1788).

34.   Weinert, *Constitutions,* 256; Muhlenberg, *Journals,* III, 551; Mitchell and Flanders, *Statutes at Large,* X, 24–5.

35.   Anne M. Ousterhout, *A State Divided: Opposition in Pennsylvania to the American Revolution* (Westport, Conn., 1987), 2–3, finds the term "disaffected" more accurate than either Loyalist or Tory and argues that "prevailing conditions in Pennsylvania" rather than loyalty to Great Britain after 1776 determined actions. The disaffected pacifists were a "sizeable minority" but no accurate tabulations of the total number are possible.

36.   Philadelphia Yearly Meeting, Minutes, III, 356–62; Mekeel, *Relation of Quakers,* 162–4.

37.   Marietta, *Reformation,* 222–48.

38.   Mitchell and Flanders, *Statutes at Large,* IX, 109–12; Mekeel, *Relation of Quakers,* 173–184; Thomas Gilpin, *Exiles in Virginia* (Philadelphia, 1848).

39.   Mitchell and Flanders, *Statutes at Large,* IX, 304–5, 405–6.

40.   Mekeel, *Relation of Quakers,* 200–2.

41.   Charles Wetherill, *History of the Religious Society of Friends called by Some the Free Quakers* (Philadelphia, 1894).

42.   Mitchell and Flanders, *Statutes at Large,* IX, 111–13, 305. There were several forms of the test oaths. For a discussion see Ousterhout, *State Divided,* 191–4; Benjamin Rush, *Considerations on the Present Test Act* (Philadelphia, 1784), 1, 11, 15, defends colonial Quaker Pennsylvania's record of toleration and contrasts it with the results of the test acts. Rush attacked the test acts as opposed to political freedom and religious freedom.

43.   J. Taylor Hamilton, "The Recognition of the Unitas Fratrum as an Old Episcopal Church by the Parliament of Great Britain in 1749," *Transactions of Moravian Historical Society,* (Bethlehem, Pa., 1925), 1–27.

44.   "The Town Regulations of Lititz, Pa., 1912," *Pennsylvania German Society Proceedings* (1912), I, 731–5; Joseph Levering, *A History of Bethlehem, Pennsylvania* (Bethlehem, Pa., 1903), 44–5, 147, 181, 210–13, 266–9, 417–19.

45.   Hamilton, *John Ettwein,* Part II, 168–71, 174–8.

46.   Ibid., 240–1. During the French and Indian War, the Moravian definition of pacifism had allowed for watches and drills for self defense but no active fighting against Indians. Levering, *Bethlehem,* 321; John W. Jordan, "Bishop Augustus Gottleib Spangenberg," *PMHB* 8(1884): 236–8.

47.   Hamilton, *John Ettwein,* II, 191.

48.   Ibid., 197–202.

49.   Ibid., 179, 194, 212–13, 220.

50.   Ibid., 178, 181–3, 206–9, 222–3.

51.   Richard McMaster, *Land, Piety, Peoplehood: The Establishment of Mennonite Communities in America 1683–1790* (Scottsdale, Pa., 1985), 249–87.

52.   Arthur Young, "Treatment of Loyalists in Pennsylvania," (Ph.D. diss., Johns Hopkins, 1955), 399, Appendix X; Ousterhout, *State Divided,* 304–15.

53.   In 1764 Muhlenberg fumed that on Sunday "grown and half-grown boys were gathering in large crowds, stripped naked on the banks, and bathing in the river, thus giving great offense. . . ." Muhlenberg, *Journals,* II, 89.

54.   Levering, *Bethlehem,* 130–2, 150; Kenneth Hamilton, ed., *Bethlehem Diary* (Bethlehem, Pa., 1971), 16–17. *Votes of Assembly,* I, 569.

55.   Asa Earl Martin, "Lotteries in Pennsylvania Prior to 1833," *PMHB,* 47(1923): 310–19; Mitchell and Flanders, *Statutes at Large,* V, 445–8.

56.   Mitchell and Flanders, *Statutes at Large,* V, 720–2.

57.   Ibid., 184–6. The preamble was the same in both antilottery laws.

58.   *Votes of Assembly,* VI, 5197, 5223, 5332; VII, 5722, 5895, 5972, 6302, 6306, 6377, 6352.

59.   William Dye, "Pennsylvania versus the Theatre," *PMHB,* 55(1931): 339–50.

60.   *Votes of Assembly* VI, 4993, 4995; *Records of Presbyterian Church,* 293; *PMHB* 23(1899):268.

61.   J. Thomas Jable, "The Pennsylvania Sunday Blue Laws of 1779: A View of Pennsylvania Society and Politics," *Pennsylvania History* 40(Oct., 1973):420.

62.   Mitchell and Flanders, *Statutes at Large,* VIII, 544–5.

63.   Ibid. X, 315.

64.   Ibid. IX, 333–8; Jable, "Blue Laws," 423–5.

65.   Mitchell and Flanders, *Statutes at Large,* IX, 55–58, 311.

66.   Ibid., IX, 297–300, 414–17; X, 175.

67.   Dye, "Pennsylvania versus the Theatre," 359–68. The repeal was not for all plays, but allowed only those "capable of advancing morality and virtue and polishing the manners and habits of society, and it being contrary to the principles of a free government to deprive any of its citizens of a rational and innocent entertainment, which at the same time that it affords a necessary relaxation from the fatigues of business is calculated to inform the mind and improve the heart." Only theatrical representations that improved morals and manners were to be licensed. Mitchell and Flanders, *Statutes at Large,* XIII, 184–6.

68.   Owen Ireland, "The Crux of Politics: Religion and Party in Pennsylvania, 1778–1779," *WMQ* (Oct., 1985): 453–75; idem, "The Ethnic-Religious Dimension of Pennsylvania Politics, 1778–1779," *WMQ* 30(1973): 423–48; Wayne Bockelman and Owen Ireland, "The Internal Revolution in Pennsylvania: An Ethnic-Religious Interpretation," *Pennsylvania History* 41(1974): 125–59. Rosemary Warden, "Revolution in Political Leadership," (Ph.D. diss., Syracuse University, 1979, University Microfilms, Ann Arbor, Mich., 1986), 190–4.

Chapter V. Religious Liberty and the Republic

1.   Robert L. Brunhouse, *The Counter-Revolution in Pennsylvania, 1776–1790* (Harrisburg, 1942), 191–227. The new constitution abolished a unicameral legislature, ended the council of censors, and created a house and senate. The governor gained a veto power and extensive power over appointments, and the judiciary became more independent of the assembly. There were more checks and balances upon the assembly than under the 1776 constitution.

2.   Edwin Wolf 2nd and Maxwell Whiteman, *History of the Jews of Philadelphia from Colonial Times to the Age of Jackson* (Philadelphia, 1957), 82, 147–52.

3.   *The Proceedings Relative to the Calling the Conventions of 1776 and 1790. The Minutes of the Convention that Formed the Present Constitution* (Harrisburg, 1825), 216–18, 376.

4.   Ibid., 144, 195–6, 271, 274.

5.   Weinert, *Constitutions,* 212.

6.   *Purdon's Pennsylvania Statutes Annotated. Constitutions,* Articles 1 and 2 (Philadelphia, 1969), 227–34.

7.   Leonard Levy, *The Establishment Clause and the First Amendment* (New York, 1986), 84, 94, 96.

8.   *American State Papers Bearing on Sunday Legislation,* ed. William Addison Blakely, revised by Willard Allen Colcord (1911, reissued New York, 1970), 149.

9.   Weinert, *Constitutions,* 11. The 1911 constitution dropped the mention of God in the preamble. Whatever secularity that action meant did not apply to the assembly that shortly thereafter made Bible reading in schools mandatory.

10.   Mitchell and Flanders, *Statutes at Large,* X, 1779, 323–38; XII, 1786, 313–22.

11.   Ibid. XV, 1794, 110–18.

12.   Ibid. XVI, 1798, 106–8; *Acts of General Assembly of the Commonwealth of Pennsylvania,* 1816, 329; 1831, 134; 1835, 336.

13.   *Acts of General Assembly,* 1838, 525.

14.   James Wilson, "Lectures on Law," *The Works of James Wilson,* ed. James Dewitt Andrews (Chicago, 1896), I, 92–3, 99. For a general discussion of Wil-

son's views on law, see Page Smith, *James Wilson: Founding Father, 1742–1798* (North Carolina, 1950), 308–41; Geoffrey Seed, *James Wilson* (New York, 1978), 86–140.

15. Wilson, *Works,* 103–5, 125.

16. Ibid., 112–13.

17. Ibid., 121.

18. Ibid., 122–3.

19. There are no modern biographies of William White and Samuel Stanhope Smith, but essential details can be found in the *Dictionary of American Biography,* ed. Allen Johnson and Dumas Malone (New York, 1930–6), IX, 344–5; X, 121–2.

20. Jacob Cooke, *Tench Coxe and the Early Republic* (Chapel Hill, N.C., 1978).

21. David Hawke, *Benjamin Rush: Revolutionary Gadfly* (Indianapolis, Ind., 1971); *The Autobiography of Benjamin Rush,* ed. George W. Curran (Princeton, N.J., 1948).

22. Eric Foner, *Tom Paine and Revolutionary America* (New York, 1976).

23. I suspect, but cannot prove, that there was always a group in Pennsylvania who supported Thomas Paine and Joseph Priestly and opposed the sympathetic relationship between the state and the institutional church. Albert Post, *Popular Free Thought in America, 1825–1850* (New York, 1943), 24; Elizabeth M. Griffin, *Philadelphia Unitarianism, 1796–1861* (Philadelphia, 1961), 31–60.

24. William White, *A Sermon on the Reciprocal Influence of Civil Policy and Religious Duty* (Philadelphia, 1793), 13–14.

25. Samuel Stanhope Smith, *The Lectures Corrected and Improved* (Trenton, 1812), 227–8. Parts of this work were written in 1794–5.

26. Donald J. D'Elia, "The Republican Theology of Benjamin Rush," *Pennsylvania History* 33(April, 1966): 189–203.

27. Tench Coxe, "An Enquiry into the National Character of the People of the United States of America," *Democratic Press,* IX, Oct. 28, 1809.

28. William White, *A Sermon, Delivered in Christ Church, on the 21st Day of June, 1786, At the Opening of the Convention of the Protestant Episcopal Church* (Philadelphia, 1786), 5.

29. White, *A Sermon on the Duty of Civil Obedience as Required in Scripture* (Philadelphia, 1799), 5–6, 20–1.

30. Samuel Smith, *Lectures Corrected,* 227–8. The Library Company of Philadelphia owns Benjamin Rush's copy of this book.

31. White, *Sermon on Reciprocal Influence,* 13–14, 17. White carefully did not criticize the establishments of religion in New England. The state was to "aid" religion, but the manner of the aid should be left to the communities, 18.

32. D'Elia, "Republican Theology," 187; Curran, *Autobiography of Benjamin Rush,* 339–40.

33. Samuel Stanhope Smith, *Divine Goodness to the United States of America* (Philadelphia, 1795). I used the London, 1795 edition, 27.

34. Coxe, "An Enquiry," VI, Oct. 21, 1809; VII, Oct. 24, 1809.

35. Samuel Smith, *Divine Goodness,* 25, 28.

36. *Jefferson's Extracts from the Gospels, The Papers of Thomas Jefferson,* 2d Series, ed. Dickinson W. Adams (Princeton, New Jersey, 1983), 317–24, 331.

37. Benjamin Rush, *Considerations on the Present Test-Law* (Philadelphia, 1784), 20.

38. Coxe, "An Enquiry," IX, Oct. 28, 1809.

39. Ibid. VII, Oct. 24, 1809.

40. Thomas Paine, *The Age of Reason* I, *Writings of Thomas Paine*, VI, ed. D. W. Wheeler (New York, 1908), 275; Foner, *Tom Paine*, 245–9.

41. Paine, *Writings*, VII, 61, 70, 137–8.

42. Ibid. VII, 18.

43. Ibid. VI, 30, 87.

44. George Washington, "Farewell Address," reprinted in Noble E. Cunningham, ed., *The Early Republic* (New York, 1968), 52–53.

Chapter VI. Politicians Debate Religious Liberty

1. William Loughton Smith, *The Pretensions of Thomas Jefferson to the Presidence Examined; And the Charges against John Adams Refuted* (Philadelphia, 1796), 36–7.

2. *To the Electors of Pennsylvania. Take your Choice! Thomas McKean or James Ross* (Philadelphia, 1799); "Franklin," *To the Citizen of the County of Philadelphia* (Philadelphia, 1799); Roberdeau Buchanan, *Life of Hon. Thomas McKean, L.L.D.* (Lancaster, Pa., 1790); Jacob Cooke, *Tench Coxe and the Early Republic*, 349–61; Harry Tinkcom, *Republicans and Federalists in Pennsylvania, 1790–1801* (Harrisburg, Pa., 1950); Richard G. Miller, *Philadelphia: the Federalist City* (Port Washington, New York, 1976). Most of the secondary literature on politics ignores the religious freedom debate. Exceptions are Gary Nash, "American Clergy and the French Revolution," *WMQ*, 3d Series, 22(July, 1965): 392–412, and Charles O. Lerche, Jr., "Jefferson and the Election of 1800: A Case Study in the Political Smear," *WMQ*, 3d Series, 5(1948):470, 472–5.

3. *Diary and Autobiography of John Adams*, L. H. Butterfield, ed., *The Adams Papers* (New York, 1964), I, 8, 14, 22.

4. A good bibliography and the best survey of Jefferson's religious beliefs is in Eugene Sheridan, "Introduction," in Dickinson W. Adams, *Jefferson's Extracts from the Gospels*, 3–42.

5. Thomas Jefferson, *Notes on the State of Virginia* (Philadelphia, 1801), 312.

6. John Mitchell Mason, *The Voice of Warning to Christians on the Ensuing Election of a President of the United States* (New York, 1800), 19.

7. Robert Hall, *Modern Infidelity, Considered with Respect to Influence on Society, in a Sermon* (Philadelphia, 1800), 22–6, 38–41. Hall, a Baptist, made no direct reference to Jefferson but his anti-French and anti-Republican tone was clear.

8. Mason, *Voice of Warning*, 7–8, 30–6.

9. Ibid., 34; William Linn, *Serious Considerations on the Election of a President* (New York, 1800), 24–8, 32.

10. Dickinson N. Adams, *Jefferson's Extracts From the Gospels*, 11.

11. *Aurora*, Aug. 27, 1800.

12. Ibid. June 27, 1800. On October 14, 1800 the *Aurora* described Jefferson as a churchgoer.

13. Ibid. Feb. 22, March 31, Aug. 27, 1800.

14. *To the Republican Citizens of the State of Pennsylvania, Lancaster,* Sept. 17, 1800, 5, 13. This pamphlet was signed by the most prominent Republican politicians in Pennsylvania. *Aurora,* March 31, Sept. 18, 1800.

15. *Aurora,* Feb. 22, Sept. 1, 1800.

16. Ibid. April 9, Sept. 6, 1800; *To the Republican Citizens,* 13; *To the Friends of Freedom and Public Faith* (Philadelphia, 1799) pictured Penn as offering a haven to immigrants.

17. *Aurora,* Aug. 11, 18, Sept. 22, Oct. 17, 1800.

18. Frost, "William Penn's Experiment in the Wilderness," 588–9, 605.

19. *To the Republican Citizens,* 6; *Aurora,* Aug. 18, Sept. 6, 1800. The *Aurora* had a variety of names: *The Philadelphia Aurora, Aurora, For the Country,* and *Aurora, General Advertiser.* William Duane succeeded Benjamin Franklin Bache as editor in 1798 and vigorously supported the Jeffersonian Republicans.

20. *Aurora,* Aug. 7, Aug. 18, 1800.

21. One author drew a careful distinction between Presbyterians and Congregationalists. Another said the laity were unaware of what a few Presbyterian clergy were doing. *Aurora,* July 31, Aug. 23, Oct. 17, 1800.

22. Ibid. April 21, Oct. 17, 1800.

23. Ibid. June 27, 1800.

24. Ibid. April 8, 9, 1800.

25. Ibid. Aug. 11, 1800.

26. Ibid. Sept. 1, 1800; *Philadelphia Gazette,* Aug. 30, 1800. Abercrombie's "fast day" sermon had previously provoked the *Aurora.*

27. *Aurora,* Sept. 1, 1800.

28. Ibid. Aug. 31, 1800.

29. John Cozens Ogden, *A View of the New England Illuminati* (Philadelphia, 1799); idem, *A Sermon Upon Peace, Charity, and Toleration Delivered in St. Paul's Church, in Philadelphia...* Feb. 23, 1800. (Philadelphia, 1800). Ogden dedicated his sermon to John Adams, showing that for him the Illuminati were not a partisan issue.

30. *Aurora,* March 1, 31, April 17, June 30, July 31, Aug. 23, 1800.

31. Ibid. Feb. 22, 1800.

32. Ibid. July 8, July 9, 1800.

33. Ibid. July 7, 11, 25, 30, 1800.

34. Ibid. July 19, 30, Aug. 4, 1800.

35. Blakely, *American State Papers,* 202; Levy, *Establishment Clause,* 94–107. Robert S. Alley, ed., *James Madison on Religious Liberty* (Buffalo, N.Y., 1985), 35–94.

36. Blakely, *American State Papers,* 174.

37. Ibid., 201–2; Levy, *Establishment Clause,* 96–100.

38. Blakely, *American State Papers,* 158–9.

39. Ibid., 121–3, 243.

40. Dickinson W. Adams, *Jefferson's Extracts from the Gospels,* 36.

41. Blakely, *American State Papers,* 136–7.

42. Sheridan, "Introduction," in Dickinson W. Adams, *Jefferson's Extracts,* 13.

43. Blakely, *American State Papers,* 174, 205; Madison in 1823 referred to the

"consummation" of the divorce between religion and law in Pennsylvania. Jefferson called Pennsylvania the "cradle of toleration and freedom of religion." *The Writings of Thomas Jefferson,* ed. A. W. Lipscomb and A. E. Bergh (Washington, D.C., 1905), XIV, 129.

44. William L. Smith, *Pretensions of Thomas Jefferson,* quoted from Jefferson's second inaugural.

45. Jefferson once claimed he never received a Quaker's vote. Lipscomb and Bergh, *Writings,* XII, 346. This statement was an exaggeration. See the contrary sentiment expressed by Miers Fisher in 1798. Harry Tinkcom, *Republicans and Federalists,* 173. I am grateful to Edwin Bronner for calling attention to Fisher's statement.

46. Foner, *Tom Paine,* 254–63.

47. Sanford Higginbotham, *Keystone in the Democratic Arch: Pennsylvania Politics 1800–1816* (Harrisburg, 1952); Philip Klein, *Pennsylvania Politics 1817–1832* (Philadelphia, 1940); Raymond Walters, *Alexander James Dallas* (Philadelphia, 1942); Charles Snyder, *Jacksonian Heritage: Pennsylvania Politics, 1833–1848* (Harrisburg, Pa., 1958).

48. John Coleman, *Thomas McKean* (N.J., 1975).

49. Glatfelter, *Pastors and People* II, 125.

50. *Dictionary of American Biography,* ed. Allen Johnson and Dumas Malone (New York, 1930), VII, 309–12.

51. *Aurora,* Jan. 9, 1821. The Quids in 1805 termed Duane an "enemy of religion."

52. *Franklin Gazette,* Nov. 17, 18, 1818; *Democratic Press,* Nov. 20, 1818. "William Penn," writing in the *Gazette,* thought the issue involved the factions in the Democratic-Republican party, because Binns had supported Governor Snyder's similar proclamation in 1813.

53. *Franklin Gazette,* Nov. 17, 1818; There was no follow-up mention as to the content of the meeting.

54. Edwin Bronner, *Thomas Earle as a Reformer* (Philadelphia, 1948).

55. *Mechanics Free Press,* April 26, May 10, June 4, 1828; Oct. 10, 1829; Feb. 3, July 31, 1830; Feb. 5, April 2, 1831. The official name was *The Philadelphia Times, Mechanic's Free Press and Working Men's Register.*

56. Ibid. May 10, July 26, Nov. 22, Dec. 20, 1828; Feb. 27, April 24, 1830; Feb. 5, 1831.

57. Ibid. April 2, 1831.

58. *Temple of Reason* (1836), "To the Reader," 22, 57.

59. Ibid., 68, 93, 130–1, 135, 158–9, 165, 175.

60. Larry Ingle, *Quakers in Conflict: the Hicksite Reformation* (Knoxville, Tenn., 1986), 61.

61. *Delaware Free Press,* 1832, 42, 43, 46, 61, 70. The paper was published from 1830–3.

62. Ibid. Oct. 2, 1831, 28.

63. Ibid. Jan. 21, 1832, 30.

64. *Priestcraft Unmasked* published in New York and Philadelphia, 1830; Justus E. Moore, *The Warning of Thomas Jefferson; or a Brief Exposition of the Dangers to be Apprehended to our Civil and Religious Liberties from Presbyterians*

(Philadelphia, 1844); Abel C. Thomas, *Strictures on Religious Tests, with Special References to the Late Reform Convention* (Philadelphia, 1838); William Heighton, *An Address to the Members of the Trade Societies* (Philadelphia, 1827).

65. Edwin Wilbur Rice, *The Sunday School Movement, 1780–1917, and the American Sunday School Union 1817–1917* (Philadelphia, 1917).

66. David Brion Davis, "Some Themes of Counter-Subversion: An Analysis of Anti-Masonic, Anti-Catholic, and Anti-Mormon Literature," *Mississippi Valley Historical Review* 48(Sept., 1960): 205–24.

67. Philip Klein, *Pennsylvania Politics 1817–1832.*

68. There is no good history of the Presbyterian Church, U.S.A. in Pennsylvania in the period. I have relied on *Minutes of the General Assembly* and *The Christian Advocate.*

69. Methodist, *Christian Advocate* (New York 3/28/1828) II, 82; *Journal of the Proceedings of the . . . Convention of the Protestant Episcopal Church* (Philadelphia, 1840, 1850) vol. 56, 19; vol. 60, 29; *Letter to the Rt. Rev. Alonzo Potter, D.D. . . . In Vindication of the Principle of Christian Union for the Propagation of the Gospel* (Philadelphia, 1850), 19, 24–5. 34.

70. *Journal of the Thirty-Fifth House of Representatives* (Harrisburg, Pa., 1824–5) II, 55–6.

71. Ezra Stiles Ely, *The Duty of Christian Freeman to Elect Christian Rulers* (Philadelphia, 1828), 5, 7–8.

72. Ibid., 5, 9.

73. Ibid., 8–10.

74. Ibid., 10–11.

75. Ibid., Appendix, 19.

76. Ibid., 20.

77. Ibid., 22. Prints the debate as extracted from "The Harrisburg Chronicle," *Democratic Press* Feb. 13, 1828; *Paulson's American Daily Advertiser,* Feb. 19, 1828; Ely, *The Duty of Christian Freedmen,* 19–20, reprints the speech of General Duncan.

78. *Journal of the Thirty-Seventh House of Representatives of the Commonwealth of Pennsylvania* (Harrisburg, Pa., 1827), 18, 328; *Journal of the Thirty-Eighth House of Representatives of the Commonwealth of Pennsylvania* (Harrisburg, Pa., 1828), 80, 153, 166, 357; *Journal of the Thirty-Eighth Senate of the Commonwealth of Pennsylvania* (Harrisburg, Pa., 1828), 287.

79. Martin introduced nine negative petitions on one day. *Journal of the Thirty-Eighth Senate,* 77; *Journal of the Thirty-Eighth House,* 178, 191, 209, 216, 224, 316, 329, 323, 338, 345, 351, 366, 395, 436.

80. Samuel Hazard, ed., *Register of Pennsylvania* (Philadelphia, 1828), I, 77. In 1845, without any controversy, the state incorporated the American Sunday School Union. *Laws of Pennsylvania of the Session of 1845,* 454–5.

81. *Proceedings and Debates of the Convention of the Commonwealth of Pennsylvania to propose Amendments to the Constitution* (Harrisburg, Pa., 1837–9), V, 317–31.

82. Ibid., 318–19.

83. Ibid., 323, 325–6.

84. Ibid., 320–2. In Philadelphia there was another bitter debate on the subject.

The convention, by a 57 to 33 vote, decided not to pay the clergy. The Philadelphia clergy had already indicated they did not wish to be paid.
85. Ibid. I, 12.
86. Ibid. VII, 139–44.
87. *Journal of the Senate,* 2 vols. (Harrisburg, 1835–6) II, 559–60 records a
debate over whether a person of unorthodox belief in hell could testify.
88. *Proceedings and Debates of the Convention,* VII, 139–44.
89. *Journal of the Fifty-First House of Representatives of the Commonwealth
of Pennsylvania* (Harrisburg, Pa., 1841), 453–4.
90. Ibid., 501.

Chapter VII. The Churches and Religious Liberty

1. MacMaster, *Land, Piety, Peoplehood,* 279.
2. Lyman H. Butterfield, "Elder John Leland, Jeffersonian Itinerant," *Proceedings
of the American Antiquarian Society,* 62(Oct., 1952):155–242; Robert Turbet, *A
Social History of the Philadelphia Baptist Association* (Philadelphia, 1944), 51–
3; William McLoughlin, *Isaac Backus: On Church, State and Calvinism* (Cambridge, Mass., 1968); idem, *New England Dissent,* (Cambridge, Mass., 1971) 2
vols.
3. Thomas Coke, *Four Duties of the Gospel Ministry* (Philadelphia, 1796), 18,
34; Doris Andrews, "Popular Religion and the Revolution in the Middle Atlantic
Ports: The Rise of the Methodists, 1770–1800" (Ph.D. diss., University of Pennsylvania, 1986), 152–5.
4. Thomas Coke and Francis Asbury, *The Doctrine and Discipline of the Methodist Episcopal Church in America,* ed. Frederick A. Norwood (Rutland, Vt., 1798,
reprinted 1979), 102–3, 171. There was also a strong antislavery section.
5. *A Confession of Faith, Put Forth By the Elders and Brethren of Many Congregations of Christians* (9th ed., Philadelphia, 1798), 31–6. This Confession, written in London, was adopted by Baptist meeting in Philadelphia in 1742, and first
printed with additions in 1743 and 1798.
6. Fred J. Hood, *Reformed America: The Middle and Southern States, 1783–
1837* (University: University of Alabama, 1980), 52–3.
7. Glatfelter, *Pastors and People,* II, 458; Paul Boller, Jr., *George Washington
and Religion* (Dallas, Tex., 1963), 163–94, reprints Washington's responses to
the churches. Someone should print the various churches' addresses.
8. Presbyterian Church of the United States of America, *Acts of the General
Assembly,* 1789, 4–6; Glatfelter, *Pastors and People,* II, 458.
9. Philadelphia Yearly Meeting, Minutes, 1789, 161–5. Microfilm, Friends Historical Library, Swarthmore College.
10. *Journal of the House of Representatives: George Washington Administration 1789–1791, 2nd Congress, 1st Session 1791–1792* (Wilmington, Del.,
1977), vol. 4, 36–7, 50–1, 62; *The Congressional Journals of the United States,*
Part I of the *National State Papers of the United States* Series, 1789–1817, vol. 2,
First Congress, Second Session (1790), 33–5, 47, 58–9, 60–2; vol. 3, First Congress, Third Session (1790–1), 15, 19–20, 47; Thomas Drake, *Quakers and Slav-*

ery (New Haven, 1950); *Rules of Discipline and Christian Advices of the Yearly Meeting of Friends for Pennsylvania and New Jersey* (Philadelphia, 1797), 32.

11. *Address of the Board of Managers of the American Protestant Association* (Philadelphia, 1843), 48; *Acts and Proceedings of the Coetus and Synod of the German Reformed Church in the United States from 1791 to 1816,* (Chambersburg, Pa., 1854, reprinted 1930), 3; Anson Stokes, *Church and State in the United States* (New York, 1950), I, 471–3.

12. *Acts and Proceedings,* 63; *Documentary History of the Evangelical Lutheran Ministerium of Pennsylvania and Adjacent States. Proceedings of the Annual Conventions from 1748–1821* (Philadelphia, 1898), 456–7.

13. *Acts and Proceedings,* 19; *Documentary History,* 283–6.

14. Robert Smith, *Detection Detected* (Lancaster, Pa., 1757) 25, 29, 34–5; James Brown Scouller, *A Manual of the United Presbyterian Church of North America,* (Harrisburg, Pa., 1881), 25, 37–8, 338.

15. Alexander Gellatly, *Some Observations upon a late Piece entitled The Detection Detected, or a Vindication* (Germantown, Pa., 1758); Robert Smith, *Detection Detected;* Samuel Delap, *Remarks on Some Articles of the Seceders New Covenant, and their Act of Presbytery Making it the term of Ministerial and Christian Communion,* (Belfast, reprinted Lancaster, 1754).

16. Gilbert Tennent, *The Blessedness of Peace-Makers represented; and the Danger of Persecution considered: In two Sermons, On Mat. v. 9 . . . Preached . . . May, 1759* (Philadelphia, 1765), 44–6.

17. [Robert Annan], *Exposition or Defense of the Westminster Assembly's Confession of Faith, Being the Draught of an "Overture" Prepared by a Committee of the Associate Reformed Synod, in 1783* (Cincinnati, Ohio, 1855), 197–202.

18. Robert Annan, *Brief Animadversions on the Doctrine of Universal Salvation . . . To which is added, The Connexion (sic) between Civil Government and Religion* (Philadelphia, 1787), 37.

19. Ibid., 38–9, 41, 47.

20. Ibid., 40–1.

21. Ibid., 37, 44, 49.

22. Ibid., 45–6.

23. Joseph Wilson, *Presbyterian Historical Almanac & Annual Remembrancer of the Church* (Philadelphia, 1860), vol. II, 177–8.

24. Samuel Wylie, *The Two Sons of Oil; or, The Faithful Witness For Magistracy & Ministry Upon a Scriptural Basis. Also, A Sermon on Coventry* (Greenburg, Pa., 1803), 39, 44.

25. Ibid., 40–1.

26. Ibid., 52–7.

27. Ibid., 51.

28. *No Union of Church and State; or A Letter to the Rev. James R. Wilson* (Albany, N.Y., 1832), 11.

29. Joseph Cooper, *The True Issue, or The Confession of Faith and the Associate Testimony, In Reference to the Civil Magistrate's Power in Matters of Religion Compared* (Philadelphia, 1845), 6.

30. Gilbert MacMaster, *The Moral Character of Civil Government* (Albany, N.Y., 1832), 16–17.

31. Ibid., 65.

32. Ibid., 26–8.

33. Ibid., 27.

34. J. H. McIlvaine, *A Nation's Right to Worship God. An Address Before the American Whig and Cliosophic Societies of the College of New Jersey* (Trenton, N.J., 1859), 35–9.

35. William Findley, *Observations on "The Two Sons of Oil" containing a Vindication of the American Constitution* ... (Pittsburgh, 1812), 33, 127. Findley, like James Wilson, grounded all statute law upon the moral or natural law that was immutable.

36. Ibid., 23–6, 149–51.

37. Ibid., 118–22.

38. Ibid., 124.

39. Ibid., 127, 130.

40. Ibid., 74–5, 130–4.

41. Among the many secondary works discussing religion and public policy that I have found most useful are John Bodo, *Protestant Clergy and Public Issues* (Princeton, N.J., 1954); Charles C. Cope, Jr., *Social Ideas of Northern Evangelicals, 1820–1860* (New York, 1954); and Hood, *Reformed America*. James M. Banner, Jr., *To The Hartford Convention: The Federalists and the Origins of Party Politics in Massachusetts 1789–1815* (New York, 1970), 26–8, 153–67; Linda Kerber, *Federalists in Dissent* (Ithaca, N.Y., 1970), 208–14; and James Kloppenberg, "The Virtues of Liberalism: Christianity, Republicanism, and Ethics in early American Political Discourse," *Journal of American History*, 74(1987):9–33, show religious influences on ideology, but are not directly about Pennsylvania.

42. Fred Hood has demonstrated how the Reformed writers could combine a providential interpretation of the Revolution/Constitution with an emphasis upon normal dominance of natural law. Although many Protestants in the early nineteenth century remained convinced that America was a chosen nation with a special destiny, neither premillenialism nor postmillenialism is a major theme in the writings of Pennsylvanians on religious liberty. Hood, *Reformed America*, Chapters 2 and 4; Ernest Lee Tuverson, *Redeemer Nation: The Idea of America's Millenial Role* (Chicago, Illinois, 1968).

43. Albert Barnes, *Thanksgiving Sermon. The Virtuous Public Services of William Penn.* (Philadelphia, 1845), 15–16.

44. Samuel Fisher, *Two Sermons Delivered at Moorestown, New Jersey: to which is annexed An Address to the Presbyterian Congregation of that Place* (Moorestown, N.J., 1814), 52.

45. Edward B. Davis, "Albert Barnes, 1798–1870, An Exponent of New School Presbyterians," (Th.D. diss., Princeton Theological Seminary, 1961), 79–80.

46. James Abercrombie, *A Sermon Preached in Christ Church and St. Peter's Philadelphia; On Wednesday, May 9, 1798* (Philadelphia, 1798), 4–5, 20–3, 28–31, 38. I am grateful to Deborah Mathias Gough for calling my attention to Abercrombie's significance.

47. James Abercrombie, *Two Sermons: The First, Preached on Thursday, July 30; The Second Preached on Thursday, August 20, 1812; Being Days of Fasting, Humiliation, and Prayer, Appointed by Public Authority* (Philadelphia, 1812), Preface, iii.

48. Ibid., iv–v, 23–5, 32–3. The minutes of the Lutheran ministerium and Reformed coetus discuss many congregational complaints against the clergy, but preaching of politics is not mentioned as a cause of disaffection.

49. Richard Pointer, "Philadelphia Presbyterians, Capitalism, and the Morality of Economic Success, 1825–1855." *PMHB* 112(July, 1988): 349–75; Bruce Lawrie, *Working People of Philadelphia* (Philadelphia, 1980), Chps. 2, 6.

50. Othniel Alsop Pendleton, Jr., "The Influence of the Evangelical Churches Upon Humanitarian Reform: A Case Study Giving Particular Attention to Philadelphia, 1790–1840," (Ph.D. diss., University of Pennsylvania, 1945) discusses antislavery, lotteries, Sunday Schools, temperance; (Methodist) *Christian Advocate and Journal,* June 27, 1827, 82; *Extracts from the Minutes of the General Assembly of the Presbyterian Church in the United States of America* (Philadelphia, 1817), Minutes, III, 1812, 7–9, 95, 318; Ibid. New School, 1854, 503, 659; 1855, 31. All Presbyterian General Assembly minutes after 1837 will be referred to by date and whether Old School or New School.

51. *Minutes of the General Assembly of Presbyterian Church,* Minutes, IV, 1818, 90–5, 163; New School, 1833, 659; 1840, 18; 1853, 329–30; (Methodist) *Christian Advocate and Journal,* 1827, II, 127; In the *Methodist Quarterly* the Sabbath, temperance, and Roman Catholicism received frequent mention. Antislavery is the only political question receiving extended treatment, and this came in the 1850s.

52. In 1850 an address of the Pennsylvania Colonization Society about evangelism in Africa was signed by the Episcopal bishop, a Methodist, Baptists, an Old School Presbyterian and a New School Presbyterian. *Letter to the Right Rev. Alonzo Potter* (Philadelphia, 1850).

53. (Presbyterian) *Christian Advocate,* II, 1824, 158.

54. Ibid. III, 1825, 109–11, 191; IV, 1826, 47–8.

55. Ibid. IV, 1826, 192.

56. Ibid. VIII, 1830, 264.

57. Ibid. VII, 1829, 480, 576.

58. Ibid., III, 1825, 283–4; VII, 480.

59. Ibid. VI, 1828, 507–8.

60. Ibid. VIII, 1830, 264–5.

61. Ibid. IX, 1831, 264, 552; X, 1832, 560.

62. Ibid. VII, 1829, 222, 277, 446; VIII, 1830, 264, 571, 576.

63. Absalom Jones, *A Thanksgiving Sermon, Preached January 1, 1808 in St. Thomas's or the African Episcopal Church, Philadelphia* (Philadelphia, 1808), 15–16.

64. Russell Parrott, *An Oration on the Abolition of the Slave Trade* (Philadelphia, 1812), 8; idem, *An Address on the Abolition of the Slave Trade* (Philadelphia, 1816), 4–5.

65. *Constitution of the Female Association of Philadelphia for the Relief of Women and Children in Reduced Circumstances* (Philadelphia, 1803), 8; *Reports of the Female Hospitable Society of Philadelphia Since Its Commencement in 1808* (Philadelphia, 1831); *First Report of the Female Bible Society of Philadelphia* (Philadelphia, 1815), 8; *Constitution of the Female Hebrew Benevolent Society of Philadelphia* (Philadelphia, 1825).

66. Mary Still, *An Appeal to the Females of the African Methodist Episcopal Church* (Philadelphia, 1857).

67. Sarah Grimké, *Letters on the Equality of the Sexes and the Condition of Women* (Boston, 1838, reprinted New York, 1970), 106–17, 122–3.

68. *Lucretia Mott: Her Complete Speeches and Sermons,* ed. Dane Greene (New York, 1980) 126–31.

69. Ibid., 131, 155, 174.

70. W. J. Rorabaugh, *The Alcoholic Republic* (New York, 1979).

71. *Philadelphia Statutes,* 1808, 531–2. Until 1821 the sale of beer, ale, and cider by the glass was unregulated. *Pennsylvania Statutes,* 1821, 155.

72. Ibid. 1823, 10–11; 1829, 129–32; 1833, 82–4.

73. Ibid. 1819, 74–5; 1822, 4–5, 226.

74. *Report of a Committee Appointed by the Pennsylvania Society for Discouraging the Use of Ardent Spirits, To Examine and Report What Amendments Ought to be Made in the Law of the Said State for the Suppression of Vice and Immorality* (Philadelphia, 1828), 11–12.

75. The best general account of changing temperance tactics, but that devotes little attention to Pennsylvania, is in Ian Tyrrell, *Sobering Up: From Temperance to Prohibition in Antebellum America 1800–1860* (Westport, Conn., 1979). John Krout, *The Origins of Prohibition* (New York, 1925) is still useful.

76. *Laws of the General Assembly of the State of Pennsylvania, Passed at the Session of 1829–1830* (Harrisburg, Pa., James Cameron, 1830), 352–5. Similar regulations on taverns had been used in colonial Pennsylvania.

77. Ibid. 1832, 73.

78. Ibid. 1834, 117–23; 1835, 597, 604.

79. Ibid. 1846, 248–9; *Minutes of the General Assembly of the Presbyterian Church* (Philadelphia, 1852–56), New School, 1852, 181; 1855, 31.

80. Tallies were 158, 318 for and 163, 457 against. The strongest vote against came from counties with high concentrations of Germans. An analysis of voting patterns is in William E. Gienapp, "Nebraska, Nativism, and Rum: The Failure of Fusion in Pennsylvania, 1854," *PMHB,* 109(1985): 458–62. William A. Gudelunas, Jr. and William G. Shade, *Before the Molly Maguires: The Emergence of the Ethno-Religious Factor in the Politics of the Lower Anthracite Region, 1844–1872* (New York, 1976), 29, 37, 56–7, 63–5, found Methodists and Presbyterians supporting reform, while German Lutherans and Irish Catholics opposed.

81. Asa Martin, "The Temperance Movement in Pennsylvania Prior to the Civil War," *PMHB,* 49(1925): 225.

82. The annual reports of the managers of the Pennsylvania Society for Discouraging the Use of Ardent Spirits and its pledge for abstinence were secular. This was also true of the addresses of the Pennsylvania State Temperance Society. Albert Barnes, *Throne of Iniquity, or Sustaining Evil by Law* (Harrisburg, Pa., 1852), a very popular temperance pamphlet, is a reasoned political-moral discourse that could have been delivered by a lawyer. Dudley Tyng, *Voice of Blood* (Philadelphia, 1855), 15; Albert Barnes, *The Connexion of Temperance with Republican Freedom: An Oration* (Philadelphia, 1835). An example of the merging of religion and politics is in *Minutes of the General Assembly of the Presbyterian Church* (Philadelphia, 1855), New School, 31.

Chapter VIII. The Legal Implications of Religious Liberty

1. Mitchell and Flanders, *Statutes at Large*, IV, 208–10.

2. The Scots' Presbyterian Church sought incorporation in 1779. Ibid. IX, 338; *Pennsylvania Statutes*, 1791, printed in James Dunlop, *General Laws of Pennsylvania* (Philadelphia, 1847), 132–4.

3. Methodist Church versus Remington. Frederick Watts, *Reports of Cases Argued and Determined by the Supreme Court of Pennsylvania* (Philadelphia, 1834–41), I, 218–24.

4. Ibid., 218.

5. *Laws of the General Assembly of the Commonwealth of Pennsylvania Passed at the Session of 1841.* (Harrisburg, Pa., 1841), 269.

6. Presbyterian Church versus Montgomery County, 1858, Benjamin Grant, *Reports of Cases Argued and Adjudged in the Supreme Court of Pennsylvania* (Philadelphia, 1859), III, 245–7.

7. Updegraph versus the Commonwealth, 1824, Thomas Sergeant and William Rawle, *Reports of Cases Adjudged in the Supreme Court of Pennsylvania* (Philadelphia, 1820–9), II, 406.

8. Presbyterian Church versus Montgomery County, Grant, *Reports of Cases*, III, 245–7.

9. *The Doctrines and Discipline of the Methodist Church* (1798, reprinted Vermont, 1979), 173–5; *Journal of the Proceedings of... Fifty-Seventh Convention of Protestant Episcopal Convention of the State of Pennsylvania* (Philadelphia, 1841), 30.

10. Baptist Congregation versus Scannel, et al., 1854, Grant, *Reports of Cases*, III, 48–51.

11. Sutter, et al., versus Trustees First Reformed Dutch Church, 1862, Robert E. Wright, *Pennsylvania State Reports Comprising Cases Adjudged in the Supreme Court of Pennsylvania* (Philadelphia, 1861–6), 503–13.

12. Justice Thompson's dissent. Sutter versus Dutch Church, Grant, *Reports of Cases*, 1864, III, 337–50.

13. Riddle versus Stavern, Sergeant and Rawle, *Reports of Cases*, II, 542–3; Unangst versus Shortz, Thomas L. Wharton, *Reports of Cases*, V, 519–24.

14. Owen versus Henman, Sergeant and Rawle, *Reports of Cases*, I, 548–51.

15. Schriber versus Rapp, Watts, *Reports of Cases*, V, 360–5.

16. Jeremiah Foster, ed., *An Authentic Report of the Testimony in a Cause at Issue* (Philadelphia, 1831).

17. Commonwealth versus Green, Wharton, *Reports of Cases*, IV, 599–606.

18. *Mechanics Free Press* 66(April 11, 1829).

19. First Presbyterian Church of Harrisburg, 1858, Grant, *Reports of Cases*, II, 240.

20. Presbyterian Congregation versus Johnson, Watts and Sergeant, *Reports of Cases*, I, 35–41.

21. Lessee of Executors of Theodore Bowers versus Franciscus Fromm, Addison, *Reports of Cases*, I, 361–0. The results of a 1797 case at Holy Trinity in Philadelphia are less clear. The trustees fired the episcopally appointed pastor and

hired two other priests whom the bishop excommunicated. The bishop initiated the case, but the verdict is uncertain. Patrick V. Carey, *People, Priests, and Prelates,* 100–1. This book is the best discussion of the trusteeship controversy.

22. Francis E. Tourscher, *The Hogan Schism and Trustee Trouble in St. Mary's Church, 1820–1829* (Philadelphia, 1930), is superficial and often wrong on details, but it does print several documents.

23. St. Mary's Church, Sergeant and Rawle, *Reports of Cases,* VII, 517–63.

24. J. William Frost, ed., *Quaker Origins of Antislavery,* (Norwood, Pa., 1980), 299–300.

25. Gary Nash, *Forging Freedom: The Formation of Philadelphia's Black Community* (Cambridge, Mass., 1988), 12, 14, 20–4.

26. Frost, *Quaker Origins,* 292–7.

27. Magaw's sermon is printed in William Douglas, *Annals of the First African Church in the United States now Styled the African Episcopal Church of St. Thomas* (Philadelphia, 1862), 70.

28. Ibid., 85–91, 96, 99.

29. Ibid., 139–66. The clergy voted 44 to 42 against admission; the laity 51 to 16 against; in 1854 the clergy voted 70 to 28 in favor, but the motion lost because the lay members voted 40 to 32 against.

30. For general accounts see Richard Allen, *The Life Experiences and Gospel Labors of the Rt. Rev. Richard Allen* (reprinted, Nashville, Tenn., 1960), 15–31; Carol George, *Segregated Sabbaths: Richard Allen and the Rise of Independent Black Churches* (New York, 1973), 57–71; Charles Wesley, *Richard Allen: Apostle of Freedom* (Washington, D.C., 1935), 79–90, 134–48.

31. *Articles of Association of the African Methodist Episcopal Church of the City of Philadelphia in the Commonwealth of Pennsylvania* (Philadelphia, 1799), 4–5, 7, 9–10.

32. "Improving, Amending, and Altering the Articles of Association of the African Methodist Church," reprinted in R. R. Wright, *The Encyclopedia of the African Methodist Episcopal Church* (Philadelphia, 1947), 332–3.

33. Green Against African Methodist Church, Sargeant and Rawle, *Reports of Cases,* I.

34. Brief of Joseph Hopkinson, April 24, 1815; J. Emory to Samuel Shoemaker, April 6, 1815, Robert Burch, Dec. 16, 1815 in "African Church" file in Edward Carey Gardner Collection, Box 33, Historical Society of Pennsylvania.

35. Sheriff's sale for June 13, 1815; Account of Jacob Fetter, sheriff in "African Church," Gardner Collection; Daniel A. Payne, *History of the African Methodist Episcopal Church* (Nashville, Tenn., 1891), 5–8.

36. Herbert Aptheker, ed., *A Documentary History of the Negro People in the United States* (New York, 1969), I, 68; Coker says the supreme court of Pennsylvania decided the case, but in neither published records nor in the supreme court Mss. at Harrisburg is there a record of the case.

37. William T. Catto, *A Semi-Centenary Discourse, Delivered in the First African Presbyterian Church, Philadelphia, on the Fourth Sabbath of May 1857* (Philadelphia, 1857), 110.

38. Updegraph versus the Commonwealth, Sergeant and Rawle, *Reports of*

Cases, XI, 409–10. For the *Mechanics Free Press* comments upon blasphemy see June 14, 1828. The paper on May 3 listed the arrests, fines, and sentences for intoxication, swearing, and Sabbath-breaking in Philadelphia.

39. Updegraph versus the Commonwealth, Sergeant and Rawle, *Reports of Cases,* XI, 393. In 1818 Robert Murphy was convicted of blasphemy by the Philadelphia Mayor's Court and fined £10. Murphy's defense was that the law was unconstitutional, but the Mayor's Court said such a ruling was beyond its authority. *Franklin Gazette,* Nov. 17, 1818. The reasoning in Updegraff follows closely the court's arguments against Murphy.

40. Updegraph versus the Commonwealth, Sergeant and Rawle, *Reports of Cases,* XI, 394–8.

41. Ibid., 398–9.

42. Ibid., 399–403.

43. Ibid., 404–6.

44. Ibid., 408–9.

45. Frederick L. Bronner, "The Observance of the Sabbath in the United States, 1800–1865," (Ph.D. diss., Harvard, 1937) is indispensible for an understanding of the controversies.

46. *Minutes of the General Assembly of the Presbyterian Church,* 1812, 26, 1815, 126; Alfred Hamilton, *The Christian Sabbath: An Argument from the New Testament for the Divine Authority of the Christian Sabbath* (Philadelphia, 1846), 20; John H. Agnew, *A Manual on the Christian Sabbath* (Philadelphia, 1852), vii, 87–9; Justin Edwards, *Permanent Sabbath Documents* (Philadelphia, 1844), 6, 11.

47. John Bodo, *The Protestant Clergy and Public Issues 1812–1848* (Princeton, 1954) sees the advocates of the Sabbath laws as "theocrats," a term he carefully defines but that still seems more applicable to New Englanders than to Pennsylvania's clergy.

48. Hamilton, *Bethlehem Diary,* 16–17; Brother Lamech, *Chronicon Ephratense,* 44–5; Levering, *A History of Bethlehem,* 130–3, 211–12.

49. *Report Relative to the Observances of the Sabbath Made to the House of Representatives* (Harrisburg, 1850).

50. Bronner, "Observance of the Sabbath," 59–67.

51. *Minutes of Presbyterian General Assembly,* 1815, 256–7; *Christian Advocate,* IV, 1826, 336; VI, 1828, 507–8; VII, 1829, 576.

52. Johnson and Malone, *Dictionary of American Biography* (1933), V, 114–16; *Mechanics Free Press,* Jan. 24, 31, 1829.

53. Kepner versus Keefer, Watts, *Reports of Cases,* IV, 231–5; Berrill versus Gibbs, Clark, *Report of Cases,* I, 313.

54. Logan versus Mathews, *Pennsylvania State Reports,* VI, 417.

55. Huidekoper versus Cotton, Watts, *Reports of Cases,* III, 58–9; Omit vs. Commonwealth, *Pennsylvania State Reports,* XXI, 426–37.

56. Commonwealth versus Eyre, Sergeant and Rawle, *Reports of Cases,* I, 346–51.

57. *Proceedings of the Sabbath Convention at Hollidaysburg* (Philadelphia, 1846) 7–8.

58. *Laws of Pennsylvania* (Session, 1845), 364.

59. Murray versus Commonwealth, *Pennsylvania State Reports,* XXIV, (1855), 270.

60. *Proceedings of the Sabbath Convention at Hollidaysburg* (Philadelphia, 1846), 7; George Wharton Pepper and William D. Lewis, *Pepper and Lewis's Digest of Decisions and Encyclopedia of Pennsylvania Law, 1754–1898* (Philadelphia, 1898–1904), XX, 35, 434.

61. Updegraff versus Commonwealth, Sergeant and Rawle, *Reports of Cases,* II, 394; Sprecht versus Commonwealth, *Pennsylvania State Reports,* VII, 312, 325; the dissent here would become a majority in the 1850s.

62. Commonwealth versus Eyre, Sergeant and Rawle, *Reports of Cases,* I, 352. There was a dissent that did not consider Sabbath-breaking a breach of the peace.

63. Huidekoper versus Cotton, Watts, Reports of Cases, III, 59.

64. Ibid.; Sprecht versus Commonwealth, *Pennsylvania State Reports,* VII, 325.

65. Johnston versus Commonwealth, *Pennsylvania State Reports,* XXII: 111, 115.

66. Ibid., 102.

67. Ibid., 109–11.

68. Ibid., 115.

69. Commonwealth versus Nesbit, 34, *Pennsylvania State Reports,* XXIV, 405–7.

70. Ibid., 407–8.

71. Ibid., 405–6.

72. Ibid., 406.

73. Ibid., 407, 411.

74. Commonwealth versus Jeandell, Grant, II, 506, 510; Wharton and Pepper, XX, 35486.

75. Sparhawk versus Union Passenger Railway Company, *Pennsylvania State Reports,* LIV, 422–4.

76. Ibid., 424–8.

77. Ibid., 432–43.

78. Ibid., 443.

79. Ibid., 450–1.

80. *Purdon's Pennsylvania Statutes Annotated,* Title 18: Crimes and Offenses, 346–76.

81. *Proceedings of the Anti-Sabbath Convention* (Boston, 1848), 15; *Sunday Mails: or, Inquiries into the Origin, Institution, and Proper Mode of Observance of the First Day of the Week* (Philadelphia, 1830), 24–5.

82. Moore, "The Warning of Thomas Jefferson," *Aurora,* Jan. 9, 1821.

83. Abel Thomas, *A Century of Universalism in Philadelphia and New York* (Philadelphia, 1872), 91–7, 107; Lucretia Mott, "Progress of the Religious World," in Dana Greene, ed., *Lucretia Mott: Her Complete Speeches and Sermons* (New York, 1980), 59–70.

84. *Mechanics Free Press,* Jan. 17, 24, 31, 1829; Feb. 28, 1829; May 10, 1828; April 26, 1828. The editor, son of a Quaker, was a strong opponent of clerical power. The newspaper insisted that the burden of Sabbath legislation fell disproportionately on the poor.

85. Bodo, *Protestant Clergy,* ix.

Chapter IX. Religious Liberty and the Catholic and Jewish Minorities

1. Morris Schappes, *A Documentary History of the Jews of the United States, 1654–1875* (New York, 1950), 26–30 reprints the act.

2. "Extract from the Council of Censors, Dec. 23, 1782," in *Independent Gazeteer or the Chronicle of Freedom* #116, Jan. 17, 1784.

3. Wolf and Whiteman, *History of the Jews,* 149–50.

4. *Poulson's American Daily Advertiser,* LIV, #15, 27, Jan. 25, 1825.

5. *Poulson's,* XLVIII, #13, 415, Nov. 24, 1819.

6. Wolf and Whiteman, *History of Jews,* 299.

7. "Religion and Public Schools," *The Occident* 17(April, 1859): 59. Moshe Davis, *Emergence of Conservative Judaism* (Philadelphia, 1965), 91; Leon Jick, *Americanization of the Synagogue* (Hanover, N.H., 1976).

8. "Religious Equality," *Occident* 5(Jan. 1848): 225.

9. Ibid., 5: 217–25, 265–75; 16(Sept., 1858): 270–1.

10. Ibid. 6(Dec., 1849): 403–10.

11. Marcus Jastrow quoted in Moshe Davis, *Emergence,* 91. When writing to the State Department in 1840, Philadelphia Jews exalted in "equality of civil and religious rights" and "lack of danger of persecution." Quoted in Jacob Jacobs "The Damascus Affair of 1840 and the Jews of America," in *Jewish Experience in America,* ed. Abraham J. Karp (New York, 1969), 271–80.

12. Joseph Casino, "Anti-Popery in Colonial Pennsylvania," *PMHB,* 105(1981): 279–309; Charles Metzger, *Catholics and the American Revolution* (Chicago, 1962), III, Chapter 11.

13. Jay P. Dolan, *The American Catholic Experience: A History from Colonial Times to the Present* (New York, 1985), 105–9; Joseph P. Kirlin, *Catholicity in Philadelphia* (Philadelphia, 1909).

14. Kirlin, *Catholicity,* 94–5, 118. Jacob Duché, an Episcopal clergyman, described in print Father Harding as "much esteemed by all denominations of Christians in this city for his prudence, his known attachment to British liberty, and his unaffected pious labours among the people, to whom he officiates." Dolan, *American Catholic Experience,* 102.

15. Kirlin, *Catholicity,* 161, 276; *American Daily Advertiser,* Feb. 9, 1828; Dale B. Light, "Rome and the Republic: Francis Patrick Kenrick and the Devotional Revolution in Philadelphia Catholicism, 1830–1851," Philadelphia Center for Early American Studies, Sept. 12, 1986. My interpretation of the history of the Catholic church in Philadelphia draws heavily upon Light's insights, and I am grateful to him for several long discussions in which he suggested the most valuable sources to read.

16. Joseph M. McShane, "John Carroll and the Appeal to Evidence a Pragmatic Defense of Principle," *Church History* 57(1988): 298–309.

17. Dale B. Light, "The Reformation of Philadelphia Catholicism, 1830–1860," *PMHB* (July, 1988): 376–7, 384; Patrick Carey, *People, Priests, and Prelates: Ecclesiastical Democracy and the Tensions of Trusteeism* (South Bend, Ind., 1987) Chapters 3, 9.

18. Hugh J. Nolan, *The Most Reverend Francis Patrick Kenrick, Third Bishop of*

Philadelphia, 1830–1851. Catholic University of America Studies in American Church History, ed. Peter Guilday and John Tracy Ellis, XXXVIII (Washington, D.C., 1948),310–11.

19.   Dolan, *American Catholic Experience* and Carey, *People, Priests* have excellent introductions to this period.

20.   Robert F. McNamara, "Trusteeism in the Atlantic States, 1785–1855," *Catholic Historical Review* 64(1978): 357–76; Patrick Dignam, *History of Legal Incorporation of Catholic Church Property in the United States, Catholic University of America Studies in American Church History,* XIV (Washington, D.C., 1933), 73, 75, 78, 82.

21.   Francis J. Herktorn, *A Retrospective of Holy Trinity Parish* (Philadelphia, 1914), 24–5, 34; Dignam, *Legal Incorporation,* 2–3.

22.   Mathew Carey, *Sundry Documents Submitted to the Consideration of the Pewholders of St. Mary's Church, by the Trustees of That Church* (Philadelphia, 1812), 14–15; idem, *Address to the Right Reverend The Bishop of Pennsylvania, and the Members of St. Mary's Congregation,* (Philadelphia, 1820), 3–4; idem, *A Desultory Examination of the Reply of Reverend W. V. Harold to Catholic Layman's Rejoinder* (Philadelphia, 1822); Richard W. Meade, *An Address to the Roman Catholics of the City of Philadelphia, In Reply to Mr. Harold's Address* (Philadelphia, 1823) 5–6, 11–12; William Hogan, *A Short Address to the Roman Catholic Congregation of St. Mary's* (Philadelphia, 1822); "Minute Book of St. Mary's Church, Philadelphia," *Records of the American Catholic Historical Society,* IV (1898), XLII (1931); Tourscher, *The Hogan Schism,* reprints several important documents.

23.   Nolan, *Kenrick,* 75–9 on Fathers Ryan and Harold's appeal to the United States government against the bishop's decision to transfer them. Hogan, *A Short Address.*

24.   Patrick Carey, "Arguments for Lay Participation in Philadelphia Catholicism," *Records of the American Catholic Historical Society* 92(1981):45–58. See also the citations in fn. 12.

25.   Nolan, *Kenrick,* 118–26.

26.   Ibid., 127–8, 143, 183; Dignam, *Legal Incorporation,* 103–4, 152, 160.

27.   Herktorn, *Retrospective of Holy Trinity Parish,* 44.

28.   Nolan, *Kenrick,* 138.

29.   Feb. 26, 1848 letter quoted in Nolan, *Kenrick,* 398–9. Kenrick had made the same argument against the religious exercises in public schools.

30.   Ibid., 258; Edith Jeffrey, "Reform, Renewal, and Vindication: Irish Immigrants and the Catholic Total Abstinence Movement in AnteBellum Philadelphia" *PMHB,* 112(July, 1988): 407–431.

31.   Nolan, *Kenrick,* 413–4.

32.   Ibid., 159.

33.   Ibid., 346, 355; Light, "Rome and the Republic," 39, fn.65; Francis Patrick Kenrick, *The Primary of the Apostolic See . . . In a Series of Letters addressed to the Right Reverend J. H. Hopkins* (Philadelphia, 1838).

34.   *The Controversy between the Rev. John Hughes, of the Roman Catholic Church and the Rev. John Breckinridge, of the Presbyterian Church, Relative to* *the Existing Differences in the Roman Catholic and Protestant Religion* (Philadelphia, 1833), 2. Some passages that relate to religious liberty are 56, 67, 72–5, 110–13, 115–19, 126–7.

35.   Mathew Carey, *To the Reverend John M. Mason, Editor of the Christian's Magazine* (Philadelphia, 1808) xvi–xvii; idem, *A Roland for an Oliver, Letters on Persecution* (Philadelphia, 1826); John McCaffrey, *Church and State: A Lecture Delivered before the Catholic Institute of Baltimore* (Baltimore, 1854), 3, 16, 22.

36.   *Address of the Board of Managers of the American Protestant Association* (Philadelphia, 1843), 7, 13, 20, 23–5; *First Annual Report of the American Protestant Association Together with a Sketch of the Address at the First Anniversary, Nov., 1843* (Philadelphia, 1844), 15–18, 21–3; T. V. Moore, *The Relative Influence of Presbytery and Prelacy on Civil and Ecclesiastical Liberty* (Philadelphia, 1845), 4–5, 11–14; Joseph H. Martin, *The Influence, Bearing, and Effects of Romanism on the Civil and Religious Liberties of Our Country* (New York, 1844), 3–4, 14, 16.

37.   Nolan, *Kenrick,* 220; Michael J. Curley, *Bishop John Neumann, C.SS.R.* (Philadelphia, 1952), 204–5, 260.

38.   Priscilla Ferguson Clement, *Welfare and the Poor in the Nineteenth Century City: Philadelphia, 1800–1854* (Philadelphia, 1985), 20, 23,162–4; John Alexander, *Render Them Submissive: Responses to Poverty in Philadelphia, 1760–1800* (Amherst, Mass., 1980), stresses the social control element in private and public charity.

39.   "Report of the House of Refuge," *Journal of the Senate of the Commonwealth of Pennsylvania* (Harrisburg, Pa., 1835–6) II, 458–9. The annual reports of the Philadelphia Bible Society were printed in the Senate Journals.

40.   Jacqueline Thibaut, " 'To Pave the Way to Penitence': Prisoners and Discipline at the Eastern State Penitentiary, 1829–1835," *PMHB* 106(1982):187–94; "Report of the Eastern State Penitentiary," *Journal of the Senate of the Commonwealth of Pennsylvania* (Harrisburg, Pa., 1835–6) II, 469, 471, 532, 550.

41.   Dunlop, *General Laws,* 428, 759.

42.   James Wickersham, *A History of Education in Pennsylvania* (Lancaster, Pa., 1886) remains the only survey of Pennsylvania education in this period.

43.   In 1840, 220 school districts still used the Bible as a reader; this was approximately one-half of the reporting, or one-fifth of the total districts. *Journal of the Senate of the Commonwealth of Pennsylvania* (Harrisburg, Pa., 1840), 641.

44.   *Acts of the General Assembly of Pennsylvania* 1824, 137–45; 1834, 170–9.

45.   "Report of Superintendent of Common Schools," *Journal of the Senate,* 1836–7 (Harrisburg, Pa., 1837) II, 341–2; *Pennsylvania Statutes,* 1835–6, 532; 1837–8, 336, 342. Before the 1830s the state never discussed the curriculum of the schools or colleges that it subsidized in order to educate poor scholars. *Acts of Assembly,* 1812, 378; 1818, 124; 1819, 200; 1821, 131; 1822, 110; 1837, 336–7.

46.   Vincent P. Lannie and Bernard C. Diethorn, "For the Honor and Glory of God: The Philadelphia Bible Riots of 1840," *History of Education Quarterly* (Spring, 1968):44–106.

47.   Michael Feldberg, *The Philadelphia Riots of 1844: A Study of Ethnic Conflict* (Westport, Conn., 1975), 126.

48. Kenrick's letter to the Board of Controllers is printed in Kirlin, *Catholicity,* 312–14; Nolan, *Kenrick,* 288–303. The American Protestant Association also printed Kenrick's letter in their Annual Report, in an edition of 20,000 copies.

49. Diane Ravitch, *The Great School Wars: New York City 1805–1973* (New York, 1974), 9, 42–57.

50. Kenrick's successor, Bishop John Neumann, also opposed sending Catholic children to a public school. Like Kenrick, he disliked any religious exercises held outside the auspices of the Catholic church. Curley, *Neumann,* 208–9.

51. There were only 500 Catholic children in parochial schools at the end of Kenrick's tenure in Philadelphia. His successor, Neumann, increased that number to 5,000. Curley, *Neumann,* 194, 211.

52. In 1834 the Board issued an instruction against "religious instructions" in the public schools. Kirlin prints the statement in *Catholicity,* 311–12. To the board, Bible reading, hymn singing, and prayers were not sectarian.

53. Nolan, *Kenrick,* 189; Curley, *Neumann,* 225. The standard history of American pre-Civil War nativism is Ray Billington, *The Protestant Crusade 1800–1860* (New York, 1938). Chapter IX, 220–37, discusses Philadelphia. Whatever anti-Catholic sentiments existed in Philadelphia in early 1844 were not reflected in Harrisburg. The assembly in February, 1844 gave to Kenrick and his successors the right to hold in trust any Roman Catholic church property in the State. *Laws of Pennsylvania . . . of the Session of 1844,* 62–3.

54. Nolan, *Kenrick,* 324–7.

55. Nolan, *Kenrick,* 336–7. The Catholic suit was based on an 1841 Pennsylvania law.

56. *The American Woman,* vol. I, #1 (August 1, 1844), speech of Mrs. Catharine Shurlock. I am indebted to Judith Hunter for calling this source to my attention.

57. Ibid., Aug. 1, 1844; Aug. 6, 1844; Sept. 38, 1844; Jan. 1, 1845; Feb. 1, 1845.

58. Ibid. Speech of Lewis Levin reprinted Sept. 14, 1844.

59. William E. Gienapp, "Nebraska, Nativism, and Rum, 440–5, 460–3; James Huston, "The Demise of the Pennsylvania American Party," *PMHB* 109(1985): 473–80, 489–95; Michael F. Holt, "The Antimasonic and Know Nothing Parties," in Arthur M. Schlesinger, Jr., ed., *History of United States Political Parties* I, 593–620.

60. Gienapp, "Nebraska, Nativism and Rum," 447–8.

61. Huston, "The Demise," 479–80, 493.

62. Addison, *Reports of Cases,* I, 362; Curley, *Neumann,* 226–7.

63. Curley, *Neumann,* 221–7, 253–5; Dignam, *Legal Incorporation,* 198–200.

Epilogue: The Dismantling

1. *Purdon's Pennsylvania Statutes Annotated* Constitution: Articles 1 to 4 (Philadelphia, 1961) 106–11.

2. *Purdon's Pennsylvania Statutes Annotated* Title 18: Crimes and Offenses, 346–76.

3. Minersville, Pa. (PA) School District vs. Gobitis, 310 US 586 (1940), in Joseph Tussman, *Supreme Court on Church and State* (New York, 1962), 80–90.

4. John Wilson, *Public Religion in American Culture* (Philadelphia, 1979)

161–3; Joseph Tussman, *Supreme Court on Church and State,* 80–90, 142–70. The concurrence of Justice Murphy and the dissent by Justice Frankfurter, who had written the majority opinion in Gobitis, drew upon history. Frankfurter cited Franklin along with Jefferson and Adams and claimed that the Revolution decreed equality for all religious bodies and no special privileges for any. "The Constitutional protection of religious freedom terminated disabilities, it didn't create new privileges."

5. Murdock versus Commonwealth of Pennsylvania, 319 US 105 (1943); Tussman, *Supreme Court,* 112–118.

6. John Wilson and Donald Drakeman, eds., *Church and State in American History* (Boston, 1987) 230–4 gives excerpts from several recent Supreme Court decisions. Two excellent discussions of the implications of recent Supreme Court decisions on religion are Michael E. Smith, "The Special Place of Religion in the Constitution," *Supreme Court Review* (1983), 83–124 and Michael W. McConnell, "Accommodation of Religion," *Supreme Court Review* (1985), 1–59. The most recent important church and state case, involving a Pennsylvania practice again, concerned a nativity scene and a menorah displayed on public property in Pittsburgh. The court condemned the creche but allowed the menorah. County of Allegheny versus American Civil Liberties Union and Chabad versus American Civil Liberties Union, *United States Law Week* (6/27/89), 57 LW 5045-73.

Bibliography

American Patterns of Church and State

John F. Wilson, *Church and State in America*, 2 vols. (Westport, Conn.: Greenwood, 1986–7) is a comprehensive annotated bibliography discussing both the relationships between government and institutionalized church and the impact of religious values on American society from colonial days until the present. Among very useful secondary sources are Thomas J. Curry, *The First Freedoms: Church and State in America to the Passage of the First Amendment* (New York: Oxford University Press, 1986); William Lee Miller, *The First Liberty: Religion and the American Public* (New York: Knopf, 1987); Leonard Levy, *The Establishment Clause: Religion and the First Amendment* (New York: Macmillan, 1986); Mark DeWolfe Howe, *The Garden and the Wilderness: Religion and Government in American Constitutional History* (Chicago: University of Chicago, 1965).

Primary source collections are John Wilson, and Donald L. Drakeman, eds., *Church and State in American History* (Boston: Beacon Press, 1967); Robert T. Miller, and Ronald B. Flowers, eds., *Toward Benevolent Neutrality: Church, State, and the Supreme Court* (Waco, Tex.: Baylor University Press, 1977); William Addison Blakely, ed. *American State Papers Bearing on Sunday Legislation,* revised by William Allen Colord (1911, reprinted New York: Da Capo Press, 1970). Colonial laws of religion are printed in Nicholas Trott, *The Laws of the British Plantations in America, Relating to the Church and Clergy, Religion, and Learning* (London: B. Cowle, 1721); for the pre-Civil War period see Ransom Hebard Tyler, *American Ecclesiastical Law: The Law of Religious Societies, Church Government, and Creeds, Disturbing Religious Meetings, and the Law of Burial Grounds in the United States* (Albany: W. Gould, 1866). Francis N. Thorpe, ed., *The Federal and State Constitutions, Colo-*

nial Charters, and Other Organic Laws..., 7 vols. (Washington, D.C.: Government Printing Office, 1909) prints all colonial charters and state constitutions.

Religion and society in Pennsylvania in the colonial period are dealt with in many secondary sources including Patricia U. Bonomi, *Under the Cope of Heaven: Religion, Society, and Politics in Colonial America* (New York: Oxford University Press, 1986); Jon Butler, *Power, Authority, and the Origins of American Denominationalism: English Churches in the Delaware Valley, 1680–1730. Transactions of the American Philosophical Society,* Feb. 1978, vol. 68, Part 2; Dietmar Rothermund, *Layman's Progress: Religious and Political Experience in Colonial Pennsylvania 1740–1770* (Philadelphia: University of Pennsylvania Press, 1962); Sally Schwartz, *"A Mixed Multitude": The Struggle for Toleration in Colonial Pennsylvania* (New York: New York University Press, 1987); Otto Reinher, ed., *Quest for Faith, Quest for Freedom: Aspects of Pennsylvania's Religious Experience* (New Jersey: Associated University Press, 1987).

Books and articles on nineteenth century religion that either focus on or are relevant to Pennsylvania are John Bodo, *Protestant Clergy and Public Issues, 1812–1848* (Princeton, N.J.: Princeton University Press, 1954); Frederick Bronner, "Observance of the Sabbath in the United States, 1800–1865," (Ph.D. dissertation, Harvard University, 1937); William A. Gudelunas, Jr., and William G. Shade, *Before the Molly Maguires: The Emergence of the Ethno-Religious Factor in the Politics of the Lower Anthracite Region, 1844–1872* (New York: Arno Press, 1976); Fred Hood, *Reformed America: The Middle and Southern States, 1783–1837* (University: University of Alabama Press, 1980); moral reform issues are discussed in Asa Earl Martin, "Lotteries in Pennsylvania Prior to 1833," *Pennsylvania Magazine of History and Biography* 47(1923): 307–27, 48:(1923): 66–92, 159–80; the same author's article, "The Temperance Movement in Pennsylvania Prior to the Civil War, *PMHB* 49(1925): 194–230; Othniel Alsop Pendleton, Jr., "Influence of the Evangelical Churches upon Humanitarian Reform: A Case Study Giving Particular Attention to Philadelphia, 1790–1840," (Ph.D. dissertation, University of Pennsylvania, 1945); Ian Tyrrell, *Sobering Up: From Temperance to Prohibition in Antebellum America, 1800–1860* (Westport, Conn: Greenwood, 1979). Gary Nash, *Forging Freedom: The Formation of Philadelphia's Black Community* (Cambridge, Mass.: Harvard , 1988) has several chapters on blacks' religion.

Pennsylvania government records containing information on religious liberty include *Statutes at Large of Pennsylvania, 1682–1801,* vol. 1, compiled by Gail McKnight Beckman (New York: Vantage, 1976); Ibid, vols. 2–14, edited by James T. Mitchell, and Henry Flanders (Harrisburg,

Pa.: Harrisburg Publishing Co., 1906); *Laws of the Commonwealth of Pennsylvania, 1700–1810* 4 vols. (Philadelphia: 1810); *Acts of the General Assembly of the Commonwealth of Pennsylvania, 1805–1860* (Harrisburg, Pa.: 1806–1861); *A Digest of the Ordinances of the Corporation of the City of Philadelphia, and the Acts of Assembly Relating Thereto* (Philadelphia: J. Crissy, 1841); Robert A. Weinert, *Constitutions of Pennsylvania, Constitution of the United States* (Harrisburg, Pa.: Legislative Reference Bureau, 1964); *The Proceedings Relative to Calling the Convention of 1776 and 1790: The Minutes of the Convention that Formed the Present Constitution of Pennsylvania* (Harrisburg, Pa.: J. S. Wiestling, 1825); *Proceedings and Debates of the Convention of the Commonwealth of Pennsylvania, to Propose Amendments to the Constitution* 14 vols. edited by Packer, Barrett, and Parke (Harrisburg, Pa.: Packer, Barrett, and Parke, 1837–9). Legislative records include *Minutes of the Provincial Council of Pennsylvania, Colonial Records* 16 vols. (Harrisburg and Philadelphia: 1838–53); the assembly records are in *Votes and Proceedings of the House of Representatives of the Province of Pennsylvania, Pennsylvania Archives* 8th Series, 8 vols. (Harrisburg, Pa.: 1931–5). After 1790 in the General Assembly, both the House of Representatives and the Senate published a journal of their proceedings. After 1844 records of the Pennsylvania Supreme Court are in the *Pennsylvania State Reports;* earlier records are in *Reports of Cases Argued and Determined in the Supreme Court of Pennsylvania: Adjudged in the Courts of Pennsylvania,* edited by A. J. Dallas (1798–1807), Horace Binney, (1809–15), Jasper Yeates (1817–19), Thomas Sergeant and William Rawle (1818–29), William Rawle (1829–36), Frederick Watts (1834–41); Thomas Wharton, (1839–41), Frederick Watts and Henry J. Sargeant (1842–3). Additional cases are in Benjamin Grant, *Reports of Cases Argued and Adjudged in the Supreme Court of Pennsylvania,* 3 vols. (Philadelphia: 1859–64); Alexander Addison, *Reports of Cases in the County Courts and . . . Appeals of the State of Pennsylvania* (Washington: 1860); Thomas L. Wharton, *A Digest of Reported Cases Among the Several Courts Held in Pennsylvania* 2 vols., 4th edition (Philadelphia: R. and J. W. Johnson, 1843); *Pepper and Lewis's A Digest of Decisions and Encyclopaedia of Pennsylvania Law, 1754–1898* 23 vols. edited by George Wharton Pepper, and William D. Lewis (Philadelphia: R. Welsh, 1898–1904).

Primary and Secondary Works on Individual Denominations: Quakers

The records of Philadelphia Yearly Meeting and the Meeting for Sufferings are available at the Friends Historical Library, Swarthmore College and at the Quaker Collection, Haverford College. Hugh Barbour, and J. William Frost, *The Quakers* (Westport, Conn.: Greenwood, 1988) is a general history. The best biography of William Penn is in the introduction to each section of *The Papers of William Penn* 4 vols., edited by Mary Maples Dunn, and Richard Dunn, (Philadelphia: University of Pennsylvania Press, 1981–7). Penn's collected printed works were published in London in 1726 and again in 1825. Mary Maples Dunn, *William Penn: Politics and Conscience* (Princeton, N.J.: Princeton University Press, 1967) focuses on religious liberty.

During the colonial period, Quakers played so influential a role in Pennsylvania that scholars link the meetings' history with that of the colony. Edwin B. Bronner, *William Penn's Holy Experiment* (New York: Temple University Press, 1962) and Gary Nash, *Quakers and Politics: Pennsylvania, 1680–1726* (Princeton, N.J.: Princeton University Press, 1968) cover the early history of Quakers; Nash has a broader scope but Bronner is more reliable. Alan Tully, *William Penn's Legacy: Politics and Social Structure in Pennsylvania, 1726–1755* (Baltimore, Md.: Johns Hopkins University Press, 1977) sees political harmony as dominant. Conflict is more apparent in Jack Marietta, "The Growth of Quaker Self-Consciousness in Pennsylvania, 1720–1748," in *Seeking the Light: Essays in Quaker History,* edited by J. William Frost, and John M. Moore (Wallingford, Pa.: Pendle Hill Publications, 1986), 79–104. Articles by Alan Tully, Hermann Wellenreuther, and J. William Frost in the *PMHB,* 107 (1983) focus on Quakers and politics as do essays by Tully and Richard Ryerson in *Power and Status: Officeholding in Colonial America,* edited by Bruce Daniels (Middletown, Conn: Wesleyan University Press, 1986). See also James H. Hutson, *Pennsylvania Politics, 1746–1770: The Movement for Royal Government and Its Consequences* (Princeton, N.J.: Princeton University Press, 1972). Jack Marietta, *The Reformation of American Quakerism, 1748–1783* (Philadelphia: University of Pennsylvania Press, 1984); Richard Baumann, *For the Reputation of Truth: Politics, Religion, and Conflict Among the Pennsylvania Quakers, 1750–1800* (Baltimore, Md., Johns Hopkins University Press, 1971); and Arthur Mekeel, *Relation of Quakers to the American Revolution* (Washington, D.C.: University Press of America, 1979) focus on Quaker responses to the French and Indian War and the American Revolution. These books should be supplemented by two general histories of the Revolution in Pennsylvania: Richard Ryerson, *The Revolution Is Now Begun: The Radical Committees of Philadelphia, 1765–1776* (Philadelphia: University of Pennsylvania 1979) and Anne M. Ousterhout, *A State Divided: Opposition in Pennsylvania to the American Revolution* (Westport, Conn.: Greenwood, 1987). There is no good history of Friends in the post-Revolutionary age. Larry Ingle, *Quakers in Conflict: The Hicksite Reformation* (Nashville: University of Tennessee Press, 1986) is the best description of events in the schism.

Baptists

Official records are Abram D. Gillette, ed., *Minutes of the Philadelphia Baptist Association from A.D. 1707 to A.D. 1807* (Philadelphia: American Baptist Publication Society, 1851); *Minutes of the Philadelphia Baptist Association, 1809–1859* (Philadelphia: 1809–59); Morgan Edwards, *Materials Toward a History of the Baptists in Pennsylvania* (Philadelphia: 1770, facsimile reprint, Ann Arbor: University of Michigan Microfilms, 1978); a useful secondary source is Robert Torbet, *A Social History of the Philadelphia Baptist Association, 1707–1940* (Philadelphia: Westbrook, 1944).

Lutheran and Reformed

Official records are *Documentary History of the Evangelical Lutheran Ministerium of Pennsylvania and Adjacent States, Proceedings of the Annual Conventions from 1748–1821* (Philadelphia: Board of Publications of the General Council of the Evangelical Lutheran Church in North America, 1898); *Minutes and Letters of the Coetus of the German Reformed Church in Pennsylvania, 1747–1792* (Philadelphia: Reformed Church Publishing Board, 1903); *Acts and Proceedings of the Coetus and Synod of the German Reformed Church in the United States from 1791 to 1816 Inclusive* (Chambersburg, Pa.: M. Kieffer, 1854, reprinted 1930). Theodore G. Tappert, and John Doberstein, *Journals of Henry Melchoir Muhlenberg,* 3 vols. (Philadelphia: Evangelical Lutheran Ministerium of Pennsylvania and Adjacent States and Muhlenberg Press, 1945) is the most valuable primary source. Theodore E. Schumauk, *A History of the Lutheran Church in Pennsylvania,* 2 vols. (Philadelphia: General Council Publications House, 1903) covers the eighteenth and nineteenth centuries, but the definitive history of Lutheran and Reformed in colonial Pennsylvania is Charles H. Glatfelder, *Pastors and People: German Lutheran and Reformed Churches in the Pennsylvania Field, 1717–1793* 2 vols. (Breinigsville, Pa.: Pennsylvania German Society, 1981). Paul Eller, "Revivalism and the German Churches in Pennsylvania," (Ph.D. dissertation, University of Chicago, 1933); and John B. Frantz, "Revivalism in the German Reformed Church in America to 1850, with Emphasis on the Eastern Synod," (Ph.D. dissertation, University of Pennsylvania, 1961) cover the pre-Civil War period.

Methodists

Official records are *Minutes of the Annual Conference of the Methodist Episcopal Church, 1788–1851; Methodist Magazine* (London, 1778–,

Philadelphia, 1797–98, New York, 1818–28) retitled *The Methodist Magazine and Quarterly Review,* 1830–40, retitled *Methodist Quarterly Review* 1841–60; Thomas Cope, and Francis Asbury, *Doctrines and Discipline of the Methodist Episcopal Church, in America, with Explanatory Notes,* edited by Frederick Norwood, 1798 facsimile, (Rutland, Vt.: Academy Books, 1979). Secondary accounts include Doris Andrews, "Popular Religion and the Revolution in the Middle Atlantic Ports: The Rise of the Methodists, 1770–1800" (Ph.D. dissertation, University of Pennsylvania, 1986); *The History of American Methodism* 3 vols. (Nashville, Tenn.: Abington Press, 1964) has several chapters on events in Pennsylvania. Carol V. R. George, *Segregated Sabbath: Richard Allen and the Rise of Independent Black Churches* (New York: Oxford University Press, 1973) tells the story of the creation of the African Methodist Episcopal Church.

Presbyterians

Records of the Presbyterian Church in the United States Embracing the Minutes of the General Presbytery and General Synod, 1706–1788 (Philadelphia: 1904, reprinted New York: Arno Press, 1969); *Extracts from the Minutes of the General Assembly of the Presbyterian Church in the United States of America* (Philadelphia, 1789–1860). After the schism, the Old School continued to issue minutes under the same title. The New School dropped the term "extracts." The most important periodical was the Presbyterian *Christian Advocate,* vols. 1–12 (Philadelphia: 1823–34). Guy Klett, *Presbyterians in Colonial Pennsylvania* (Philadelphia: University of Pennsylvania, 1937); and Leonard Trinterud, *The Forming of an American Tradition: A Reexamination of Colonial Presbyterianism* (Philadelphia: Westminster, 1949) are the essential histories for the colonial period. Martin Lodge, "The Great Awakening in the Middle Colonies" (Ph.D. dissertation, University of California, 1964); Marilyn Westerkamp, *Triumph of the Laity: Scots-Irish Piety and the Great Awakening, 1625–1760* (New York: Oxford University Press, 1988); and Milton J. Coulter, *Gilbert Tennent, Son of Thunder* (Westport, Conn.: Greenwood, 1986) trace the antecedents and impact of the Great Awakening. Elizabeth Ingersoll, "Francis Alison: American 'Philosophe' 1705–1799" (Ph.D. dissertation, University of Delaware, 1974) is very valuable. There is no good secondary source describing the history of Presbyterians in Pennsylvania in the antebellum period. Edward B. Davis, "Albert Barnes, 1798–1870: An Exponent of New School Presbyterians" (Th.D. dissertation, Princeton Theological Seminary, 1961) discusses the most important New School minister. The comments on religion and social norms in Robert Doherty, "Social Basis of the Presbyterian Schism,

1837–1838: The Philadelphia Case," *Journal of Social History* 2(Fall, 1968):69–79; Bruce Lawrie, "Working People of Philadelphia, 1800–1850 (Philadelphia: Temple University Press, 1980); and David Montgomery, "The Shuttle and the Cross," *Journal of Social History* 5(Summer, 1972):411–15 need to be balanced with Richard Pointer, "Philadelphia Presbyterians, Capitalism, and the Morality of Economic Success, 1825–55," *PMHB* 112(1988):349–74.

Roman Catholics

Joseph L. Kirlin, *Catholicity in Philadelphia from the Earliest Missionaries down to the Present Time* (Philadelphia: J. J. McVey, 1906) is the best local history. More general accounts containing useful information on Pennsylvania Catholics include Jay P. Dolan, *The American Catholic Experience: A History from Colonial Times to the Present* (Garden City, N.Y.: Doubleday, 1985); Patrick J. Dignam, *A History of the Legal Incorporation of Catholic Church Property in the United States, 1784–1932, Catholic University of America Studies in American Church History* vol. 14 (Washington, D.C.: Catholic University of America, 1933) and Patrick Carey, *People and Prelates: Ecclesiastical Democracy and the Tensions of Trusteeism* (South Bend, Ind.: Notre Dame University Press, 1987) contain much information on Pennsylvania. Hugh J. Nolan, *The Most Reverend Francis Patrick Kenrick, Third Bishop of Philadelphia, 1830–1851, Catholic University of America Studies in American Church History,* vol. 37 (Washington, D.C.: Catholic University of America, 1948) and Michael J. Curley, *Venerable John Neumann, C.SS.R., Fourth Bishop of Philadelphia* (Washington, D.C.: Catholic University of America Press, 1952) are sympathetic biographies. Dale Light, "The Reformation of Philadelphia Catholicism, 1830–1860," *PMHB,* 112(1988): 375–406 is a revisionist look at Kenrick. Edith Jeffry, "Reform, Renewal, and Vindication: Irish Immigrants and the Catholic Total Abstinence Movement in Antebellum Philadelphia," *PMHB* 112(1988): 407–22 shows that Catholics and Protestants shared antialcohol sentiments. Dennis Clark, *The Irish in Philadelphia: Ten Generations of Urban Experience* (Philadelphia: Temple University Press, 1973) discusses the influence of Catholicism on one immigrant population. Vincent P. Lannie, and Bernard Diethorn, "For the Honor and Glory of God: The Philadelphia Bible Riots of 1844," *History of Education Quarterly* 8(Spring, 1968):44–106, and Michael Feinberg, *Philadelphia Riots of 1844: A Study of Ethnic Conflict* (Westport, Conn.: Greenwood, 1975) supplement the materials on nativism in Ray Billington, *The Protestant Crusade, 1800–1860: A Study of the Origins of American Nativism* (New York: Macmillan, 1938).

Anglicans or Episcopalians

William Stevens Perry, ed., *Papers Relating to the History of the Church in Pennsylvania, A.D. 1680–1778* (n.p., 1871) contains primary sources. Deborah Matthias Gough, "Pluralism, Politics, and Power Struggles: The Church of England in Colonial Philadelphia" (Ph.D. dissertation, University of Pennsylvania, 1978) is the closest to a history of Pennsylvania Anglicans and supplements the material in Jon Butler, *Power, Authority, and the Origins of American Denominationalism*. Many of the letters of William Smith are reprinted in Horace Wemyss Smith, *Life and Correspondence of Rev. William Smith D.D.* (Philadelphia: S.A. George, 1874, reprinted New York: Arno Press, 1972). Albert F. Gegenheimer, *William Smith: Educator and Churchman, 1727–1803* (Philadelphia: University of Pennsylvania Press, 1943); Hubertis Cummings, *Richard Peters: Provincial Secretary and Cleric, 1704–1776* (Philadelphia: University of Pennsylvania Press, 1944); and Joseph Fairbanks, Jr., "Richard Peters (ca. 1704–76), Provincial Secretary of Pennsylvania" (Ph.D. dissertation, University of Arizona, 1972) are only adequate. There is no good biography of William White or history of the Episcopalians in Pennsylvania after the Revolution. I relied on the *Journal of the Convention of the Protestant Episcopal Church of the State of Pennsylvania* (Philadelphia: 1813–1855).

Sectarians and Rationalists

Charles Henry Smith, *Mennonite Immigration to Pennsylvania in the Eighteenth Century, Pennsylvania German Society Proceedings* vol. 35 (Norristown, Pa.: Pennsylvania German Society, 1929) is less useful than Richard MacMaster, *Land, Piety, Peoplehood: The Establishment of Mennonite Communities in America, 1683–1790, Mennonite Experience in America* vol. 1 (Scottsdale, Pa.: Herald Press, 1985). *Conscience in Crisis, Mennonites and other Peace Churches in America, 1739–1789: Studies in Anabaptist and Mennonite History* vol. 20, edited by Samuel R. Horst, Richard MacMaster, and Richard Ulle, (Scottsdale, Pa.: Herald Press, 1979) deals with pacifists and war. Histories of denominations include Howard Kriebel, *Schwenkfelders in Pennsylvania. Pennsylvania German Society Proceedings* vol. 13 (Lancaster, Pa.: 1904); Donald Durnbaugh, ed., *The Brethren in Colonial America* (Elgin, Ill., Brethren Press, 1967); Jacob Sessler, *Communal Pietism Among Early American Moravians* (New York: AMS, 1971, reprinted, 1973); Joseph Levering, *A History of Bethlehem, Pennsylvania, 1741–1892* (Bethlehem, Pa.: Times Publishing Co., 1903); Kenneth G. Hamilton, *John Ettwein and the Moravian Church During the Revolutionary Period* (Bethlehem, Pa.: Times Publishing Co., 1940); J. Taylor Hamilton, and Kenneth G. Hamilton, *History of the*

Moravian Church (Bethlehem, Pa.: Interprovincial Board of Christian Education, Moravian Church in America, 1967); Linda Gollin, *Moravians in Two Worlds: A Study of Changing Communities* (New York: Columbia University Press, 1967); Brother Lamech, *Chronicon Ephratense,* translated by J. Mack Hark (Lancaster, Pa.: S. H. Zaln, 1889).

Unitarians and Universalists

See Abel Thomas, *A Century of Universalism in Philadelphia and New York* (Philadelphia, Collins, 1872); Elizabeth M. Geffen, *Philadelphia Unitarianism, 1796–1861* (Philadelphia: University of Pennsylvania, 1961); Eric Foner, *Tom Paine and Revolutionary America* (New York: Oxford University Press, 1976); Albert Post, *Popular Freethought in America, 1825–1850* (New York: Columbia University Press, 1943). Anticlericalism is found in a series of nineteenth-century, short-lived newspapers: *The Philadelphia Times, Mechanics Free Press and Working Men's Register, The Temple of Reason,* and *Delaware Free Press.*

Jews

Pennsylvania's Jewish Community is described in Edwin Wolf 2nd and Maxwell Whiteman, *History of the Jews of Philadelphia from Colonial Times to the Age of Jackson* (Philadelphia: Jewish Publication Society of America, 1957) and Leon Jick, *Americanization of the Synagogue, 1820–1870,* (Hanover, N.H.: Brandeis University Press, 1976).

Sermons, tracts, religious periodicals, newspapers, manuscripts, and secondary sources not focusing directly on Pennsylvania are cited only in footnotes.

Index

214

97–9, 108, 114, 121, 125, 127, 135,
138, 141, 146, 152, 178, 182
Price Bill, 158
Priestly, Joseph, 58, 91, 93, 186
Princeton, 91, 97, 112; *see also* College of
New Jersey
prohibition, 122, 160; *see also* alcohol
Proprietary party, 33, 35, 37–9, 43, 47–9;
51–2; 56, 60–2, 174
Protestants, 11, 28, 48, 53, 143, 147; liberty for all, 50; service in government
limited to, 21; *see also* individual
denominations

Quaker party, 32, 35, 40, 42, 44, 48–9, 51–
2, 60, 62, 64, 174; policies, 32–3
Quakers, 5, 10–19, 22–48, 51–2, 54, 56,
59, 60–4, 66, 69–70, 72, 84, 89–90,
92–6, 100, 105–7, 109, 119–20, 124,
127, 130, 144, 148, 156, 162, 165,
174; antislavery protest, 82; in Assembly, 28, 38; English, 10, 39–40;
Hicksite, 97, 122, 126–7, 142; and
higher education, 49; ministers in government, 19, 23; Orthodox, 126–7;
pacifism, attitude to Revolution, 63;
peace testimony, 17–18, 31–9; Philadelphia Yearly Meeting, 32, 39, 127; in
politics, 38–9; politics, withdrawal
from, 62; principles incompatible with
government, 31; and the Revolution,
66; sectarian mentality, 4; testimonies
in early Pennsylvania law, 17; view of
conscience, 11, 14–19; view of direct
revelations, 11; view of Pennsylvania,
34; women ministers, 15, 119; *see also*
affirmation; pacifism; sectarians
Quary, Colonel Robert, 21

railroads, 140–1
Rakestraw, William, 36
Ranters, 10
Rapp, George, 126
Rapp, Heinrich, 46
Read, John Meredith, Justice, 140–1
reason, 11, 53, 78–9, 81, 143, 151, 160; *see
also* natural law
Reformed. *see* German Reformed Church
Reformed Presbyterian Church, 6, 53, 93,
108–13
religious liberty, 4, 8, 13, 23, 27, 30, 32,
35–6, 38, 43, 52–3, 58, 64–5, 69, 88–
9, 112, 138, 149, 152; autonomy for
the churches, 4, 8; catechism, 147; in
charter and early laws of Pennsylvania,
13; courts, 124; definition, 4, 33, 72;
freedom of conscience, 4; goals of,

124; laws of, 124; and reason, 53, 54;
and royal government, 52; sectarian
definition, 72; *see also* conscience;
church and state; religious toleration;
Penn, William
religious pluralism, 3, 82, 162
religious tests, 75, 77, 88, 145; for office, 6,
8, 20, 95, 102–3, 132, 160
religious toleration, 4, 11, 13–15, 18, 22,
25, 36, 45, 56, 80, 107, 113, 115; 1681
statute, 15; 1705 statute, 22; *see also*
church and state; conscience; religious
liberty
republican religious liberty, 78–85, 106,
147–8
Republicans, Democratic or Jeffersonian, 6,
80, 88, 91, 94–5, 97, 104, 162
Rhode Island, 35
riots, 153, 156–57
Roman Catholic Church. *see* Catholic
church
Ross, James, 86, 94
royal government, 43, 48, 52
Rush, Benjamin, 5, 78, 80–3, 147

sabbath, *see* Sunday
St. Thomas's African Episcopal Church,
charter, 130
Saur, Christopher, 28, 37, 59, 176
schism, 126–7; Keithian, 15
Schlatter, Michael, 37, 46–7
School District of Abington Township ver-
sus Schempp, 161
schools, 15, 26, 75, 91, 100, 107–8, 153–
7, 161; Bible reading in, 155–7, 202;
charity, 37, 49; laws on, 143, 154, 165;
parochial, 155, 164, 202; prayer in,
146, 161, 164; public, 7, 144, 146,
153; religious instruction, 155
Schulze, John Andrew, 94
Schwenkfelders, 68
Scotland, 50, 57
Scots-Irish, 5, 32, 39, 41–2, 50, 60, 98
Scottish Covenanters, 6, 53, 108
Seabury, Samuel, 89
Second Continental Congress, 64
Second Great Awakening, 7, 121
secret societies, 151
sectarians, 4, 47, 52, 56, 59–60; *see also*
Mennonites; Moravians; Quakers
Seixas, Rabbi Gervase, 145.
self-defense, 30
separation of church and state, *see* church
and state
Sergeant, John, 102
Seventh-Day Adventists, 146
Seventh-Day Baptists, 93, 135, 142